W9-BZT-757

RH
(✓)
(9−
41710
HA

Hadassah and the Zionist Project

Hadassah and the Zionist Project

Erica B. Simmons

ROWMAN & LITTLEFIELD PUBLISHERS, INC.
Lanham • Boulder • New York • Toronto • Oxford

ROWMAN & LITTLEFIELD PUBLISHERS, INC.

Published in the United States of America
by Rowman & Littlefield Publishers, Inc.
A wholly owned subsidiary of The Rowman & Littlefield Publishing Group, Inc.
4501 Forbes Boulevard, Suite 200, Lanham, Maryland 20706
www.rowmanlittlefield.com

PO Box 317
Oxford
OX2 9RU, UK

Copyright © 2006 by Rowman & Littlefield Publishers, Inc.

All rights reserved. No part of this publication may be reproduced, stored in a
retrieval system, or transmitted in any form or by any means, electronic, mechanical,
photocopying, recording, or otherwise, without the prior permission of the publisher.

British Library Cataloguing in Publication Information Available

Library of Congress Cataloging-in-Publication Data

Simmons, Erica.
  Hadassah and the Zionist project / Erica Simmons.
    p. cm.
  Includes bibliographical references and index.
  ISBN 0-7425-4937-2 (cloth : alk. paper) —ISBN 0-7425-4938-0 (pbk. : alk. paper)
  1. Hadassah, the Women's Zionist Organization of America. 2. Zionism—United
States—History—20th century. 3. Palestine—Social conditions—20th century. 4.
Israel—Social conditions—20th century. 5. Jewish Agency for Israel. Youth Aliyah
Dept. I. Title.
DS150.H4S56 2005
369'.25694'0820973—dc22   2005013372

Printed in the United States of America

∞™ The paper used in this publication meets the minimum requirements of
American National Standard for Information Sciences—Permanence of Paper for
Printed Library Materials, ANSI/NISO Z39.48-1992.

Contents

Abbreviations

AZMU	American Zionist Medical Unit
CZA	Central Zionist Archives
FAZ	Federation of American Zionists
HMO	Hadassah Medical Organization
HNI	*Histadrut Nashim Ivriot,* or Federation of Hebrew Women
HWZOA	Hadassah, the Women's Zionist Organization of America, Inc.
IDF	Israel Defense Forces
JDC	American Jewish Joint Distribution Committee (or "Joint")
JPS	Jewish Publication Society
NCJW	National Council of Jewish Women
OETA	Occupation of Enemy Territories Administration
SHS	Straus Historical Society
SSC	Sophia Smith Collection, The Jane Addams Papers
UPA	United Palestine Appeal
WIZO	Women's International Zionist Organization
WZO	World Zionist Organization
ZOA	Zionist Organization of America

Acknowledgments

I wish to thank Professor Harold Troper for his encouragement, scholarly guidance, and general good humor during the various stages of researching and writing the dissertation that led to this book. I also appreciate the assistance provided by Professor David Levine, Professor Grace Feuerverger, and Professor Molly Ladd-Taylor. Susan Woodland, Hadassah archivist at the Center for Jewish History, shared her knowledge of Hadassah's history and guided me through a wealth of archival materials during research trips I made to New York. My understanding of Hadassah's work was also enriched by my conversations with women who have personal experience with the organization. For their willingness to share their thoughts and memories, I thank Mrs. Mira Bramson, Ms. Alisa Poskanzer, Professor Yaffa Schlesinger, Mrs. Bernice Tannenbaum, Mrs. June Walker, and Mrs. Edna Warsawe. Many thanks also to my affable editor, Brian Romer, for his enthusiasm and patience.

I appreciate the encouragement and support I received from my parents, Harvey and Eileen Simmons. My sister, Leah Levin, offered editorial advice and shared her knowledge of the subject. I would also like to thank my brother, Daniel Simmons, and my brother-in-law, Avner Levin, for their help, as well as Itzhak and Miki Levin, and Lilac Levin, for their hospitality during a research trip to Israel. For their good cheer and friendship I thank Bushra Junaid, Frieda Forman, Pauline Peters, and Stella Walker.

Finally, I am very grateful for the research funding I received from the Hadassah-Brandeis Institute and the Center for Jewish History, the Memorial Foundation for Jewish Culture, the Ontario Graduate Scholarship program, and the Social Sciences and Humanities Research Council of Canada.

This book is dedicated to my parents, Harvey and Eileen Simmons.

CHAPTER ONE

~

Introduction:
American Maternalists in
Palestine and Israel

In the pre-state era before Israel's establishment in 1948, when most Zionist organizations concentrated on political lobbying and land development to advance the Zionist cause, Hadassah, the Women's Zionist Organization of America, adopted a radically different—and at the time, controversial— strategy: it sought to improve living conditions in the Yishuv (the Jewish community of pre-1948 Palestine) through providing hands-on social services to the local population.[1] Under the leadership of Henrietta Szold, Hadassah first sent public health nurses to Palestine in 1913. From this point on, Hadassah slowly and methodically laid the groundwork for the medical and social welfare systems of the future Jewish state.

Hadassah was an extraordinarily successful organization by any measure: funds raised, size of membership, or projects realized. Moreover, from the mid-1920s through the end of the Second World War, it was the largest Zionist organization in the United States. Surprisingly, however, Hadassah has received relatively little scholarly attention until now. One possible explanation for this is Hadassah's roots in two sociopolitical movements: Progressivism and Zionism. Not all American Zionists shared the values and goals of the Progressive movement, but Hadassah's founders saw in the project to build a Jewish state the chance to design a society that would represent the best of American Progressive ideals.

What were these ideals? Progressivism was based on a faith in social improvements through reform activities. The rapid pace of late-nineteenth-century industrialization, urbanization, and immigration had given rise to

1

crowded slums with poor sanitation, widespread ill health, and poverty. Progressives regarded science—very broadly defined—as the driving force of modernization and progress, and were guided by the principles of efficiency, accountability, systematization, and respect for professional expertise. From the late nineteenth century through the 1930s, reformers worked to integrate immigrants, create protective health and safety legislation, end child labor, improve working conditions and housing, and protect food supplies. They pressured government to enlarge its responsibility for social welfare programs and services. To show government what should be done, Progressives set up demonstration projects and launched a wide variety of initiatives, from public health programs to urban sanitation measures, domestic science classes, juvenile courts, parks, and playgrounds. In short, Progressives created many of the elements of the American welfare state.

At the time, educated women had few professional avenues open to them, and many were making their first tentative steps toward a more public role. Deprived of the vote and thus a role in electoral politics, women found other channels to make their voices heard. By setting up and staffing settlement houses or creating voluntary associations, women took a leading role in reform activities. Forced to justify their activities in terms that were socially acceptable, they claimed to be taking an interest only in those domestic types of issues in which they were already expert—issues, that is, that were widely considered to be within women's "sphere." As women kept their homes clean and their children healthy, so they would try to extend these responsibilities to the larger society. In this way, Progressive women reformers presented their activities as a natural extension of women's domestic and maternal concerns into the public realm. For this reason, historians describe them as "maternalists," and their activist work is sometimes called "social"—or sometimes "municipal"—housekeeping.[2]

This exploration of Hadassah's social welfare work shows not only how deeply some American Jews identified with Progressivism but how a group of American Jewish women started the Hadassah organization to turn Progressive ideas into a plan of action that they employed to advance the Jewish nationalist struggle in Palestine. Hadassah developed a synthesis of Progressive maternalist and Zionist ideas, which is called here "Zionist maternalism." The core of Zionist maternalism was the idea that Jewish women bore a specific responsibility for social welfare in the Yishuv. Guided by this principle, Hadassah then imported to Palestine not only the sociopolitical ideology but also the roster of projects characteristic of American Progressive maternalism. For this reason, I argue that Hadassah's early work in Palestine is best understood not in the context of the American Zionist movement but rather as an offshoot of the maternalist politics and "child-saving" agenda of the Progressive reform movement in the United States.

From the beginning, Hadassah's founders aimed to create a medical *system* in Palestine rather than merely supplying emergency medical relief services. Countrywide public health services would be the foundation of this medical system. Every Hadassah program, from the early milk stations to school luncheons and organized playgrounds, was designed to fit into this overarching goal.

As the beneficiaries of a full century's worth of public health programs and measures, it is hard for us now to grasp just how revolutionary the concept of public health was in the early twentieth century. Public health nurses working in the community pioneered popular education techniques that spread the latest scientific knowledge about how better nutrition, hygiene, and sanitary measures might improve people's health and quality of life. Poor people who could not afford a doctor's services were given the tools to improve their families' chances of good health and got access to nursing care in their own homes.

This book examines the specific American field-tested projects that Hadassah transplanted to the Yishuv: pasteurized milk depots, maternal education, health care and health education in the schools, school lunches, nutrition education, organized playgrounds, model flats, sanitary reform, and domestic science education. Through the analysis of Hadassah's archival materials, including publicity brochures, newsletters, and correspondence, I show how Hadassah set up and administered these projects and also how, through a carefully crafted publicity campaign, the organization persuaded many American Jewish women to support its innovative social welfare agenda.

Hadassah's founder, Henrietta Szold, was a dynamic and tireless activist compared by her colleagues to Jane Addams, the well-known Progressive activist who founded the Hull House Settlement in Chicago.[3] Szold moved to Palestine permanently in 1927 and was thereafter a powerful political force in the Yishuv. Throughout her life, however, Szold remained deeply American in her outlook, as she herself acknowledged. At a celebration of her seventy-fifth birthday held in New York City, Szold attributed her interests and achievements to "the inspiration I received through my American schooling, my contact with American civilization and through my identification with public and civic work in the United States."[4] The American influence on Szold is key to understanding her political views and her determination to ensure that Hadassah's activities in the Yishuv were guided not only by Zionist imperatives but by American democratic ideals. Despite relinquishing her official position as Hadassah president, Szold remained the organization's guiding force until her death in 1945.

Many of the early members of Hadassah in New York City were women of a new leisure class; like Szold, they were relatively well off and well educated—the American-born, English-speaking daughters of German Jewish immigrants. They were interested in Jewish affairs and were committed to self-education on Jewish topics. Like many other American women of their class, they felt a sense of social responsibility which they expressed through volunteer work and philanthropy.

Hadassah was designed according to Szold's ideas of how to recruit women to the Zionist cause. She decided the best approach would be through an appeal to their maternal instincts and concerns and a "practical" mandate of support for the development of modern, American-style health and education services in the Yishuv. As a women's organization, Hadassah regarded its activities in the areas of education, health, social work, and child welfare as the vital contribution of women to the Zionist cause.

But other American Zionist organizations did not share Hadassah's priorities. In the American Zionist press and at meetings and conferences, Hadassah was repeatedly excoriated for diverting attention, energies, and funds from what others regarded as the more urgent Zionist needs of agriculture and settlement. Despite such criticism, Hadassah stood firm and, over time, enabled American Jewish women to play a leading role in the Zionist creation of a Jewish state-in-the-making in Palestine.

As an American Jewish women's organization that worked in the Yishuv, Hadassah's early history in effect straddles two separate worlds: that of American Jews in the Progressive-era United States and that of the Jewish community of Palestine in the pre-state period. The first half of the twentieth century was a formative era in the development of each community. In Palestine, Jews built the institutions and political apparatus of self-government and, in 1948, saw Zionist hopes realized with the declaration of the State of Israel. At the same time, the complexion of American Jewry was transformed from a largely foreign-born, Yiddish-speaking, immigrant community to a native-born English-speaking community with a greater sense of security about their status as Americans.

Thus, this book covers a distinct era in the history of American Jews and their relationship to the Jewish state, from the era of the First World War through the early years of Cold War tensions and beyond. Palestine was still a backwater of the Ottoman Empire when Hadassah was founded in 1912. By the time the first Hadassah nurses arrived in Palestine the following year, the country was on the brink of war. Although Hadassah was forced to suspend its medical activities due to the disruptions caused by the First World War, it sent the American Zionist Medical Unit (AZMU) to Palestine at the war's end, on the heels of the Balfour Declaration and in time for the establishment of the British Mandate. By doing so, Hadassah established its presence in Palestine at a pivotal moment in the Yishuv's trajectory toward statehood. From then on, Hadassah worked steadily to advance its vision of a democratic, egalitarian, and pluralistic Jewish state.

Hadassah brought two decades worth of experience in child welfare work to its 1935 commitment to become the sole American sponsor of Youth Aliyah—the effort to save children from Nazi-occupied Europe and bring them to Palestine. Here, Hadassah's familiarity with the cultural and social differences among Jews from European countries—gleaned from its social welfare work in the Yishuv—stood the organization in good stead. During the Second World War, and in its aftermath, Hadassah helped Youth Aliyah to rescue, house, and educate thousands of young European (Ashkenazi) Jewish refugees. This work, in turn, prepared Hadassah for its role in helping Israel to absorb the children of the Middle Eastern and North African (Oriental or *Mizrahi*) Jews who arrived, en masse, during the first decade of statehood.

Through decades of work, Hadassah succeeded in building permanent links between the Jewish communities of America and Palestine (later Israel). In the early years, Hadassah took pains to reassure its members that they could be both patriotic Americans and active Zionists. Indeed, Hadassah said that as good Americans, Jews were duty bound to support Zionist goals of creating a democratic national state for a persecuted minority. Hadassah eagerly sought the support of American Jewish leaders like Louis Brandeis, Stephen Wise, and Judah Magnes who conceived of an American Zionist ideology in the spirit of the American pioneers and infused with Progressive reformist idealism.

Despite the growth of Hadassah, Zionism in the United States never attracted the support of more than a minority of American Jews. Without serious fears of domestic anti-Semitism, American Jews were more inclined to regard Palestine as a necessary safe haven for other Jews: refugees from Europe or elsewhere. But even without strong Zionist sentiment, in times of crisis, as during the First and Second World Wars, American Jewry responded generously to requests for help and funds for Palestine. Recognizing this potential, Hadassah wisely aimed from the beginning to draw into its fold as many Jewish women as possible whether through appeals to their humanitarian sentiments, Jewish identification, or Zionist commitments.

For Hadassah's leaders, Zionism was not only the Jewish struggle for statehood, it was also a path to spiritual and cultural enrichment for American

Jews and a way to unite a far-flung community around a common cause. For Jewish women in particular, so often denied professional and intellectual outlets, Hadassah also offered broader horizons. "Every woman and girl in America who participates" in Hadassah, said the American Zionist magazine *The New Palestine* in 1922, "begins to live in a wider world, in the Orient as well as in America; her sympathy is capable of being aroused . . . she feels a part of the Jewish people the world over."[5]

Despite Hadassah's formidable contribution to the Zionist state-building enterprise, most histories of American Zionism deal with Hadassah only briefly and regard it of interest primarily for its occasional clashes with other Zionist organizations.[6] Given Szold's powerhouse personality and her overwhelming influence on Hadassah, scholars have naturally focused primarily on her and only secondarily on Hadassah itself.[7] There are a handful of essays discussing Szold's life and ideas: historians Michael Brown and Allon Gal, in particular, stress the influence of American liberal traditions and Progressive ideas on Szold and, concomitantly, on Hadassah.[8] But very few scholars have addressed the repercussions of what historian Mary McCune calls Hadassah's "gender-based Zionism."[9] The few who have discussed the gender issue include McCune, Joyce Antler, and Michael Berkowitz, who analyzes the "cold embrace" of women's organizations by both American and European Zionists.[10]

This history focuses on Hadassah itself, on its character as a women's organization and its social welfare work in the Yishuv. This necessitates not only a reassessment of the relationship between Hadassah and the rest of the American Zionist movement but also appraisal of the exact nature of the influence of American Progressive ideas on Hadassah's activities in Palestine. Here, the concept of Zionist maternalism helps to give shape to Hadassah's unique interpretation of American maternalist ideology. Through this approach, I hope to shed light on a subject mostly overlooked by historians: the contributions of organized Zionist women to the evolution of Zionism as both an ideology and a movement, as well as to the development of the Yishuv. Why did Hadassah decide to focus on social welfare and why did it choose specific social welfare projects? How did it explain and promote these projects to its American members? What did it hope these projects would contribute to the Zionist struggle? What, in the end, did Hadassah's social welfare work achieve?

For the most part, the history of the Yishuv has been told in terms of political conflict and military struggles. The quiet work of creating social welfare institutions in Palestine—work undertaken primarily by Hadassah along with other women's organizations—is a less dramatic but equally crucial part of the history of the Zionist state-building project. Hadassah took responsibility for a nation's education and public health and, by doing so, forced the provision of social services onto the Zionist agenda. As each of Hadassah's programs took root in the Yishuv, the Progressive American ideals enshrined within the programs also took hold and made their mark on Yishuv society. If Hadassah's many projects in the Yishuv comprised the building blocks of statehood, then the organization's continued involvement in supporting Israeli social welfare programs after 1948 shows how well Hadassah understood that the full realization of Zionist hopes required a commitment to state-building as an ongoing process.

Notes

1. *Yishuv* ("settlement" or "community" in Hebrew) is the term used for the Jewish community of pre-1948 Palestine.

2. For the history of maternalist politics in the United States, see Molly Ladd-Taylor, *Mother-Work: Women, Child Welfare, and the State, 1890–1930* (Urbana and Chicago: University of Illinois Press, 1994). For a comparative examination of maternalism in different countries, see Seth Koven and Sonya Michel, eds., *Mothers of a New World: Maternalist Politics and the Origins of Welfare States* (New York and London: Routledge, 1993); Seth Koven and Sonya Michel, "Womanly Duties: Maternalist Politics and the Origins of Welfare States in France, Germany, Great Britain, and the United States, 1880–1920," *American Historical Review* 95, no. 4 (October 1990): 1076–1108.

3. In 1924, Louis Brandeis wrote that Szold "has been called the Jane Adamms [sic] of our Jewish world—and not without reason." Melvin I. Urofsky and David W. Levy, eds., *Letters of Louis D. Brandeis*, vol. 5 (Albany: State University of New York Press, 1978), 107. Rabbi Stephen Wise made the same comparison at Szold's seventy-fifth birthday celebration in New York City. See "Women Here Honor Hadassah Founder," *New York Times*, 23 December 1935, sec. 2, 5.

4. "City and Zionists Honor Miss Szold," *New York Times*, 10 January 1936, 15.

5. Mignon Rubenovitz, "Our Tenth Birthday," *The New Palestine*, 10 March 1922, 150.

6. See, for example, Naomi Cohen, *American Jews and the Zionist Idea* (New York: Ktav, 1975); Daniel Elazar, *Community and Polity: The Organizational Dynamics of American Jewry* (Philadelphia: Jewish Publication Society, 1976; rev. ed. 1995); Samuel Halperin, *The Political World of American Zionism* (Detroit: Wayne State University Press, 1961); Mark Raider, *The Emergence of American Zionism* (New York: New York University Press, 1998). Research that does focus on Hadassah includes Marlin Levin, *It Takes a Dream: The Story of Hadassah* (Jerusalem: Gefen, 1997); Carol Bosworth Kutscher, "The Early Years of Hadassah, 1912–1921" (Ph.D. diss., Brandeis University, 1976); Donald Herbert Miller, "A History of Hadassah, 1912–1935"

(Ph.D. diss., New York University, 1968). Many Hadassah members went to live in Palestine. See Naomi Ann Lichtenberg, "Hadassah's Founders and Palestine, 1912–1925: A Quest for Meaning and the Creation of Women's Zionism" (Ph.D. diss., Indiana University, 1996). Hadassah and other Jewish organizations involved in relief work are discussed by Mary McCune, "Charity Work as Nation-Building: American Jewish Women and the Crises in Europe and Palestine, 1914–1930" (Ph.D. diss., Ohio State University, 2000).

7. For example: Joan Dash, *Summoned to Jerusalem: The Life of Henrietta Szold, Founder of Hadassah* (New York: Harper & Row, 1979); Irving Fineman, *Woman of Valor: The Life of Henrietta Szold, 1860–1945* (New York: Simon & Schuster, 1961); Marvin Lowenthal, *Henrietta Szold: Life and Letters* (New York: Viking, 1942); Rose Zeitlin, *Henrietta Szold: Record of a Life* (New York: Dial, 1952).

8. See Michael Brown, "Henrietta Szold's Progressive American Vision of the Yishuv," in *Envisioning Israel: The Changing Ideals and Images of North American Jews*, ed. Allon Gal (Jerusalem: Magnes Press, 1996), 60–80; Michael Brown, "Henrietta Szold," in *The Israeli-American Connection: Its Roots in the Yishuv, 1914–1945* (Detroit: Wayne State University Press, 1996), 133–60; Allon Gal, "Hadassah and the American Jewish Political Tradition," in *An Inventory of Promises: Essays in American Jewish History in Honor of Moses Rishin*, ed. Jeffrey S. Gurock and Marc Lee Raphael (Brooklyn, N.Y.: Carlson, 1995), 89–114; Joan Dash, "Doing Good in Palestine: Magnes and Henrietta Szold," in *Like All the Nations? The Life and Legacy of Judah L. Magnes*, ed. William M. Brinner and Moses Rischin (Albany: State University of New York Press, 1987), 99–111. Szold's philosophy of Zionism as a spiritual mission is explored by Eric L. Goldstein, "The Practical as Spiritual: Henrietta Szold's American Zionist Ideology, 1878–1920," in *Daughter of Zion: Henrietta Szold and American Jewish Womanhood*, ed. Barry Kessler (Hagerstown: Jewish Historical Society of Maryland, 1995), 17–33.

9. Mary McCune, "Social Workers in the *Muskeljudentum*: 'Hadassah Ladies,' 'Manly Men' and the Significance of Gender in the American Zionist Movement, 1912–1928," *American Jewish History* 86, no. 2 (June 1998): 135–65.

10. Michael Berkowitz, "Cold Embrace: The Reception of Hadassah and Organized European Women Zionists," in *Western Jewry and the Zionist Project, 1914–1933* (Cambridge: Cambridge University Press, 1997), 175–79; Szold hoped Zionist activities would revitalize the lives of American Jewish women. See Joyce Antler, "Zion in Our Hearts: Henrietta Szold and the American Jewish Women's Movement," in Kessler, ed., *Daughter of Zion*, 33–55.

~

CHAPTER TWO

"The Healing of the Daughter of My People": Henrietta Szold and the Creation of Hadassah, the Women's Zionist Organization of America

One remarkable woman—Henrietta Szold—was the driving force of the Hadassah organization for over thirty years. She was born in Baltimore in 1860, the eldest of the five surviving children (all daughters) of Rabbi Benjamin Szold and Sophie Schaar Szold, German-speaking Hungarian Jews who arrived in the United States in 1859. At that time, the Jewish community of Baltimore, some seven thousand strong when Henrietta was born, consisted mostly of immigrants from Germany.

Henrietta's father had fought in the 1848 democratic uprising in Hungary and was a prominent figure in Baltimore society, known for his devotion to "the restoration of the Jewish homeland" and his liberal political views. A Lincoln supporter, Rabbi Szold was also a vocal critic of slavery and racial discrimination.[1] One of Henrietta's earliest memories was of helping her mother and other women prepare linen bandages to send to soldiers fighting in the Civil War. Another was watching Lincoln's funeral procession while hoisted up on her father's shoulders. The young Henrietta was exceptionally close to her father, studying Jewish and general topics under his tutelage and later, as a teenager, acting as his secretary.[2]

Upon graduating from high school at age sixteen, Szold began working as a schoolteacher. In the 1880s, as Russian Jewish immigrants poured into Baltimore, Szold realized that their lack of English language and literacy skills were a barrier to any possibility of economic advance. Since the immigrants worked during the day, Szold saw a need for a school that offered classes in the evening. In 1889 she opened the Russian Night School to teach English, civics, and vocational subjects like bookkeeping and dressmaking to immigrant laborers. As money was raised, the school expanded. By the time the school closed down almost a decade later, more than five thousand immigrants had attended classes at the school. Many consider the Russian Night School to be the first such school of its kind in the United States, and such schools made a major impact. A half century later, in gratitude, New York City mayor Fiorella LaGuardia told Szold:

> If I am today Mayor of New York, it is because of you. Half a century ago you initiated that instrument of American democracy, the evening school for the immigrant. . . . Were it not for such programs of education and Americanization at the time of our largest immigration waves, a new slavery would have arisen in American society perhaps worse than the first.[3]

While she was still a teenager, Szold also began to write columns for the New York *Jewish Messenger* weekly newspaper under the pen name Shulamith. In her columns she discussed the cultural and social life of Baltimore Jewry, commented on international events affecting Jews, and, occasionally, offered her views on the role of women. In this way, Szold developed both her ideas on Jewish issues and her writing skills.[4] In 1893 Szold took the position of executive secretary of the Jewish Publication Society of Philadelphia (JPS), where she was to spend the next two decades as an editor, a translator, and an essayist. While working at the JPS, Szold remained involved in teaching and in educational administration and also carved out a side career as a prolific contributor of essays to the national Jewish press.[5]

Soon after Szold began working at the Jewish Publication Society, Zionism as a modern political movement emerged in Western Europe with the 1896 publication of Theodor Herzl's visionary tract *Der Judenstaat* (*The Jewish State*). After covering the Dreyfus case in France, Herzl, a Viennese journalist, concluded that the problem of anti-Semitism required a political solution—namely, the creation of a Jewish state. In *Der Judenstaat*, Herzl laid out his vision for such a state and proposed the means by which it might be realized. He then organized the First Zionist Congress, which drew more than two hundred delegates to Basle, Switzerland, in 1897. The congress created the World Zionist Organization (WZO) to serve as the institutional representative and political center of the Zionist movement.[6]

The First Zionist Congress produced a platform which declared that "Zionism seeks to create for the Jewish people a home in Palestine secured by public law." The Basle Platform called for the promotion of Jewish settlement in Palestine, for Jews to unite in national and international organizations, for the "strengthening and fostering of Jewish national sentiment and national consciousness," and for "steps toward obtaining the consent of governments, where necessary, in order to reach the goal of Zionism."[7] This marked the beginning of Zionism as a political, rather than just sentimental, movement of national liberation with a plan of action and concrete goals. In 1898, American Zionists met in New York City and formed the Federation of American Zionists (FAZ).

Large-scale Jewish immigration to the Holy Land, however, predated the organized Zionist movement. In the 1880s, fleeing a wave of pogroms and massacres, thousands of Eastern European Jews began arriving in Palestine. Some were members of the *Hibbat Zion* (Love of Zion) movement who were influenced by Leo Pinsker's 1882 booklet *Auto-Emancipation*, which called for Jewish nationhood as the only solution to European anti-Semitism. Many of these Jewish migrants were overwhelmed by the difficulties of establishing themselves in Palestine, however, and did not stay. But thousands continued to arrive over the years before World War I, and they helped to establish not only the early agriculture settlements but also many of the institutions and organizations of the Yishuv.

Szold followed the vicissitudes of these early settlers in Palestine closely and also kept abreast of new currents in Zionist thought by reading the books and pamphlets written by Zionist ideologues like Pinsker, Ahad Ha'am, and A. D. Gordon. Szold shared Ahad Ha'am's view that the Jewish settlement of Palestine might help to revive and rejuvenate American Jewry. In a 1901 essay Szold contributed to the second issue of the FAZ magazine *The Maccabaean*, she argued that Zionism was both a spiritual and a practical ideology and that only Zionism could ensure "the re-establishment of Jewish life for the Jews."[8]

In her journalism, Szold developed her ideas about Zionism. She was also interested in what sort of Jewish society should be created and the place of women in that society. Szold first described her thoughts on the status of Jewish women in an article titled "The Education of the Jewish Girl" that she contributed to *The Maccabaean* in July 1903. "Advancement in the position of women," she claimed, "is itself the scale on which the rising culture of a people is registered." The article also shows that Szold was aware of the social reform work being done by activists like Jane Addams in Chicago and Lillian Wald in New York, whose settlement houses would be the model for the Hadassah organization's first project in Palestine a decade later. Szold wrote that Addams, in a talk given to the National Council of Jewish Women, said that she

> thinks Jewish women peculiarly well prepared to fill a place in the larger life
> . . . among all the women in the foreign quarters of Chicago none showed the

same aptitude as Jewish women for absorbing the civic and social spirit characteristic of modern life. . . . [This is the] same aptitude which, in the judgment of the social settlement worker, promises to make acceptable contributions in solving the problems of child labor, factory and sweat-shop abuses, tenement house reform, the dispensation of charity, municipal corruption, and social regeneration.[9]

In 1907, at the suggestion of her friend Dr. Judah Magnes, Szold joined a small women's study group named Hadassah, which was a chapter of an American Zionist women's movement called Daughters of Zion and met weekly to discuss Zionist writings. Lotta Levensohn came up with the idea of a women's Zionist study group in 1906 or 1907 while working as a secretary for Magnes, who was at that time honorary secretary of the Federation of American Zionists. Levensohn later recalled that although a few such groups already existed,

many, if not most of their members had only vague, romantic ideas about Zionism. Their activities were limited mostly to giving occasional Sunday afternoon teas to which speakers were invited . . . and reading. Lacking a coherent programme of Zionist education . . . the members sooner or later lost interest and drifted away.[10]

Given such instability, Magnes asked if Levensohn could "suggest ways and means of recruiting women for the Zionist organization and keeping them interested." Levensohn drew up a reading list of Zionist classics for the proposed group, including *Rome and Jerusalem* by Moses Hess; Pinsker's *Auto-Emancipation*; *Pinsker and His Brochure* by Ahad Ha'am; and *The Jewish State* by Theodor Herzl. Levensohn explained her rationale thus: "In those days, Zionism was ridiculed as a mad phantasy on the one hand, and on the other, relentlessly opposed as a menace to the Jew's citizenship. Zionist faith, therefore, had to be buttressed by a knowledge of the fundamentals of Zionism."[11]

Levensohn presented the reading list to Magnes, who suggested that she recruit twenty or more friends to join the newly formed group, and Magnes asked Szold to attend the group's first meeting. Levensohn was intimidated by Szold's reputation—"I was so dumbfounded at the idea of asking so renowned a scholar and editor to study Zionism with young girls far inferior to her in knowledge of Zionism"—but was impressed when Szold replied that she would prefer to be a working member, rather than an honorary member, of the group.[12]

The turning point in Szold's life and career came when in 1909, accompanied by her mother, she visited Palestine for the first time. At that time,

Palestine consisted of the areas we now describe as Israel, the Palestinian territories, and Jordan, and all the country's inhabitants, including Jews, were called Palestinians. Both women were appalled by what Szold described as the "misery, poverty, filth, [and] disease" they saw among the Jewish communities there. The experience, Szold acknowledged, politicized her as a Zionist. She wrote home: "There are heroic men and women here doing valiant work. If only they could be more intelligently supported by the European and American Jew." From Milan, on her way home the following month, Szold wrote to a friend: "The result is I am still a Zionist, that I think Zionism a more difficult aim to realize than I ever did before, and finally that I am more than ever convinced that if not Zionism, then nothing—then extinction for the Jew."[13]

According to Szold, after visiting the Jewish Girls' School in Jaffa, where the pupils escaped many of the diseases afflicting other local children because of regular in-school medical attention, her mother told her: "That is what your group ought to do. What is the use of reading papers and arranging festivals? You should do practical work in Palestine." Szold took her mother's advice to heart and, upon returning home to New York, "presented to us," Levensohn recalled later, "a plan for district visiting nursing patterned after Lillian Wald's project on the East Side of New York."[14]

The idea of a nurses' settlement was based on the American "settlement house" model, in which staff lived among and worked with local residents in poor communities. District nursing grew out of Lillian Wald's idea of establishing a neighborhood center where nurses would both live and work and so become an "organic" part of neighborhood life. Wald, the daughter of a middle-class Jewish family, was a trained nurse who was studying to be a doctor when she agreed to teach a class in home nursing to immigrants living in New York City's Lower East Side neighborhood. Called away from a class she was teaching by a child whose mother needed medical help, Wald was shocked by her first encounter with a poverty-stricken immigrant family.

In her 1915 memoir, *The House on Henry Street*, Wald wrote that "all the maladjustments of our social and economic relations seemed epitomized in this brief journey and what was found at the end of it." "That morning's experience," she recalled, "was a baptism of fire." When Wald discovered that some 90 percent of ill people among New York's poor stayed at home unattended because they could not afford to pay for doctors or hospital care, she decided to start a home-nursing service in the Lower East Side.[15]

In 1895, Wald and another nurse, Mary Brewster, moved into a house on Henry Street where they planned to offer free or low-cost, nonsectarian nursing services to neighborhood residents. Wald's idea was that the nurses should be socially integrated into the neighborhood and should visit people in their homes: "We were to live in the neighborhood as nurses, identify ourselves with it socially, and, in brief, contribute to it our citizenship."[16] By 1905, Henry Street had expanded dramatically: nurses working out of eighteen district centers cared for a total of 4,500 patients. The nurses responded to calls, made regular visits, and taught home-nursing classes. The nurses, Wald explained, "are the indispensible carriers of the findings of the scientists and the laboratories to the people themselves, using their sympathy and training to make as intelligible as language permits the facts of health and life."[17]

Under Wald's guidance, Henry Street began to offer classes and social activities to both children and adults and was gradually transformed into a settlement house that offered a range of social, cultural, educational, and vocational programs as well as nursing services. Possessed of a broad social vision, Wald was politically active in reform efforts and campaigned for the establishment of parks and children's playgrounds, as well as for improved housing and public sanitation measures.[18]

This was the model Szold had in mind for Hadassah's first venture into Palestine. After two years of planning and preparation, a meeting was called for February 24, 1912, in New York City, and a notice was sent out announcing: "The time is ripe for a large organization of women Zionists, and they desire to invite you to attend a meeting for the purpose of discussing the feasibility of forming an organization which shall have for its purpose the promotion of Jewish institutions and enterprises in Palestine, and the fostering of Jewish ideals."[19]

A small committee later met to draft a constitution to present at the first meeting of the proposed new organization. At the meeting, Szold and another woman described their recent visits to Palestine and told the assembled women of the desperate need for maternity services for Jewish women there. The returned travelers offered "stirring and moving accounts of the Jewish pioneers there whose task was even more difficult than that of our pioneers here in the West."[20] The meeting adopted the new constitution; the name Daughters of Zion, Hadassah Chapter; and a motto, "The healing of the daughter of my people." The constitution made provisions for non-Zionist women to join the organization as "associate members." By these means "a society founded by Zionist women with Zionist aims, serves at the same time as a philanthropic agency for those non-Zionists who can be interested in social work among women and children in Palestine."[21] The measure of Zionist loyalty was a willingness to sign a pledge supporting the Basle Platform adopted by the First Zionist Congress in 1897.

The creation of the special "associate member" category shows that despite an oft-stated desire over the years to distinguish its "political" contribution from charity work, Hadassah was from its inception willing to exploit the charitable, but apolitical, sentiments of others. Hadassah's first annual report noted: "Fortunately Jews still have a sentimental interest in the Holy Land, and it is possible to stimulate even those who are unsympathetic with Zionism to participate in the betterment of conditions among their brethren in the ancient home."[22]

Another concern for Hadassah's founders was that so many women's Zionist organizations were "apt to fade out of existence after a brief period of feverish activity at ill-attended meetings. When the original members marry, and their household duties properly absorb them, and do not permit of attendance at frequent meetings, the studies and the collections alike are neglected." To avoid this fate, Hadassah would require more active involvement from its members. Women who joined Hadassah became part of an organization devoted to "a practical philanthropy, one that occupies itself with the needs of women and children, and deals with them in a modern scientific way." Hadassah's founders hoped that this would help to win the loyalties of women: "It is Hadassah's experience that Jewish women . . . embrace eagerly the chance of doing in a systematic way what they saw their mothers and grandmothers do in the haphazard way of the tin collection boxes (*Pushkes*)." This focus on the practical was the essence of what the organization described as "the Hadassah Plan."[23]

Still, raising money for Palestinian Jews would not be easy. While some better-off American Jews supported organizations that helped Jewish immigrants to the United States during this period, and many more sent money to their families in Eastern Europe, there was little in the way of organized Jewish philanthropy directed at helping Jewish communities abroad. American Jews were first galvanized into collective action by the outbreak of World War I, when they mounted a national campaign to provide assistance to Jewish refugees in Europe. Although there were complaints that wealthy American Jews were not generous enough with donations, the organizations that were established in this period, and the fundraising techniques they developed, set the pattern that would be followed by Jewish organizations for decades to come. But even in the prewar period, the overwhelming need of European Jewry tended to eclipse the plight of the impoverished Jewish community of Palestine. Pre–World War I American Zionist organizations found that they faced stiff competition in their efforts to raise funds for Palestinian Jewry.

The fledgling Hadassah organization set the goal of expanding its membership to three hundred in order to obtain the income necessary to undertake the financing of a project. Various health-related projects were proposed, but no single suggestion was endorsed. Rose Jacobs, an early member of the group who eventually served two terms as national president, recalled later that Hadassah continued to hold regular "parlour meetings" with "a cultural program, lectures, songs, lantern slides of Palestinian scenes, etc."[24] The women passed around a popular handheld device called a stereopticon to view vivid 3-D photographs that showed the desperate plight of Jewish women and children in Palestine.

On January 1, 1913, less than a year after Hadassah's founding meeting, Szold announced that the New York philanthropist Nathan Straus had offered to pay for the first four months of the cost of sending a Hadassah-sponsored nurse to Palestine if Hadassah would guarantee to support her subsequently. Shortly after, a Hadassah member raised sufficient money from donations in Chicago to send a second nurse to Palestine and to pay her salary for five years. Two American nurses, Rose Kaplan and Rachel Landy, were hired, and sailed for Palestine on January 16, 1913. Not long after arriving, the nurses opened a small clinic in Jerusalem on March 23, 1913, to deal primarily with maternity care and cases of trachoma—a contagious disease of the eye that was rampant in Palestine and throughout the Middle East. Left untreated, trachoma causes blindness.[25]

When Hadassah could afford to send a third nurse, Szold recommended that she prepare by studying American models. The nurse, said Szold, should "spend two months closely observing the work of the Nurses' Settlement in New York [and] the health work in the schools." As founding member Alice Seligsberg explained it: "The present object is not so much to bring relief in individual cases of illness as to organize a thorough system of district-nursing throughout the towns and colonies of Palestine, beginning with Jerusalem."[26]

Szold and her fledgling organization cultivated links with Wald, and Szold also looked for advice and approval from Jane Addams, the Chicago activist who founded Hull House Settlement. In 1913, Addams visited the Hadassah nurses' settlement in Jerusalem. In 1914, Szold visited the Henry Street nurses' settlement "and spoke to Miss Rebecca Schatz, who declared that many of the principles adopted by Hadassah in its work in Palestine were the same as those that secured success for the Henry Street Settlement." Szold later asked Wald to suggest a candidate when another nurse was sought to send to Palestine.[27]

With its program beginning to take shape, Hadassah continued to draw in new members. At the first annual meeting, on March 16, 1913, the women listened to an address by Dr. Magnes on the subject "The Relation of Zionism to Americanism."[28] This was an issue of some concern to American Jews, who worried that their support for Zionism might be regarded as disloyalty to the United States.

By May of that year, Hadassah was confident enough to explain how it planned to approach its Palestinian health work in the public forum of the American Zionist movement, *The Maccabaean*:

> Keeping the needs of women and children primarily in view, they [the Hadassah nurses in Palestine] will organize the work of the midwives along the lines laid down by the State and made effective through the activity of the Nurses' Settlement and the Russell Sage Foundation. For this aspect of the work they will be furnished with the means to employ midwives . . . to supply linens to mothers and babies, and afford a modicum of relief in the shape of medicine and food. They are expected to train probationers and helpers, organize "Little Mothers" circles like those under the New York Board of Health, and give illustrated health talks to mothers and girls at the schools and elsewhere; in short, engage in all the social service and educational activities of a nurses' settlement.

In short, through these methods, Hadassah would bring to Palestine an American-style "district visiting nurses system, at once social, educational and hygienic in scope."[29] Here we see the extent to which Hadassah's approach was modeled directly on the sort of public health work being done by Wald and other American reformers. This style of nursing care included the provision not just of medicine but also of linens and food; it required that nurses recruit and train volunteer assistants as well as teaching women and girls about health.

The "Little Mothers" program that Hadassah wished to bring to Palestine was created by Sara Josephine Baker, a New York City doctor involved in public health work, after she read John Spargo's *Bitter Cry of the Children*, a muckraking exposé of child labor, hunger, and poverty in New York City published in 1906. Spargo argued that "little mothers"—youngsters looking after younger siblings—contributed to high rates of infant mortality. Baker's program sent nurses into schools to teach young girls about child rearing, health, and sanitary housekeeping. Some of these girls were already responsible for looking after their siblings and households, but it was also hoped that they would teach their mothers what they had learned from the nurses. By teaching young girls about infant safety and health, some deaths might be prevented, and the information would also be useful to these girls in their adult lives. Little Mothers programs were also set up in Chicago and other American cities.[30] Hadassah's founders thought such a program would be easily adaptable to Palestinian conditions.

Meanwhile, the nurses in Jerusalem kept in close touch with Hadassah's Board of Directors, which in turn kept a growing number of local Hadassah chapters informed of their work. By September 8, 1913, the nurses reported that they had so far treated ten thousand cases and that they planned to treat nine thousand children for trachoma. At a meeting of the board, "it was suggested that folders and extracts of the nurses' letters be sent to the members to bridge the gap between meetings," and later, a letter was sent from New York to the nurses telling them "how valuable letters from Palestine are as propaganda material."[31]

Hadassah's clinic in Jerusalem was described as a settlement house at the first annual convention of the Daughters of Zion of America, held in Rochester, New York, June 29–30, 1914. Delegates heard that along with the two nurses at the clinic, a physician was hired part time "to treat poor cases gratis" and to supervise the nurses along with the first three of six midwives who would be hired for "the Jewish poor of Jerusalem." In addition, a part-time eye doctor was hired to treat five thousand children in thirty-six Jerusalem schools.

Also on the agenda at the convention was the addition of the phrase "to foster Zionist ideals in America" to Hadassah's mandate, which would then read: "The purpose of this Association is to promote Jewish institutions and enterprises in Palestine and to foster Zionist ideals in America." After a "lively and long discussion," the members agreed to rename their organization "Hadassah, the Women's Zionist Organization of America" or "Hadassah." Policy was to be decided at annual conventions; a central committee would make decisions for the organization between conventions. Given that there were now seven chapters of the society outside New York (in Baltimore, Boston, Chicago, Cleveland, Newark, Philadelphia, and St. Paul), it was now possible to speak of "a tentative national organization."[32]

In 1915, Hadassah's Central Committee reported:

> Our Zionist organization . . . consists not of the leisure classes of women but of the working women, who are busy all day as teachers, as shopgirls, as workers at trades, as stenographers. We must remember that Zionism is a democratic movement, that its success depends upon the mass of Jewish women.[33]

Because the members of the organization thought it vital that women be educated "not only to Judaism but to a realization of their civic and national responsibilities," efforts were made to incorporate educational features into many activities. The leadership urged every chapter to make a commitment to self-education by forming a reading or study circle. Member Jessie Sampter launched the School of Zionism as a vehicle for spreading the Zionist message; she wrote educational material for use by Hadassah's study circles, trained speakers, and enrolled hundreds of women as students in a correspondence course on Zionism.[34]

The First World War interrupted Jewish immigration to Palestine and had a devastating impact on the Yishuv—crop failure, rampant starvation and disease, rising rates of infant mortality—culminating in scenes of horror described in vivid detail by the American Zionist press of this period. The ruling Turkish authorities, fearing the dismemberment of their domain, cracked down and expelled Jewish nationalists: many thousands of Jews were forced out or fled the country. Communication between Hadassah in the United States and Jews in Palestine was cut off. With Palestine then part of the Ottoman Empire and allied to Germany, it was impossible for Hadassah to continue its work. The nursing station was closed in September 1915. One nurse stayed in Jerusalem, and the other went to help Palestinian Jews in the refugee camps in Alexandria, Egypt.[35]

An American government representative stationed in Copenhagen managed to speak with Hadassah's Dr. Thon in Jerusalem and described the grim scene in Palestine in a terse cable to New York: "Inform Miss Szold situation poor Jewish population Jerusalem terrible. Hundreds Jewish girls, women, fall by hunger, in disease and shame." But there was little Hadassah could do. With its Palestinian activities on hold, Hadassah's leaders worried that its members might lose steam. The solution? Hadassah advised intensive self-education in Zionist topics and cautioned: "During these months, when planning for the Palestinian work cannot occupy us, we ought to be busy making thoroughgoing Zionists of ourselves. Our organization ought to be firmly consolidated, so that it may be a fine, pliant instrument for all the uses it may be called upon to serve, and whenever it may be called upon for such services." Hadassah's Central Committee also reminded members that the organization's efforts in Palestine had a political goal: "We Zionists may not rest satisfied with philanthropic undertakings in Palestine. These are in line with our aim, but we aim beyond them. We must constantly keep national unity before our eyes, and national progress."[36]

In July 1916, at the organization's third annual national convention, held in Philadelphia, Hadassah's membership was reported to be nearly two thousand. In response to the crisis in the Yishuv, the World Zionist Organization issued an urgent appeal for a medical force to be sent to Palestine. The Federation of American Zionists agreed to provide most of the estimated $265,000 budget for this venture but asked Hadassah to contribute $25,000 and to administer the project. Szold announced this fundraising goal at the Hadassah convention, and by 1917, the organization had raised $30,000.[37]

As the United States entered the war in 1917, Hadassah continued to expand its membership, and its coffers.

In order to secure Jewish support for the British war effort, in 1917, a scant few weeks before the British army arrived in Jerusalem, the British foreign minister issued the Balfour Declaration, which affirmed the right of Jews to a "national home" in Palestine. Hadassah, like other Zionist organizations worldwide, hailed this as a major victory for the movement: "The will to live of the Jewish people," said a Hadassah editorial, "has been given official recognition by one of the Great Powers."[38]

The British army conquered Jerusalem in December 1917, and was allowed to run the country under the Occupation of Enemy Territories Administration (OETA). In 1920, representatives of the Allied countries met at the San Remo conference and agreed to allow a British mandate over Palestine based on the principles of the Balfour Declaration. Britain organized a new civil administration to govern the country, which was still suffering from the effects of the war. Malnutrition, disease, poverty, and military conflict had taken their toll on the whole population.[39]

Hadassah's leaders made preparations for the organization to send representatives back to Palestine; all were eager to build on the work so abruptly halted. With the end of the war, it was now possible for Hadassah to carry through with the FAZ's request that it lead the effort to send a forty-five-member medical team—the American Zionist Medical Unit (AZMU)—to establish hospitals and clinics across Palestine.[40] At home in the United States, there was Zionist business to attend to. Hadassah joined the FAZ, which was soon renamed the Zionist Organization of America (ZOA).

Alice Seligsberg was put in charge of the AZMU's personnel and administration. Hadassah was soon choosing from among four hundred applicants to their newly established Nurses' Training School in Jerusalem: "The requirements were only a high school education, general cultural background and good moral character." Thirty-five students were accepted. There were no classrooms and no textbooks in Hebrew, and copies of lecture notes had to be delivered to students who lived in different parts of the country. A few years later, Colonel G. W. Heron, director of health in the British Mandatory government, told the fourth group of graduates from the school:

> You must remember the centuries it took Europe to adopt scientific measures of prevention of disease. Prejudices exist in this country, stronger prejudices than in Europe or America where education has advanced further. Therefore the graduating nurses that go out into Palestine must remember that it is by their example and precept that these prejudices may be gradually overcome—

not only by their advice on medical questions but also by their personality and character.[41]

To its appeals for donations from Americans, Hadassah now added a request for Hebrew-language textbooks and other supplies for the nursing school.

Buoyed by her organization's success in attracting Jewish women to the Zionist cause, Szold wrote to Seligsberg in 1920: "Isn't it curious how the Hadassah idea has taken hold of women? . . . It is necessary to invent, actually invent, a specific Hadassah task to satisfy them."[42] Szold also confided to Seligsberg her apprehensions about her upcoming departure for Palestine, where she intended to help the AZMU (which was renamed the Hadassah Medical Organization, or HMO, in 1921) become more independent of American control: "We ought to show by our acts," Szold wrote, "that we expect to drop 'American' from our title as soon as may be; and then 'Zionist,' and then 'Unit'—so transforming a purely American undertaking into a Palestinian Jewish Medical Department."[43]

At first, in Palestine, Szold was shocked by the disorganization of the Yishuv: "I love order," Szold wrote on April 27, 1921. "Disorder nauseates me. And they [Zionist settlers in Palestine] are systemless. They hate efficiency— almost because it is efficient."[44] Once in Palestine, Szold administered an ever-expanding network of Hadassah-funded health facilities and social welfare programs. These included the School Luncheons program launched in 1923, which provided both meals and nutrition education to four thousand schoolchildren, and the *Tipat Halav* (Drop of Milk) program, which distributed pasteurized milk to mothers and children.[45]

In a 1923 letter to a Chicago supporter on AZMU letterhead, Szold listed Hadassah's many activities: four hospitals; dispensaries and clinics; laboratories; medical inspection in Jewish schools (fifteen thousand children); sixtysix rural clinics; immigration services in Haifa and Tel Aviv; three child welfare stations; home visiting; outside obstetrical services, and a nurses' training school.[46] The services supplied by Hadassah were, as they had been from the beginning, available to all without religious or national restrictions.

By providing health services on a nondenominational basis, Hadassah's leaders, and its American Progressive supporters like Nathan Straus, hoped to build mutual respect and goodwill between Arabs and Jews in Palestine. Arguing that such egalitarianism was in the best spirit of both the American and Jewish traditions, these supporters were convinced that if Arabs saw concrete benefits—in the form of health and other services—from the Jewish presence in Palestine, they would be less inclined to oppose continued Jewish immigration. Szold herself believed in the possibility of Arab-Jewish coexistence

and, along with Judah Magnes and other Zionists, was involved in two organizations that advocated binationalism in Palestine—first *Brit Shalom*
(Covenant of Peace) and later *Ihud* (Union).[47]

Never complacent, Hadassah's leaders remained very interested in expanding their reach among American Jewish women, and their organization's skillful use of publicity (or as it was called at the time, propaganda) is
evident even in this early period of Hadassah's development. Seligsberg acknowledged that "we were making propaganda in those first years not only
through the spoken but also through the printed word." Further, she explained that as early as 1913, when Hadassah's budget allowed for the hiring
of a third nurse to send to Palestine, they looked for a candidate who had not
only strong nursing and clerical skills, but also some skill in taking photographs: "Photography was stressed not only here but later on again, because
we sorely needed pictures for American propaganda."[48] With this in mind,
Hadassah's Central Committee also made copies of the New York chapter's
large collection of lantern slides depicting Palestinian conditions in order to
make these real-life images available to Hadassah chapters in other parts of
the country.[49]

Propaganda meant not only the promulgation of gripping images of Palestinian life but also the art of persuasion through personal contact between
Hadassah members and other women. The organization's first annual report
shows how much thought was put into the best strategy for holding a parlor
meeting:

> The usual procedure was for the hostess of the occasion to issue written invi-
> tations to her friends, asking them to come to her home on a given afternoon
> to hear an address on Palestine, illustrated by stereopticon views. At these
> gatherings one or more speakers described modern conditions in Palestine and
> made a plea for Zionism. Then with a view to breaking the audience up into
> small groups and promoting informal discussion, refreshments were served. . . .
> Not only do these stereopticon views interest and instruct, but they intensify
> the emotional response of the audience to a presentation of Zionism.

In its first year of parlor meetings and sending speakers to other organizations, Hadassah expounded on Zionism to about two thousand people and recruited 156 regular and 37 associate members.[50] Years later, Alice Seligsberg
recalled that because she wanted to build a broadly based organization, Szold

> from the outset was insistent upon drawing together the women who were not
> Americanized and those others who were far removed in time from their im-

migrant forbears. We were not permitted to have more than one chapter in a city, and that chapter had to include rich and poor, Americanized socially elite and foreign born.[51]

In her account of the early history of the organization, Rose Jacobs asserted that "Hadassah aimed to set a pattern in Jewish women's organizations that would be entirely new. . . . Through its practical projects in Palestine it would aim at a constructive contribution to future political statehood."[52] While this aim now seems unremarkable, it provoked hostility and criticism from many American Zionists at the time.

These critics believed that Hadassah's philanthropic efforts were just a continuation of *halukah* (the charitable almsgiving that supported the community of indigent and pious Jews who lived in the Old Yishuv) under another name. Thus Hadassah was accused of perpetuating the Yishuv's dependent status rather than contributing to the more worthy effort of fighting for political independence, national self-reliance, and state building. Such accusations dogged Hadassah from its inception: as Szold wrote in a letter to the 1921 Hadassah convention in Pittsburgh, the organization was from the first "contemptuously charged with being, not practical,—that would have been kindly censure—but philanthropic, which, from a Zionist point of view, was the last word in malice."[53]

Hadassah also fought to have its work acknowledged as a reflection of women's unique contribution to the Zionist effort. In 1913 the organization declared that "American Jewish womanhood ought to make the establishment of the district visiting nurses system its contribution to the modern development of Palestine."[54] As Szold announced at the annual convention of the World Zionist Organization in 1915: "We go to Palestine equipped as American Jewish women particularly are, with philanthropic and social work, with the purpose of bringing to Palestine the results of American healing art." Szold reiterated that "criticism has been made of the Hadassah movement, that it is a charitable movement. I deny it!"[55] Alice Seligsberg, later Hadassah's national president from 1921 to 1923, mounted a defense in the pages of the official magazine of the ZOA, *The New Palestine*:

Hadassah is creating the nucleus of a national Board of Health. Our Government in Palestine is the Mandate Government.

 . . . What is Hadassah's relation to it and what is the future of Hadassah? It is the future of every private enterprise with a public purpose, to initiate, to set standards and maintain them, and then gradually to be absorbed by the public guardians of common welfare. So began public education, public sanitation, public welfare in every country.[56]

Again, at the Twelfth Zionist Congress (held in Carlsbad, Czechoslovakia, September 1–14, 1921) Hadassah was criticized for its sponsorship of the AZMU. In a letter to a friend, Szold remarked that the suggestion, at the Congress, "that we are doing nothing for the *halutzim* [pioneers] and the working-man, the 'productive' Jewish population, is false." Further, according to Szold, "Some of our critics went to the Congress with the intention of proposing that our hospitals be given up and all our available funds be devoted to the immigrants, the proper charge of the Zionist Organization."[57] To such critics, Szold insisted that Hadassah, alone among American Jewish organizations, "grasped the opportunity offered by the Balfour Declaration and the San Remo Decision, and aimed at by the Basle Platform." Hadassah women, Szold argued, "are working according to a definite plan towards a definite end. There is no talk—there is action, action, action."[58]

The debate over whether public health work should be considered "productive" or "unproductive" was also carried on in the American Zionist press, where the AZMU's Dr. Katznelson criticized what he called the World Zionist Organization's "primitive attitude" for classifying public health work in Palestine as "unproductive." What could be more productive, Katznelson asked, than "expenditures which aim not only at the care of the sick, but essentially at the creation of sanitary and hygienic conditions to enhance the healthy development of the population, and, in our case, to make the pioneering efforts of the restoration of Eretz Israel possible."[59]

Similarly, the AZMU's Dr. Alexander Salkind argued that "the colonization work of the Zionist Organization would have been impossible if Hadassah's work had not gone along hand in hand with it." It was, apparently, a point that needed to be made more than once. Szold told the same magazine curtly: "The medical work is not a relief measure; it is part of the constructive Keren Hayesod [Palestine Foundation Fund] program, and it is a political necessity."[60]

If some criticized Hadassah, many more—both in the United States and in the Yishuv—praised the organization's efforts to bring modern American-style medical facilities and services to Palestine. These endorsements were promptly used by Hadassah in its publicity material and in-house newsletters. When Hadassah was congratulated, however, there was often some ambivalence about whether credit for the organization's achievements was due to American Jews in general or American Jewish women in particular. Judge Julian Mack, for example, credited Hadassah with making "the first distinctive

American Jewish contribution to the land," and Rabbi Stephen S. Wise announced: "As an American Jew and Zionist, I proudly and joyously claim that the victory over curable disease and preventable squalor has been won in part by reason of the heroic service of Hadassah and its American Zionist Medical Unit, a pioneering and constructive achievement of the highest order."[61] The FAZ's Louis Lipsky wrote: "There is women's work to be done in Zionism, which the men cannot do. Hadassah has added color and quality to the Zionist movement."[62] The eminent liberal, American Zionist, and Supreme Court Justice Louis Brandeis was also a loyal supporter and outspoken advocate of the Hadassah organization.[63]

Scholars agree that Szold brought American political and social values to her work in Palestine. But historian Michael Brown argues that "her Americanizing influence on the *yishuv* and the nature of that influence have not been at all adequately considered." He points out that Szold's frames of reference for interpreting political events were derived from her American experience and, in all matters, "the solutions she favored were also American-made." Indeed Brown concludes that Szold's "contributions to [Palestine] were in large measure those of American Progressivism."[64] While Szold took her Progressive views to her Zionist work abroad, her friends and colleagues in American Zionist circles like Brandeis, Wise, and Mack were actively involved in Progressive reform efforts in the United States.

Brandeis has been described as conflating Zionist and Progressive ideals. For Brandeis, writes historian Naomi Cohen, "Zionist ideals meant primarily social reform, and he spoke of the efforts of the Palestinian *halutzim* in the same terms that he used for American reformist ventures."[65] Historian Yonathan Shapiro concurs that "what Brandeis called Jewish ideas were in reality the basic principles of the American progressive movement, even though he claimed that these values were shared by both cultures."[66] Indeed, Brandeis wrote to a friend in 1916 that in his view, Zionism had come to "represent in Jewish life what Progressivism does in general American life." Aware that Jewish support for Zionism might be regarded as unpatriotic, Brandeis hastened to assure the American public that "there is no inconsistency between loyalty to America and loyalty to Jewry. . . . Indeed loyalty to America demands that each American Jew become a Zionist."[67]

Like Brandeis, Mack, a Circuit Court judge, was involved in both the Progressive and the Zionist movements. Mack was instrumental in developing the juvenile court system in the United States and was involved in many Progressive social welfare projects, including the Juvenile Protection Association, the Playground Association, the Society for Social Hygiene, and the Immigrant Protective League. Mack also regarded Zionism and

Americanism as harmonious, rather than competing, ideologies. His vision for the Jewish homeland was one in which "we shall have room only for the best there is in the Jew in the light of the progressive ideals that animate the progressive peoples of the world."[68] Summing up the prevailing sentiment of American Zionists like Brandeis and Mack, Judah Magnes asserted that "this alternative, America or Zion . . . is by no means necessary. For myself I would say: America and Zion. America for the thousands who can live as Jews here, Zion for the thousands who must live as Jews there. . . . Zion is the complement to, the fulfillment of America, not its alternative."[69]

Hadassah's founders certainly saw no incompatibility between their American and their Zionist loyalties. By bringing Progressive maternalist ideas and projects to Palestine, Hadassah members believed that they were bringing the best of American values and skills to help their coreligionists abroad and building a Jewish state that reflected the founding principles of the United States. But many other Zionists were not convinced that Hadassah's methods were the right strategy for achieving Zionist goals. It took many years, much debate, and much lobbying on the part of Hadassah to convince other Zionist organizations that social welfare services were not simply charity but rather as important a part of the state-building effort as land settlement and agricultural schemes.

Hadassah was also caught up in a larger battle within the Zionist movement that culminated in 1920 with the rift between the faction led by Louis Brandeis and that of Chaim Weizmann. Brandeis preferred a cautious program of gradually building up Palestine in an organized way to make it more hospitable to Jewish settlement through encouraging small-scale capitalist enterprise and industrial development. In contrast, Weizmann, the de facto leader of the European Zionists, urged immediate settlement by as many Diaspora Jews as possible, especially the *halutzim*.[70]

While most scholars have described the dispute between Brandeis and Weizmann as stemming from the ideological differences between the American and the European Zionist movements, historian Michael Berkowitz argues rather that "it was a struggle about fundraising and the control of money" in the Zionist movement.[71] Brandeis, like Szold and other prominent American Zionists, was concerned about the lack of financial accountability in both the Yishuv and the Zionist movement and about the Zionist movement's increasingly intense emphasis on fundraising to the exclusion of all other forms of activity.

Brandeis was one of three members of the Reorganization Commission who went to Palestine in November 1920 to evaluate the progress of Zionist work there and to investigate how donated funds were being spent. Their report painted a dismal picture of financial mismanagement, disorganization, and self-serving bureaucracies. Projects were undertaken with more consideration for their propaganda value in further fundraising efforts than for their utility. But Weizmann and his allies in the movement rejected the commission's findings and dismissed the report's call for greater administrative and financial accountability.[72]

Following on the heels of this struggle, the Zionist Organization of America (ZOA) administration, under Louis Lipsky, accused Hadassah of fundraising outside of the authority of Keren Hayesod (the fundraising arm of the WZO). But Hadassah's Central Committee refused to submit to Keren Hayesod, and on July 12, 1921, ZOA told Hadassah that its Central Committee was dissolved. Hadassah protested, the groups negotiated, and the committee was reinstated.[73] This was just one in an ongoing series of battles in Hadassah's larger struggle for autonomy within the American Zionist movement. An agreement made between the ZOA and Hadassah following this dispute allowed Hadassah the independence to continue raising funds for its own projects in Palestine. At its 1921 convention, Hadassah also asked the ZOA to recognize the Hadassah organization "as the sole Zionist agency in America for Zionist work and propaganda among women."[74]

These sorts of struggles for autonomy and control among American Zionist organizations were endemic. According to historian Deborah Lipstadt, Zionist groups "were often characterized by fierce organizational individualism" and frequently "did not wish to relinquish any of their independence to the national organization."[75] Indeed, Hadassah affirmed its right to control the fundraising and financing of its own projects, declaring at its 1921 convention that "Hadassah requires all its energies and efforts for the administration of its own affairs" and that "no outside power shall have the right to prevent their [national officers of Hadassah] functioning."[76] The compromise worked out with the ZOA allowed Hadassah to raise funds solely for its own projects and to control the use of these funds. In return, Hadassah agreed that monies so raised would be recorded as part of Keren Hayesod's budget. A similar dispute was to occur in 1935 when Hadassah took on responsibility for funding Youth Aliyah.

That Hadassah needed the autonomy to control its own projects was always a crucial point for Szold, who declared that she was

of the opinion that women can produce the best results of which they are capable, if they assume a specific responsibility within the frame of the upbuilding program for Palestine . . . for which women will collect the whole budget, in exchange for which service they shall have the right and the duty of laying out and determining the plan and the policy.

Similarly, Szold persistently asserted that the guiding principle of the Hadassah organization was "the psychologic value of a specific task for women."[77] For Hadassah's leaders, organizational integrity, a commitment to principle, and a tightly focused mandate were all vital elements of the organization's success, and its success, in turn, vindicated Hadassah's organizing principles:

> Why a separate women's organization? Be our theories what they may, the facts prove that it works. Many women who would be passive Zionists or no Zionists at all, have been drawn actively into the ranks by the practical work of Hadassah. Hadassah is concrete, definite, unswerving. For ten years it has concentrated on the one task of bringing health to Palestine. That constancy is its ideal, is its spiritual strength. And devotion to its stake in Palestine, fear lest its precious structure fall to pieces in the fierce struggle of politics and personalities, saved Hadassah from disruption when all through the Zionist ranks ran the fire of dissension. Hadassah has kept its members together no matter what were their individual political views. Every penny of every donation collected by Hadassah goes to the medical work in Palestine.[78]

Whether Hadassah was criticized or praised, there seemed to be a consensus in this period (shared by Hadassah members) that the Zionism of women was naturally different in both style and substance from that of men. Accordingly, the Zionism of the Hadassah organization was understood to be qualitatively different from that of other male-dominated American Zionist organizations. "Hadassah is the woman in Zionism," a Hadassah editorial in *The Maccabaean* proclaimed in 1917. "That is our quality and our character. The principles we have laid down for ourselves are the principles of womanliness translated into terms of public service." The editorial continues with a description of the nature of women: "It is true that women are more minutely practical than men, with an eye constantly alert to detail, because they are kept close to the facts of life, birth and bread and shelter and disease." At the same time, however, women are idealists with a "capacity to see large, to see the whole" that enables them to struggle for "the big ideal." The editorial concludes:

> Hadassah therefore in insisting . . . upon our ultimate aim, in holding to the national vision and the big national way of doing things, is acting only the woman's part. So too in constantly dealing with practical details . . . a specific piece of work well done, she is acting only in accordance with her age-long habits, and like all women she is often misunderstood.[79]

While men might be convinced of Zionism through politics or debate, explained Hadassah, women were drawn in through the exercise of their domestic talents:

> To many women Zionism has been brought home through an apparently trivial activity—the sewing circles, which have made hundreds of garments for the children of Palestine. Little by little, as they sat together and plied their needles, the thought of the children who would wear the very dresses or shirts that were taking shape in their hands drew them nearer to the Jewish homeland, and before they knew it sentiment had passed into conviction, and the Basle Platform seemed the one natural and inevitable answer to the Jewish question.[80]

It is clear that the Hadassah organization for many years walked a fine line as it tried to position itself on the side of philanthropy rather than charity, and social work rather than political work. The effort to remain apart from political debate and divisions was essential for Hadassah's survival. Given the constant threats to Hadassah's autonomy, first within the FAZ and later within the ZOA, there was a real danger that unless Hadassah carved out a distinct agenda in Palestine, it might be too easily subsumed by these federations. Having repeatedly battled to retain its independence from the ZOA and keep its own fundraising and project-oriented system alive, Hadassah became politically independent and, within the larger Zionist world, politically astute and effective.

In 1926, Szold formally resigned from the position of Hadassah president, passing the mantle to Irma Lindheim. Nonetheless, Szold was named honorary president of the organization, and continued to have a hands-on role in Hadassah's decision making, policy formation, and administration. In 1927 Szold was asked to be one of three representatives on the Palestine Executive of the World Zionist Organization, a position she held until 1930. Szold's portfolio was Health and Education. Given Szold's continued close relationship with Hadassah, the organization was, in effect, given a voice in the Yishuv's nascent apparatus of self-government.

But despite its important role in the Yishuv and greater popular acceptance of its specialized mandate at home in the United States, Hadassah still faced periodic public criticism from male Zionist leaders like Louis Lipsky, who complained in the Zionist press that

> what was formerly a Jewish women's movement—auxiliary, complementary, aiding and comforting the main stem of the movement—became an organization animated by the sense of women's rights. Like all other women's movements of

this sort, it represented resistance to the domination of men, which resistance was turned into a demand for equality which, as soon as it was attained, became a desire to dominate and control.[81]

Similarly, a Boston Zionist leader cast doubt on Hadassah members' intellectual capacities:

> I do not believe that the membership of Hadassah, by and large, really grasps the implications of the Basle program. It should be kept in mind that a great many members of Hadassah are not Zionists in the usually-accepted sense of the word. They were attracted to Hadassah work by its humanitarian appeal. . . . This type of woman should have been permitted to carry on this work unburdened by the manifold problems of Zionism itself, to whose basic principles many of them would not subscribe if they could comprehend them.[82]

In an address to the delegates at the convention of the Zionist Organization of America in Pittsburgh, Szold reflected on her organization's struggle for recognition and acceptance in the American Zionist movement:

> For all that Hadassah was called the Women's Zionist Organization of America, there had been no warm feeling for Hadassah in the general organization. There had been constant criticism because it was not political enough, or because it was too political—either it didn't think or it thought too independently. Is it possible that we wanted recruits, but we did not want their minds?[83]

In 1930, the administrative committee of the Jewish Agency met in London and decided to begin the process of transferring jurisdiction from the Jewish Agency to the Va'ad Leumi (National Council). The Va'ad Leumi was the executive arm of the elected National Assembly of the Jewish community of Palestine. As Szold explained it, the decision was made "with the intent to place the burden of public welfare work on the Yishub [sic], and to set free the Keren Ha-Yessod [sic] collections primarily for colonization and related purposes."[84]

At the same time, Hadassah prepared for the process of transferring control of its medical services to the local authorities. But when the Hadassah Medical Organization's Dr. Yassky mentioned this inevitability to a representative of the Tel Aviv municipality, wrote Szold, he received what she described as a "characteristic" response. According to Szold, the representative said, "Why this? We are perfectly satisfied with Hadassah! We have no objection to Hadassah." Szold's acid comment on this exchange was: "Such a reply when the constant boast of Tel-Aviv is that it is not a Halukah-taker. Nor is it from anyone except Hadassah. The Yishub [sic], in other words, has a very pleasant relation to Hadassah, a sisterly relation, and sees no reason why Hadassah should not go on forever doing as it has done."[85]

In February 1931, the first session of the third National Assembly adopted a resolution that "places on record its view that the present state of social service work in the Yishub [sic]—lack of adequate social legislation, lack of regulation and co-ordination in social work, lack of communal supervision of the administration of many institutions" made it essential to establish a Department of Social Services as part of the Va'ad Leumi that would "exercise central control over social welfare activities." The department would not itself provide services but would instead serve as "an organ of information, guidance and supervision."[86]

In March 1931, while on a visit to the United States, Szold was elected as one of the seven members of the Va'ad Leumi. Szold returned to Palestine in May 1931 to take up the Social Welfare portfolio. In this position, Szold's role was to help in the transfer of health and education services from the World Zionist Organization to the Va'ad Leumi.[87] Szold took this as an opportunity to begin laying the foundations of a modern national system of social services and to stake a claim for organized Zionist women to take the leading role in this process. Szold set out her ideas in a document titled "The Future of Women's Work for Palestine."

In Palestine, Szold wrote, she confronted "a formless aggregation of public welfare activities, especially social institutions, within which the modern jostles the antiquated." Still very much a product of her Progressive roots, Szold's immediate aim was to organize and rationalize these services and, ultimately, to bring social services in Palestine up to the level of such services in the United States. After pointing out that many of the Yishuv's social service organizations were "organized, maintained, and managed by women," Szold declared: "This is the psychologic moment for the federated Zionist women of the world to decide and announce that they are prepared for an enlarged responsibility." She argued that "the Zionist women of the world have an important part to play in this binding of the Diaspora to Palestine." What sort of Zionist state would these women help to create? Szold envisioned "a Jewish centre whose educational institutions shall rank with the most exalted of the world and be worthy of Jewish tradition; whose hygienic and sanitary habits and health standards shall be in accord with the last word in science; whose social institutions shall be the creations of sociologic insight and justice."[88]

In particular, Szold called for "the organization of family case work . . . as the first step towards the coordination of the existing agencies and institutions"; the extension of preventative medicine and health education and the establishment of a medical center attached to the Hebrew University;

fundraising for educational facilities including those "for the care of the handicapped and defective [sic]" and "for music, for physical training and recreational activities, for vocational training for boys and girls, and [for] the development of arts and crafts."[89]

Szold wrote that Zionist women must prepare themselves for "taking over a larger, a more unified responsibility, of longer term, for the upbuilding of Palestine than they have borne hitherto." She also declared that "the time has come to assign to women and their activities for Palestine an officially defined and accepted place in the Zionist hierarchy and system of work." In an itemized memorandum laying out the process by which her plan could be carried out, Szold specified that she wanted Hadassah to "ask for a recognized official position with reference to the Palestinian activities they are responsible for . . . through an Advisory Council in Palestine."[90]

Underlying these demands was Szold's concern that the American Zionist movement still did not understand both that Hadassah had established a real presence in the Yishuv and its status as the primary provider of essential social services in Palestine. Instead, Hadassah was always subject to being treated as just one more American charitable group. True, said Szold, Hadassah leaders in the United States "at a distance of 6[000]–7000 miles cannot execute details in Palestine. They must depend upon some agency in Palestine itself," but this necessity, argued Szold,

> does not, to my mind, tend to destroy the identity of Hadassah and along with it its ability to carry a specific responsibility (which is the essence of its identity). What does destroy its identity is having to merge itself as a specific collecting agency for its specific purpose with a general Palestine collecting agency such as the U.P.A. [United Palestine Appeal].[91]

The transfer of responsibilities to the Yishuv meant an end to what Szold described as "the evils of absentee management." But she counseled that in order to avoid becoming "pure collection agencies" Zionist women's organizations should participate in "budget-making in which is involved policy-making," and so remain both informed about, and involved in, developments in Palestine. By these means, Szold intended that the women would "achieve intimacy with their interests in Palestine." Women's contributions to Zionist development, moreover, "constitute the bond between the Diaspora and Palestine, which must be strengthened for the sake of both."[92]

These views of the role of women explain Szold's inclination to suggest not only that the Hadassah organization get involved in practical work in Palestine, but also that its first project should be to supply medical help. While

Zionist men were involved with the political side of the state-building effort, the Zionist women of Hadassah would stick to what Szold argued women did best: ministering to women, children, the needy, and the ill. Despite Hadassah's successes in building social welfare programs and institutions in Palestine, other Zionist organizations persistently dismissed such philanthropic work as trivial, as a distraction from the crucial political struggle for statehood, and even as a perpetuation of the charity-dependent status of the Jewish community of nineteenth-century Palestine.

But the idea that social welfare was the province of women, and that social welfare work in Palestine was the particular concern of Zionist women, was not Szold's alone. Other Zionist women's organizations concurred. The London-based Women's International Zionist Organization (WIZO), for example, was the European counterpart of Hadassah with a similar mandate focused on education and social welfare for women and children. In 1922, Szold served as one of the five members of WIZO's Palestine Executive. In a memorandum submitted to the General Council of the World Zionist Organization and to the Administrative Committee of the Jewish Agency for Palestine at their meetings in March and April 1930, WIZO called for recognition of "the importance of women's work for the upbuilding of Palestine and of the necessity of Jewish women participating in this work within the particular sphere of activity suitable to their special qualifications." WIZO also asked for "the inclusion of women representatives in the bodies dealing with those particular branches of activity."[93]

Despite the condescension and criticism from other Zionist organizations, and in the face of the declining fortunes of the American Zionist movement overall, Hadassah itself went from strength to strength. In the interwar period, Hadassah had the largest membership of all the Zionist organizations in the United States. In 1927, for example, Hadassah claimed 34,466 members while the ZOA reported 21,806. In 1928, Hadassah had a budget of $1 million. With the Great Depression, Hadassah's membership began to decline, but it still remained larger than the ZOA until 1946.[94]

After 1931, Szold was immersed in the task of developing and organizing the Yishuv's social services in preparation for the transfer of administrative authority to the Va'ad Leumi. Her horizon expanded beyond Hadassah's Yishuv activities as she suddenly confronted a hodgepodge of often competing services and agencies working in Palestine. Szold observed:

> It is curious that with so many sorts of social service functioning in Palestine . . . there should not have been anywhere provision for ordinary relief. Relief of the destitute is still a matter of hysteria. . . . The needy are driven to

begging. . . . It is the old Lady Bountiful system, based on evanescent emo-
tionalism, and not on justice to the unfortunate. It is pure almsgiving or
complete neglect of elementary human needs. The result is that much
money is spent and little is accomplished.[95]

But the biggest obstacle to Szold's efforts was the Yishuv's poverty. As Szold
wrote: "We of the Vaad [sic] Leumi are caught in a vicious circle—no money,
hence no organization of the local communities, hence no tax levy, hence no
money."[96]

High on Szold's list of priorities was deciding how to deal with the problem of local "juvenile offenders" who were, she observed, "very juvenile and
not offenders at all, but sick, defective, undernourished, mentally and physically starved children." When the British authorities began a crackdown on
these youths, Szold worried that "all that the little wretches need is larger
opportunity for recreation and for education of the hand."[97] Szold's ideas
about the environmental causes of juvenile delinquency were typical of
American Progressive views. In the United States, the development of separate juvenile courts and the use of institutional placements for youth were
two efforts to deal with this problem. Settlement house activists and
women's clubs, along with some of Szold's colleagues and friends in the
American Zionist movement, like Brandeis and Julian Mack, were very involved in these issues. Szold was also aware that an estimated ten thousand
school-age children in Palestine were not receiving an education.[98] Given
the deficit in the Va'ad Leumi's education budget, Szold proposed soliciting
funds from Jewish women's organizations in the United States to support a
stipend fund (twenty-five dollars per pupil for one year of schooling) for students in Palestine.[99]

In a series of reports, Szold continued to develop her ideas about what type
of social services youth and others needed and how to begin laying the
groundwork for a coordinated social welfare system. The situation was complicated. Not only was there disorganization and duplication among the
newer social services but Szold also dealt with the many uncoordinated traditional religious and communal institutions serving the communities of the
Old Yishuv. These institutions included the rabbinate, the Free Loan societies, the burial societies, the orphanages, the religious seminaries, the homes
for the aged, and the like. Each ethnic or religious subgroup was likely to have
its own institutions, which were supported through donations from Jewish
communities abroad. The often secular-inclined *landsmannschaften* groups, set
up by people from a particular European village or locale, operated as mutual
aid societies that helped out those in need who came from the same place.

The religiously based *kollelim* (communities) depended on foreign donations, and shared the proceeds with all members of the *kollel*, whether rich or poor. These donations were often solicited by emissaries sent from Palestine.

Juxtaposed with these traditional methods of social support, commented Szold, "the psychology of life in Palestine has been completely changed by the Zionist movement with its modern implications and aims. Its influence is visible in the more recently formed welfare organizations, which approximate in method and purpose what the Western world endorses in the way of social service."[100] The traditional Jewish systems of relief did not require, as did modern social services in the United States, a "scientific" assessment of the degree and type of an individual or family's problems and needs. It was this more rigorous scrutiny and organization that Szold hoped the newer social services in Palestine might adopt.[101]

A Central Information Bureau was established. Its first task was to compile a register of all the different services and agencies. Help was sought from the Jewish Social Research Bureau in New York to design questionnaires to guide the investigators who would visit all the agencies on the list in order to find out what services each provided. A Palestinian committee was set up as a liaison between the bureau in New York and the Department of Social Services in Palestine. The committee members were Harry Viteles, Dr. M. Hoxter, Dr. A. Katznelson, Judah Magnes, and Helena Hanna Thon. Their first recommendation was that Szold join the committee and that the bureau in New York provide a twelve hundred dollar subsidy to the Va'ad Leumi's Central Information Bureau. Such close ties between the New York organization and the Department of Social Services were also important not only to keep American Jews informed about the urgent need for funding for Palestine's social services but also to facilitate the continued inflow of donations.[102]

While social services in the United States now used the "family casework" model, Szold found that in Palestine, not only were the agencies uncoordinated but

> each agency goes its own way and practically all of them deal with the individual and his need. The family as a unit is considered by none. Yet it is a fact of social service science, confirmed by the experience of the casual observer, that in a multitude of cases of misfortune the ills of the individual are rooted in conditions bound up with the family to which he belongs.

Szold explained that "basing our plan on the experience of social agencies wherever the service is systematically established, basing it, indeed, on common sense, we made it revolve around family welfare work as the central undertaking." Szold concluded that "the Department [of Social Service] knows its duty of mobilizing the facts and the forces that are calculated to influence social legislation." This report was submitted to the February–March session of the National Assembly.[103]

In 1933, Szold reported that the survey conducted by the New York bureau found 445 social service organizations in Palestine. Nonetheless, "families fallen upon evil times had no public agency to turn to." As a result, Szold explained,

> those suddenly stricken by misfortune became the object of house-to-house collections instituted for their benefit by sympathetic members of the community, or, taking matters into their own hands, they carried their applications for loans or for out-and-out help to the houses and shops of the same sympathetic persons. The category of pensioners who, in default of health, unemployment and old age insurance and widows' aid, are recognised as legitimate wards of society, does not exist. Instead there has grown up a multitudinous community of beggars who go from door to door at least once a week, before the Sabbath, or extend their open palms to the Sabbath purchasers at the market on Thursdays, or sit at the Wailing Wall or walk the streets soliciting pennies. In the varied array of social agencies, there was none charged with the problem of the destitute or the troubled family.

The first thing that needed to be done, it appeared, was to establish an inclusive and professional "family welfare institution" that employed the family casework model. Three trained social workers (all women) were found—two of them were trained in Germany and one in England. Szold noted with some surprise that "the volunteer communal workers who had hitherto done the social work of the community were not aware that social work is a profession and that there exist schools and colleges offering academic and practical courses."[104]

On April 1, 1932, the British Mandatory government appointed a probation officer to deal with "male youth offenders." The Va'ad Leumi's Department of Social Services offered to take over the Jewish cases and asked the newly appointed social workers to make the needs of children and youth their priority. Unfortunately, explained Szold, although the Jewish social services were able to investigate juvenile cases and make recommendations to the juvenile courts,

> for lack of the needed institutions and the required means, we find ourselves incapable of executing what we ourselves have proposed. We haven't the

means for a home-placement system enabling removal of a child maladjusted to its parental environment . . . we have no systematic evening classes; we have no buildings with facilities for club work and recreational occupations.[105]

In 1936, the Va'ad Leumi established a fund for a social service purpose in honor of Szold's seventy-fifth birthday and asked her to decide how the money should be spent. Szold asked that the fund be "devoted to the welfare of the child and the youth" and outlined both the problem and her proposed solutions in a document titled *The Cry of the Children of Palestine*. Szold first explored the traumatic impact of immigration on relationships between parents and children:

> The Jewish groups which . . . are catapulted into Palestine from the Asiatic East must make the painful adjustment of static habits and the psychology of a past epoch to advanced modern standards coupled with a hectic progressiveness that brooks no delay. The process hews a wide cleft between parents left behind in the race and the children oblivious of the pangs of adjustment. They, the parents and their children, do not speak the same language; they have different behavior standards; they stand opposed to each other not only with the traditional antagonism of fathers and sons, there is the added virus injected by the total lack of comprehension on the side of the bewildered elders and lack of filial reverence on the side of the youngsters. Parental authority is lost in the shuffle.[106]

The array of social services and institutions devoted to children and youth testified to the fact that the Yishuv was concerned about the welfare of its young, but there was a lack of coordination and concern for professional standards. As a result, there were many serious gaps in service and many children whose needs were not being met. Only an estimated one-third of children completed eight years of elementary education; another one-third left school at the age of eleven or twelve, and many girls of North African or Middle Eastern Jewish origin—called Oriental Jews—received no formal education at all. School fees were too expensive for many poor families, who also often required the small income that their children were able to earn.[107]

A Social Service Conference held in 1934–1935 determined that one way to prevent boys from leaving school early was to provide a system of prevocational manual training "by reason of its promise of a lead straight into practical life."[108] Szold reported that some steps were made in this direction. On another front, efforts to provide recreational programs were seen as a way to counteract the "dangers of the street." Once again, Szold looked to

the recreational and vocational programs developed by the American settlement houses as the relevant model for Palestine:

> A movement is on foot to deepen and extend the settlement idea with the
> view to devising ways and means of counteracting the meretricious pleasures of
> the street and giving content to the long afternoon hours during which the
> schools do not claim their pupils; and related to it the existing Guggenheimer
> Playgrounds are under consideration as the focal points.[109]

Although Szold declared that "the problem of the girl forms the apex of
our subject" and "requires a chapter in itself," she said rather little on the subject. A survey conducted by the *Noar Oved* (Working Youth) organization
found that

> hundreds of girl children from the age of nine up to the time of release through
> an early marriage—a release which often opens the door to a servitude of an
> even worse kind—are engaged for a pittance from seven to seven daily in the
> scrubbing of floors and similar work in homes and public places, without the
> possibility of acquiring elementary schooling.

Like boys, such girls also needed access to vocational training and employment opportunities. The few homes for working girls offered clubs, classes,
lectures, and entertainments for some, but "they still leave the problem of
the protection and the advancement of the young girl unsolved."[110]

While limited progress was made in some of these areas, Szold, echoing an
earlier Progressive motif, argued that "the lacunae in child and youth legislation are so serious and the enforcement of the laws as formulated is so halt-
ing that pioneer work is called for." This meant the immediate establishment
of a compulsory education law; public supervision and coordination and adequate funding of all services dealing with the young; social legislation to en-
trench the rights of children and youth; and, finally, the establishment of a
coordinating body, under the auspices of the Va'ad Leumi, representative of
and with authority over the organizations and institutions dealing with children and youth.[111]

The term "pioneer work" used by Szold in this context meant not only
"groundbreaking" but also that such social welfare work, like the work of
building roads and draining swamps, was part of the Zionist pioneering work
of building a new society. Szold had described the problems and proposed
some solutions. While the Yishuv was still struggling to come up with the
funds to pay for a more comprehensive system of social services, Hadassah—
with its American know-how and money—was there to bridge the gap.

Through its bold social service initiatives, Hadassah had carved out a unique social role for itself in the Yishuv. As long as tensions between Hadassah and the mainstream American Zionist movement remained in check, Hadassah could focus its attention on the work ahead.

Notes

1. Isaac M. Fein, "Baltimore Jews during the Civil War," in *The Jewish Experience in America*, vol. 3, ed. Abraham J. Karp (Waltham, Mass.: American Jewish Historical Society, 1969), 328. See also Henrietta Szold, "Early Zionist Days in Baltimore," *The Maccabaean*, June–July 1917, 256–65.

2. Irving Fineman, *Woman of Valor: The Life of Henrietta Szold, 1860–1945* (New York: Simon & Schuster, 1961), 20. For other descriptions of Szold's early family life, see Joan Dash, *Summoned to Jerusalem: The Life of Henrietta Szold, Founder of Hadassah* (New York: Harper and Row, 1979); Alexandra Lee Levin, *The Szolds of Lombard Street: A Baltimore Family, 1859–1909* (Philadelphia: Jewish Publication Society of America, 1960); Bertha Szold Levin, "Rooms in Our House: Written by Her Sister on the Occasion of Henrietta Szold's 75th Birthday," *Hadassah Newsletter*, December 1945, 10–13; Marvin Lowenthal, *Henrietta Szold: Life and Letters* (New York: Viking, 1942); Rose Zeitlin, *Henrietta Szold: Record of a Life* (New York: Dial, 1952).

3. Benjamin H. Hartogensis, "The Russian Night School of Baltimore," *American Jewish Historical Society* 31 (1928): 225–28; Shulamit S. Nardi, "Henrietta Szold: Reflections on her 25th Yahrzeit," *Hadassah Magazine*, June 1970, 8. See also Lotta Levensohn's tribute to Szold in the *American Jewish Year Book* 47 (1945–1946): 51–70.

4. Dash, *Summoned to Jerusalem*, 15–16.

5. For a discussion of Szold's tenure at the JPS, see Jonathan Sarna, "The Henrietta Szold Era," in *JPS: The Americanization of Jewish Culture, 1888–1998* (Philadelphia: Jewish Publication Society, 1989), 47–94. In her capacity as editor and translator at the JPS, Szold first published English translations of Ha'am in 1904.

6. For more on Herzl's ideas and activities, see Ernst Pawel, *The Labyrinth of Exile: A Life of Theodor Herzl* (New York: Farrar, Straus and Giroux, 1989); Jacques Kornberg, *Theodor Herzl: From Assimilation to Zionism* (Bloomington: Indiana University Press, 1993). For general histories of Zionism, see Walter Laqueur, *A History of Zionism* (New York: Holt, Rinehart and Winston, 1972); Shlomo Avineri, *The Making of Modern Zionism: The Intellectual Origins of the Jewish State* (New York: Basic Books, 1981); David Vital, *Zionism: The Formative Years* (New York: Oxford University Press, 1982).

7. Rafael Medoff and Chaim I. Waxman, *Historical Dictionary of Zionism* (London: Scarecrow, 2000), s.vv. "Herzl, Theodor"; "Basle Program."

8. Paula Hyman and Deborah Dash Moore, eds., *Jewish Women in America: An Historical Encyclopedia* (New York: Routledge, 1997), s.v. "Henrietta Szold" by Michael Brown; Henrietta Szold, "The Internal Jewish Question: National Dissolution or Continued Existence," *The Maccabaean*, November 1901, 58.

9. Henrietta Szold, "The Education of the Jewish Girl," *The Maccabaean*, July 1903, 5, 9.

10. Lotta Levensohn, "Recollections Concerning the Origin and Activities of the Hadassah Women's Zionist Study Group of New York," Jerusalem, January 1967, 1, RG 1/B 2F 17, HWZOA.

11. Lotta Levensohn, "Miss Szold as a Leader of Women," 17 November 1930, 1, RG 1/B 2/F 17, HWZOA.

12. Levensohn, "Recollections," 1.

13. Henrietta Szold to Alice Seligsberg, Milan, 12 December 1909, in Lowenthal, *Life and Letters*, 65; Henrietta Szold to Alice Seligsberg, Jerusalem, 16 November 1909, in Lowenthal, *Life and Letters*, 64; Henrietta Szold to Elvira N. Solis, Milan, 12 December 1909, in Lowenthal, *Life and Letters*, 67.

14. Levensohn, "Recollections," 3.

15. The movement began in England but was soon taken up by Americans. For an analysis of the personalities and ideologies associated with the Settlement House movement in the United States, see Mina Carson, *Settlement Folk: Social Thought and the American Settlement Movement, 1885–1930* (Chicago: University of Chicago Press, 1990). Robin Muncy discusses how some women used the Settlement House movement as a base from which to move into positions of national political influence in her *Creating a Female Dominion in American Reform, 1890–1935* (Oxford: Oxford University Press, 1991). See also Lillian Wald, *The House on Henry Street* (New York: Dover, 1971), 6–8.

16. Wald, *The House on Henry Street*, 6–8.

17. Lillian Wald, *Windows on Henry Street* (Boston: Little, Brown, 1941), 73. In this memoir, Wald wrote that she and Brewster, having begun sending visiting nurses into people's homes, had "defined this service as 'public health nursing'" (72).

18. Wald (1867–1940) is often described as the founder of public health nursing in the United States, and Henry Street Settlement became a center of nursing education for nurses from around the world. See Doris Groshen Daniels, *Always a Sister: The Feminism of Lillian Wald* (New York: Feminist Press at the City University of New York, 1989), 25–26; Karen Buhler-Wilkerson, *False Dawn: The Rise and Decline of Public Health Nursing, 1900–1930* (London: Garland, 1989). For a discussion of Wald's political activism, see Linda Gordon Kuzmack, *Woman's Cause: The Jewish Women's Movement in England and the United States, 1881–1933* (Columbus: Ohio University Press, 1990).

19. "Invitation," 14 February 1912, RG 1/B 2/F 20, HWZOA; Rose Jacobs, "Beginnings of Hadassah," in *Early History of Zionism in America*, ed. Isidore S. Meyer (New York: American Jewish Historical Society, 1958), 32–34. The best sources on the early history of the Hadassah organization are unpublished dissertations: Carol Bosworth Kutscher, "The Early Years of Hadassah, 1912–1921" (Ph.D. diss., Brandeis University, 1976); Naomi Ann Lichtenberg, "Hadassah's Founders and Palestine, 1912–1925: A Quest for Meaning and the Creation of Women's Zionism" (Ph.D. diss., Indiana University, 1996); Mary McCune, "Charity Work as Nation-building:

American Jewish Women and the Crises in Europe and Palestine, 1914–1930" (Ph.D. diss., Ohio State University, 2000); Donald Herbert Miller, "A History of Hadassah, 1912–1935" (Ph.D. diss., New York University, 1968).

20. Rebekah Kohut, "Jewish Women's Organization in the United States," *American Jewish Year Book* 33 (1931): 182. Kohut's remark is an early example of the American Zionist tendency to compare the Zionist pioneers with the pioneers of the American frontier.

21. "Report: The Healing of the Daughter of My People," *The Maccabaean*, May 1913, 135, 138.

22. "Report: The Healing of the Daughter of My People," 135, 138.

23. "Report: The Healing of the Daughter of My People," 135, 138.

24. Alice Seligsberg, "Chronicle of Hadassah: 1912–1914. Part I," *Hadassah News Letter*, February 1937, 4, HWZOA; Jacobs, "Beginnings of Hadassah," 235.

25. Seligsberg, "Chronicle of Hadassah: 1912–1914, Part I," 5; Marlin Levin, *Women of Valor: The Story of Hadassah, 1912–1987*, ed. Yossi Avner (Tel Aviv: Beth Hatefutsoth, The Nahum Goldmann Museum of the Jewish Diaspora, 1987), unpaginated.

26. Alice Seligsberg, "Chronicle of Hadassah: 1912–1914, Part II," *Hadassah Newsletter*, March 1937, 7.

27. Seligsberg, "Chronicle of Hadassah: 1912–1914, Part I," 5, 11.

28. For a discussion of the close personal and ideological ties between Magnes and Szold, see Allon Gal, "Hadassah and the American Jewish Political Tradition," in *An Inventory of Promises: Essays on American Jewish History in Honor of Moses Rishin*, ed. Jeffrey S. Gurock and Marc Lee Raphael (Brooklyn, N.Y.: Carlson, 1995), 89–114; Joan Dash, "Doing Good in Palestine: Magnes and Henrietta Szold," in *Like All the Nations? The Life and Legacy of Judah L. Magnes*, ed. William M. Brinner and Moses Rischin (Albany: State University of New York Press, 1987), 99–111.

29. "Report: The Healing of the Daughter of My People," 137–38.

30. See S. Josephine Baker, *Fighting for Life* (New York: Macmillan, 1939).

31. Gertrude Rosenblatt, "Extracts from the Diaries of Mrs. Bernard A. Rosenblatt of the Years 1911–1914," 15, RG 1/B 2/F 17, HWZOA.

32. "Report of the Proceedings of the First Annual Convention of the Daughters of Zion of America, held in Rochester, N.Y., June 29 and 30, 1914," *The Maccabaean*, July 1914, 10. See also Jacobs, "Beginnings of Hadassah," 237.

33. "Abridged Report of the Central Committee," *Hadassah Bulletin* 12, July 1915, 7.

34. The New York City–born Sampter (1883–1938) was a close friend of Szold and lived for a time in a settlement house on the Lower East Side. She was a prolific writer of propaganda for the Zionist cause. In 1919 she moved to Palestine permanently. For a brief biography, see Hyman and Moore, *Jewish Women in America*, s.v. "Jessie Ethel Sampter" by Baila R. Shargel.

35. Dash, *Summoned to Jerusalem*, 111; "Extracts from Miss Kaplan's Letter," *Hadassah Bulletin* 29, February 1917, 4.

36. *Hadassah Bulletin* 36, October 1917, 1; Gertrude Rosenblatt, "Dear Sister Hadassahs," *Hadassah Bulletin* 6, January 1915, 1; Gertrude Rosenblatt, "Dear Sister Hadassahs," *Hadassah Bulletin* 7, February 1915, 1.

37. Marlin Levin, *It Takes a Dream: The Story of Hadassah* (Jerusalem: Gefen, 1997), 60–61.

38. Editorial, *Hadassah Bulletin* 37, November 1917, 1.

39. See Naomi Shepherd, *Ploughing Sand: British Rule in Palestine, 1917–1948* (London: John Murray, 1999), 27ff; Laqueur, *A History of Zionism*, 446ff; Martin Gilbert, *Israel: A History* (London: Doubleday, 1998), 30ff.

40. For a detailed examination of the early history of the AZMU and especially the clashes between the American head of the AZMU, Dr. Rubinow, and local Palestinian Jews, see Shifra Shvarts and Theodore M. Brown, "Kupat Holim, Dr. Isaac Max Rubinow, and the American Zionist Medical Unit's Experiment to Establish Health Care Services in Palestine, 1918–1923," *Bulletin of the History of Medicine* 72, no. 1 (1998): 28–46.

41. Anna Kaplan, "The First Nine Years," *Hadassah News Letter*, April 1938, 128; Haim Yassky, "Pioneering for Public Health," *Hadassah News Letter*, February 1937, 14; "Hadassah in Palestine," *The New Palestine*, 26 December 1924, 460.

42. Henrietta Szold to Alice Seligsberg, New York, 7 January 1920, in Lowenthal, *Life and Letters*, 119.

43. Levin, *Women of Valor*, unpaginated.

44. Henrietta Szold, 27 April 1921, in Lowenthal, *Life and Letters*, 170.

45. Levin, *Women of Valor*, unpaginated.

46. Henrietta Szold, Jerusalem, to Mrs. Shure, Chicago, 7 March 1923, RG 7/HS/B 10, HWZOA.

47. See Rafael Medoff, *Zionism and the Arabs: An American Jewish Dilemma, 1898–1948* (Westport, Conn.: Praeger, 1997).

48. Seligsberg, "Chronicle of Hadassah: 1912–1914, Part II," 7.

49. *Hadassah Bulletin* 5, December 1914, 3.

50. "The Healing of the Daughter of My People," *The Maccabaean*, May 1913, 135.

51. Alice Seligsberg, "The Miss H. Szold Celebration," December 1935, RG 1/B 2/F 17, HWZOA.

52. Jacobs, "Beginnings of Hadassah," 238. Jacobs served two terms as national president of Hadassah: 1930–1932 and 1934–1937.

53. The "Old Yishuv" is the term for the Jewish community of Palestine that predated Zionist immigration, most of whose members were both pious and impoverished. The term was used during the British Mandate period to refer to the non-Zionist religious Jews of various ethnic communities who lived in Palestine. Henrietta Szold, "Address to the Convention of Hadassah," Jerusalem, 26 October 1921, 5, RG 7/HS/B 18/F 174, HWZOA.

54. "Report: The Healing of the Daughter of My People," *The Maccabaean*, May 1913, 139.

55. "Address of Miss Henrietta Szold, The Joint Opening of the Annual Conventions of the Zionist Organization of America," *The Maccabaean*, July 1915, 6.

56. Alice L. Seligsberg, "Hadassah 1912–1923: A Review of Its Aims and Achievements," *The New Palestine*, 10 March 1922, 149.

57. Henrietta Szold, Jerusalem, 7 October 1921, in Lowenthal, *Life and Letters*, 192.

58. Szold, "Address to the Convention of Hadassah," 5.

59. Dr. A. Katznelson, "Our Health Policy: Palestine's Medical Situation and Its Relation to the Government," *The New Palestine*, 2 December 1927, 452.

60. Dr. Alexander Salkind, "Stamping Out Disease: Hadassah's Work in Palestine, Interview with Dr. Alexander Salkind," *The New Palestine*, 22 August 1924, 129; "Approaching the Goal: An Interview with Henrietta Szold," *The New Palestine*, 11 December 1925, 484. Keren Hayesod was established in 1920 as the fundraising arm of the World Zionist Organization. While Palestine was under the British Mandate, Keren Hayesod financed various aspects of the Yishuv's development including immigration, absorption, education, and housing.

61. Hadassah, the Women's Zionist Organization of America, *What Is Hadassah?* RG 17/B 3, HWZOA.

62. Louis Lipsky, "Hadassah's Anniversary," *The Maccabaean*, February 1917, 145.

63. In 1916, Brandeis helped to set up a fund to provide Szold with an annuity enabling her to devote herself full-time to Zionist work. Melvin I. Urofsky and David W. Levy, eds., *Letters of Louis D. Brandeis*, vol. 5 (Albany: State University of New York Press, 1978), 115.

64. Michael Brown, "Henrietta Szold: Health, Education, and Welfare, American-Style," in *The Israeli-American Connection: Its Roots in the Yishuv, 1914–1945* (Detroit: Wayne State University Press, 1996), 134, 139. See also Michael Brown, "Henrietta Szold's Progressive American Vision of the Yishuv," in *Envisioning Israel: The Changing Ideals and Images of North American Jews*, ed. Allon Gal (Jerusalem: Magnes Press, 1996), 79.

65. Naomi W. Cohen, *American Jews and the Zionist Idea* (New York: Ktav, 1975), 16.

66. Yonathan Shapiro, *Leadership of the American Zionist Organization, 1897–1930* (Urbana, Chicago, London: University of Illinois Press, 1971), 73.

67. Brandeis to Jacob Billikopf, 16 June 1916, quoted in Alpheus Thomas Mason, *Brandeis: A Free Man's Life* (New York: Viking, 1946), 448; Brandeis speech, "The Jewish Problem and How to Solve It," April 1915, quoted in Mason, *Brandeis*, 448.

68. Julian W. Mack, "A Message to the Jews of America from Judge Julian Mack," *The Maccabaean*, September 1918, 261. For a discussion of the relationships between these American Jewish liberals and reformists, see Allon Gal, "Hadassah and the American Jewish Political Tradition." For more details about Mack's work as a reformist and as a Zionist, see Melvin I. Urofsky, *American Zionism from Herzl to the Holocaust* (Lincoln: University of Nebraska Press, 1975), 134ff.

69. Judah Leon Magnes, "The Melting Pot," in *The Zionist Movement: Selected Ideological Sources*, vol. 1, ed. Jonathan Kaplan (Jerusalem: Hebrew University, 1983), 267.

70. The dispute between Brandeis and Weizmann has been well covered in histories of the American Zionist movement. See, for example, Ben Halpern, *A Clash of Heroes: Brandeis, Weizmann, and American Zionism* (Oxford: Oxford University Press, 1987); Shapiro, *Leadership of the American Zionist Organization*. For a brief discussion of the ways in which American Zionism differed from European Zionism, see Melvin I. Urofsky, "Zionism: An American Experience," in *The American Jewish Experience*, ed. Jonathan Sarna (London: Holmes & Meier, 1986), 245–55.

71. Michael Berkowitz, *Western Jewry and the Zionist Project, 1914–1933* (Cambridge: Cambridge University Press, 1997), 74.

72 Berkowitz, *Western Jewry*, 63.

73. Berkowitz, *Western Jewry*, 66.

74. "Resolutions Adopted at Hadassah Convention, 1921," in Aaron S. Klieman and Adrian L. Klieman, eds., *American Zionism: A Documentary History*, vol. 5, *My Brother's Keeper: Fostering Projects in the Jewish National Home*, 213.

75. Deborah Lipstadt, "The History of American Zionist Organizations: An Ideological and Functional Analysis," in *Jewish American Voluntary Organizations*, ed. Michael N. Dobkowski (New York: Greenwood, 1985), 533.

76. "Resolutions Adopted at Hadassah Convention, 1921," in Klieman and Klieman, eds., *American Zionism*, vol. 5, *My Brother's Keeper*, 213.

77. Henrietta Szold, Jerusalem, to the National Board of Hadassah, New York, 23 September 1929, RG 7/HS/F 186b, HWZOA.

78. Jessie Sampter, "Constructive Healing," *The New Palestine*, 10 March 1922, 149.

79. "The Woman in Zionism," *The Maccabaean*, February 1917, 148.

80. "Hadassah in Retrospect and Prospect," *The Maccabaean*, Hadassah Anniversary Number, February 1918, 26.

81. Louis Lipsky, "What Will Hadassah Do?" *The New Palestine*, 8 June 1928, 593; "Some Zionist Fundamentals: The Relations between Hadassah and the Organization; An Interview with Elihu D. Stone," *The New Palestine*, 15 June 1928, 631.

82. "Some Zionist Fundamentals," 631.

83. Henrietta Szold, "Address to the Delegates at the Convention of the Zionist Organization of America at Pittsburgh," 11 June 1928, 4, RG 7/HS/B 18/F 187, HWZOA.

84. The Jewish Agency was created in 1929 in response to the League of Nations' 1922 request for the establishment of a "Jewish agency . . . as a public body for the purpose of advising and cooperating with the administration of Palestine in such economic, social, and other matters as may affect the establishment of the Jewish national home and the interests of the Jewish population in Palestine." The Jewish Agency worked as one with the WZO, and eventually the two bodies formally merged. According to Rafael Medoff and Chaim Waxman, "Although the Manda-

tory government maintained that the Jewish Agency had no governmental authority in Palestine, the agency managed to set up a broad administrative structure and was, in fact, viewed by the Jews of Palestine as their government." See Medoff and Waxman, *Historical Dictionary of Zionism*, s.v. "Jewish Agency"; Henrietta Szold, "The Future of Women's Work for Palestine," 1930, 4, RG 7/HS/B 18/F 189, HWZOA.

85. Henrietta Szold, Jerusalem, to Mrs. Edward Jacobs, New York City, 21 April 1930, RG 7/HS/B 12/F 127, HWZOA.

86. Henrietta Szold, "Modern Palestine Social Service," n.d., RG 7/HS/B 12/F 127, HWZOA.

87. Dash, *Summoned to Jerusalem*, 225.

88. Szold, "The Future of Women's Work for Palestine," 3, 11, 7, 13.

89. Szold, "The Future of Women's Work for Palestine," 16.

90. Szold, "The Future of Women's Work in Palestine (memorandum)," c. 1930, RG 7/HS/B 18/F 189, HWZOA.

91. Szold, "The Future of Women's Work for Palestine," 13, 14, 17.

92. Szold, "The Future of Women's Work for Palestine," 17; Szold, "The Future of Women's Work in Palestine (memorandum)."

93. Urofsky, *American Zionism*, 327.

94. Berkowitz, *Western Jewry*, 188; Urofsky, *American Zionism*, 327.

95. Henrietta Szold to Elvira N. Solis, Jerusalem, 31 July 1931, in Lowenthal, *Life and Letters*, 232.

96. Henrietta Szold, "Department of Social Service, Waad Haleumi of the Keneset Yisrael, Palestine," Jerusalem, January 1932, 8, RG 7/HS/B 12/F 127, HWZOA.

97. Henrietta Szold, Jerusalem, 2–9 June 1932, in Lowenthal, *Life and Letters*, 238–39.

98. Henrietta Szold, Jerusalem, 2 September 1932, in Lowenthal, *Life and Letters*, 240.

99. Henrietta Szold, "Department of Social Service, Waad Haleumi of the Keneset Yisrael, Palestine," 3.

100. For a history of the charity organization movement, see Kathleen Woodroofe, *From Charity to Social Work in England and the United States* (London: Routledge & Kegan Paul, 1968).

101. Henrietta Szold, "Department of Social Service, Waad Haleumi of the Keneset Yisrael, Palestine."

102. Henrietta Szold, "Department of Social Service of the Waad Haleumi," Jerusalem, February 1932, 8, 13, RG 7/HS/B 12/F 127, HWZOA.

103. Henrietta Szold, "Social Service in Palestine," Jerusalem, January 1933, 8–9, RG 7/HS/B 12/F 127, HWZOA.

104. Szold, "Social Service in Palestine," 15.

105. Henrietta Szold, *The Cry of the Children of Palestine*, Jerusalem, 1937, 6, 11–12, RG 1/B 21/F 136. Szold's choice of title echoes Spargo's *The Bitter Cry of the Children*.

106. Szold, *The Cry of the Children of Palestine*, 6.

107. Szold, *The Cry of the Children of Palestine*, 14.
108. Szold, *The Cry of the Children of Palestine*, 13.
109. Szold, *The Cry of the Children of Palestine*, 15.
110. Szold, *The Cry of the Children of Palestine*, 16ff.
111. Szold, *The Cry of the Children of Palestine*, 18ff.

CHAPTER THREE

~

"A Joyful Mother of Children": Child Welfare in the Yishuv

In the opening decades of the twentieth century, women activists and their organizations had a major impact on the development of the modern welfare state in Western countries. In France, Germany, Great Britain, and the United States, say historians Seth Koven and Sonya Michel, women played a significant role in shaping state policies on maternal and child welfare:

> In all four countries, women were usually the first to identify the social welfare needs of mothers and children and respond to them through a wide array of charitable activities. States relied on the initiatives of private-sector, largely female organizations and, in many instances, subsequently took over the funding and management of their welfare programs. Such activities thus constituted an important (but often overlooked) site of public policy and, ultimately, state formation.[1]

Women reformers were able to exert this influence on the creation of policies and programs in the United States and Western Europe precisely because, during this period, social welfare institutions and bureaucracies were in the formative stages. This was certainly the case in Palestine, where the institutions and government departments of a viable state were being organized one by one. Remarkably, in the case of the Yishuv, one woman in particular—Henrietta Szold—was instrumental in piecing together the elements of a modern social welfare system. Szold was able to achieve this not only in her capacity as head of the Hadassah organization but also through her responsibility for creating a department of social welfare, when she was appointed to the executive of the Va'ad Leumi. No single reformer in the United States could claim comparable clout.

In 1914, a year after Hadassah's nurses first arrived in Palestine, there were an estimated sixty thousand Jewish inhabitants out of an estimated total population of just under seven hundred thousand people.[2] The country was still a province of the Ottoman Empire and was on the verge of entering the First World War. There were a few hospitals and schools, run by Western charitable or missionary organizations. Some of the Jewish residents of Palestine were deeply religious and had been there for generations. This impoverished community, known as the "Old Yishuv," subsisted on a low-level economy and charitable donations (halukah) from their coreligionists abroad. More recent immigrants, often more secular and nationalist in outlook, were little better off: they too were dependent on money from abroad.

A census done by the Palestine Zionist Office for the period from 1916 to 1918 shows the ethnic breakdown of the Jewish population at just over thirty-three thousand Ashkenazim and a combined Sephardic and Oriental population of almost twenty-three thousand. Until restrictions on Jewish immigration were imposed later, during the Second World War, the Jewish population of Palestine was continually augmented by the yearly arrival of thousands of new immigrants; at the same time, the Arab population grew steadily as a result of a higher birthrate.[3]

Medical experts and visitors to Palestine alike commonly decried the lack of basic sanitation measures and the scandalously poor level of public health. Both Jews and Arabs suffered from high rates of infant mortality, infectious diseases, malnourishment, and poverty. Chronic malaria was a problem for all, punctuated by periodic outbreaks of smallpox, rabies, and even bubonic plague. Health services were inadequately provided by a patchwork of missionary hospitals, philanthropic organizations, and costly private clinics.[4]

As Mandatory authority over Palestine after World War I, Britain was reluctant to invest in developing the civic infrastructure but preferred Arabs and Jews alike to pay for and provide their own services and institutions.[5] As a result, for the Yishuv, the 1920s and 1930s were the formative decades during which the institutions and political machinery of later statehood developed. In the Jewish community, funding came from communal self-taxation as well as from the World Zionist Organization and, after its creation in 1929, the Jewish Agency. Many of the Yishuv's services were provided and funded by voluntary organizations, some of which, like Hadassah, were Diaspora based and funded. Contemporary observers were impressed by the extent of women's involvement in Palestine's social welfare services:

The striking fact in these various and not only useful, but necessary institutions is that they are run by women. Of course men collaborate with them as doctors and assistants, but the idea and the execution come from the women. Far from politics, they accomplish their real feminine duty by helping the unhappy, the needy, the abandoned and the children. It's in their tradition, but it's also quite new, because it has in no other place in the world, been done to that extent, and organized so well by women alone.[6]

Hadassah took a leading role in creating the major elements of a viable social welfare system in the Yishuv: hospitals, medical care, social services, and child welfare programs—often with American-trained staff. With justification, by 1926, the organization was able to say that "no other women's organization in the world holds the position of responsibility for the public health of an entire country as does Hadassah."[7] Indeed, the 1928 report of the Joint Palestine Survey Commission recommended that the Hadassah Medical Organization reconstitute itself as the Department of Health of the Zionist Executive.[8]

With a growing network of hospitals, health clinics, schools, trade unions, and representative political organizations, the Yishuv had the basic structures of self-government already in place decades before self-government was actually achieved. Thus, by abdicating its authority in the social service and institutional area to others, the British inadvertently encouraged the creation of the autonomous, well-organized communal infrastructure and political system of the Yishuv that would allow Palestine's Jewish community to fight successfully for independence from Britain.

Hadassah women, like Progressive women in general, explained their social welfare work by resorting to the nineteenth-century idea of separate spheres for men and women, with the domestic sphere reserved, of course, for women. This, Progressive women asserted, was the basis of their public activism. Such women often justified their involvement in public policy formation and administration by using what historians now characterize as "maternalistic" rhetoric: they claimed that the maternal, domestic role of women gave them both a particular reserve of expertise and a specific realm of social responsibility; that is, women were best able (and most obligated) to look after the needs of other women and children. Such maternalist ideas exerted an influence on women—and guided their choice of projects—across North America and Western Europe. In the United States, says historian Molly Ladd-Taylor, "motherhood was the central organizing principle of Progressive-era politics. Although it was also a unifying theme for a wide array of voluntary associations in the nineteenth century, between 1890 and 1920 it became an overtly political concern, inextricably tied to state-building and public policy."[9] Hadassah was no exception; the Jewish women's organization relied on the same maternalist rhetoric to explain that its social welfare mandate in Palestine was an inevitable extension of women's domestic concerns to the world outside the home. As Hadassah's Irma Lindheim, for example, put it:

> The Hadassah Medical Organization had, for its starting point, the deceptively simple premise that good health, for her family, and her community, is every woman's job. . . . Henrietta Szold knew well that women will best respond to the need for action when the cause touches their personal experience. As Hadassah women cared for the health and well-being of their families, so could they not be welded into a force to care for the health and well-being of the larger family, their people?[10]

The broader Zionist movement was inclined to share this view of women's expanding social role. An editorial in the Zionist magazine *The New Palestine*, for example, judged Hadassah's mandate highly appropriate for its all-female membership:

> It is peculiarly a women's organization, not simply by membership, but equally in spirit, for it has undertaken tasks which are properly associated with the best inherent abilities of women. The hospital work, the promotion of child welfare, the training of nurses, the education of the Jewish mother—all these were well and wisely chosen as within its province.[11]

Maternalist reformers in the United States were generally drawn from among more urban, middle-class, well-educated women with the time and resources to get involved in benevolent or voluntary organizations. They usually focused on helping poor and immigrant women in the urban slums. Reformers based in the Settlement House movement began with grassroots neighborhood work among the urban poor. They also set their sights on larger social change through lobbying for protective legislation or social welfare programs aimed at assisting women and children.[12]

What such American activists did at home, Hadassah did abroad. In Palestine, these American Jewish women taught the poor and immigrant women of the Yishuv modern methods of nutrition, housekeeping, hygiene, and child rearing. This instruction was based on the scientific ideas of the day, but it also reflected middle-class, moralistic, mainstream American values about how families should be organized, how husbands and wives should treat one another, how children should be raised, and what constituted a proper standard of housekeeping. As they struggled to bring the latest scientific knowledge to Palestine, Hadassah's nurses and infant welfare workers also "fought tooth and nail the superstition of the evil eye, the fetich [sic] of neighborly advice and faith in magic cures."[13]

While sharing many of the same social goals as other American women's organizations, Hadassah brought an additional, Zionist cast to its maternalist ideology. Hence, Zionist women were responsible not only for all Jewish children, but also, by extension, for the welfare of the entire Jewish people and, in particular, for the nurturing and "upbuilding" of the Jewish state-in-the-making. As a Hadassah editorial explained in 1918: "It is the woman's part in constructive national work that Hadassah seeks to stress—the mother-tasks."[14] On Hadassah's fifteenth anniversary, Irma Lindheim wrote that "Hadassah appealed to the mother instinct of the Jewish women of America, and they brought to their work a mother's love and a mother's responsibility."[15]

Hadassah publicity brochures and newsletters often described the organization as the mother of the Yishuv's children, as evidenced by titles such as *Hadassah Mothers the Children of Erez-Israel* and "Hadassah the Godmother of the Little Pioneers in Palestine."[16] Similarly, the *Hadassah Bulletin*, describing the clothes that Hadassah members sewed by hand to donate to the Yishuv, wrote: "The garments that have been sent to us give evidence of the love and affection that a Jewish mother or a Jewish sister would give to the baby clothes made for her own flesh and blood. This was to be expected, for surely the babes of Palestine are our babes."[17]

Hadassah's priority was to improve health and living conditions among women and children in the Yishuv. After the end of World War I, Hadassah began to expand its conception of health care beyond delivery of straightforward medical assistance. With thousands of immigrants constantly pouring into Palestine from a multitude of countries, Hadassah took upon itself the daunting task of trying to inculcate modern, Western ideas of health and preventive medicine. Within a few years of its arrival in Palestine, determined to build a modern medical system, the Hadassah organization was clearly operating a broadly defined American-style public health campaign. Proudly, Hadassah declared that "in the hearts of the Palestinian population. . . . [o]ur name has become identified with sanitary advance and popular education in hygienic living."[18]

In June 1921, a Mother and Infant Welfare Station was opened in Jerusalem to provide pasteurized milk and medical examinations. Emphasizing the role of education in preventive medicine, Hadassah explained to its American donors that

> the purpose of our Infant Welfare centres is to keep well babies well, and to make available to all mothers knowledge of the way to prevent needless sickness. Primarily an educational institution providing advice and teaching for mothers in the care and management of infants and little children, with a view to maintaining them in good health. Our task here consists largely in overcoming ignorance and prejudice.[19]

The infant welfare nurses tried to "encourage and prolong breast feeding" and, when this was not possible, ensure a supply of clean pasteurized milk. The nurses interviewed new mothers, examined and weighed babies, gave lectures and talks, and made follow-up visits to women in their homes. There, they ensured that the doctors' instructions were followed and that the women were properly clothing, feeding, and caring for their babies. In general, the infant welfare station was meant to be "a place where mothers will come with their troubles and receive sympathetic intelligent advice" from trained nurses.[20] Hadassah opened its twenty-first infant welfare station in 1929.[21]

In 1922, through the *Tipat Halav* (Drop of Milk) program, donkeys were used to deliver pasteurized milk in buckets labeled in Hebrew, Arabic, and English.[22] Launched in 1923, the School Luncheons program was by 1928 providing hot meals and nutrition education to fifteen hundred schoolchildren, many of whom suffered from malnutrition. Beginning in 1925, with the assistance of the Guggenheimer Playground Fund, Hadassah organized the construction of outdoor playgrounds so that both Arab and Jewish children might have a safe space for recreation.[23]

That medical work would expand in these directions was perhaps inevitable given the poor living conditions of the Yishuv's Jewish community. If the need was Palestinian, the delivery model was very American. In large American cities of the same period, visiting nurses who lived in settlement houses while working in the urban slum neighborhoods of the United States also offered a range of assistance outside the scope of conventional medical care. Indeed, as historian Mina Carson explains, Lillian Wald believed that the Henry Street Settlement nurses "must address not just the family's physical ills but also its social and economic circumstances. The nurses placed children in school and sometimes foster care, helped men find work, and put their patients in touch with philanthropies to meet their special needs."[24] Similarly, a Hadassah nurse, said the organization, "is much more than a nurse and a midwife. She is a psychologist, a teacher, a family counsellor, often family arbiter; she is the bearer of a better life."[25]

In both situations—the urban slums of American cities and the impoverished neighborhoods of Jerusalem—the press of dire circumstances, a genuine desire to help, and close proximity to the problem all contributed to the nurses' willingness to embrace an expansive notion of health care that encouraged forays into social welfare projects. But a new appreciation of the environmental—meaning, in this case, social and economic—causes of poor health was also a major contributing factor. Whereas the charity workers and "friendly visitors" of an earlier era blamed poverty on defects of character, the American-trained nurses and social workers of the 1920s were influenced by modern social thought, which drew links between poverty, lack of education, and poor health.

Hadassah nurses attributed the high infant mortality rate and poor health of surviving children to parental ignorance of the latest scientific and medical findings. And so, with missionary zeal, and more than a touch of class and ethnic superiority, Hadassah nurses taught Palestinian women "that physical motherhood brings no instinctive knowledge of infant care, and that superstitions—East European or West Asian—are no substitute for knowledge. And so, bearing and burying a baby every year or two is no longer accepted as the immutable order of things by the mothers whom Hadassah has reached."[26] Indeed, it seems that Hadassah regarded unenlightened Palestinian parents as a danger to their children's well-being. And just as children were threatened by their parents' ignorance and superstition, Palestinian mothers also needed to be protected from the hazardous folk advice furnished by their female relatives and neighbors, as this description of a session at an infant welfare station shows:

> "And don't take advice from your mothers or mothers-in-law," cautions the irreverent nurse in a parting shot. "Come and ask us your questions." The nurse knows well whereof she speaks. For a Palestinian baby who has not taken the forethought to choose intelligent parents, will need all a cat's nine lives. Else he will not escape the superstitions of his grandmothers and sundry female relatives whose chief title to run his affairs derives from the number of children they have borne—and lost.[27]

By dint of such educational efforts, Hadassah aimed to liberate Palestinian women, both Jewish and Arab, from what one infant welfare nurse described as the "superstitions and foolish customs" that enslaved them.[28] "The atmosphere is happily changing," the caption under a photo of Arab women waiting at a health clinic explains, "and the Arab woman looking to Hadassah is accepting science as a guide to health and healthful living."[29] In this way, Hadassah presented Palestinian women, Jews and Arabs, with a new version of motherhood based on science rather than superstition, and modeled on American values rather than traditional folk customs. Scientific knowledge, delivered by American (and American-trained) professionals, would substitute for shared female and communal knowledge. The Palestinian woman was, in effect, being mothered by Hadassah, for the Hadassah nurse "is the symbol of that motherhood which is being winged to Palestine from the thousands of interested Hadassah mothers in America today."[30]

Always anticipating criticism that Hadassah's infant welfare work was not, in Zionist terms, "productive," Jessie Sampter argued in the pages of *The New Palestine* that better babies made for better nation building: "Our babies are beginning to get a fair deal, and we who are perhaps too keenly conscious of the shortcomings and weaknesses of the present generation in our land, are looking forward hopefully to what a generation of healthy-minded, healthy-bodied Palestinian babies may do to save us."[31] A similar argument was made in a 1923 Hadassah fundraising pamphlet: "The greatest hope is that American Jewish women who know what Infant Care has meant in the United States wherever it has been introduced, will realize that for Palestine, Infant Care means strong healthy builders of the homeland."[32] Here, of course, the authors of the Hadassah pamphlet assume that American Jewish women not only would recognize the parallels between the public health campaign in Palestine and similar efforts in the United States but would understand the relationship between healthier infants and successful nation building: today's sturdy child is tomorrow's hardy pioneer. In this way, Hadassah tried to bolster its claim that infant welfare work was part of the productive, modern, pioneering Zionist agenda.

From the middle of the nineteenth century onward, American social workers were appalled by the high rate of infant mortality among the urban poor and particularly among the immigrant urban poor. Having observed the crowded and unsanitary conditions that obtained in the tenement housing of urban slums, the social reformers concluded that both maternal education and improvements in living conditions were the necessary basis for reducing infant mortality rates. Given that the problem was worst among immigrants, it was perhaps inevitable that the problem of infant mortality was also thought to be connected to ethnic habits, customs, and even heredity.

In the 1890s, after statistics demonstrated that digestive and nutritional disorders were the primary cause of infant mortality, the provision of clean milk became a priority for the public health movement. Reformers prevailed upon philanthropists to fund the establishment of milk stations to provide clean milk for free or at minimal cost to poor mothers. In 1893, philanthropist Nathan Straus (who later supported many of Hadassah's public health ventures in Palestine) funded one of the first public milk stations in the United States, which was set up in New York's Lower East Side neighborhood.[33]

Straus (1848–1931) was a very generous philanthropist with an inventive streak and an abiding interest in public health. Convinced that unpasteurized milk caused the devastatingly high rates of infant mortality in New York City, Straus dedicated much of his time and funds to providing clean milk to poor mothers and children. By 1917 Straus maintained eighteen milk stations in New York City that provided pasteurized "ready-to-drink" milk to mothers with infants for free or at a nominal cost. He also funded workrooms, soup kitchens, and a "preventorium" for pretubercular children and invented an apparatus for the home pasteurization of infant milk bottles. Eventually the milk stations expanded their mandate and services to dealing with overall infant welfare.

Straus's work with milk pasteurization and infant health was a model for the sort of services Szold wanted Hadassah to launch in the Yishuv. Fortunately, Straus already had one charitable commitment in Palestine: a Jerusalem soup kitchen that he opened in 1904. When Straus learned about Hadassah's plan to send American nurses to Jerusalem, he readily offered to pay the initial costs of setting up the nurses' settlement.

The wealthy philanthropist and the women's organization saw eye to eye on most issues. Both agreed on the connection between sanitation, hygiene, nutrition, and public health. Both made preventive health care, as well as maternity and child care, their priorities. Straus also shared Hadassah's commitment to nonsectarianism and insisted that the health services he funded in Palestine be accessible to Muslims, Christians, and Jews. A partnership was not long in emerging.

Straus's philanthropic work in Palestine received a lot of attention in the mainstream American press as well as in the Zionist press. In 1913, for example, the *New York Times* devoted a full-page spread to his plans, explaining that Straus, described as one of New York City's "merchant princes," was quitting business in order to devote himself to charity. In Palestine, said the newspaper, Straus would "try by wise and thorough-going works of modern sanitation and hygiene to heal the sick among his people and those who live among and around them." The *Times* mentioned that Straus would fund the "Daughters of Zion" nurses for the first four months of their venture. "But Mr. Straus's chief work in Palestine," noted the article, "and that which he plans to extend throughout the whole country, was the establishment of a Health Board at Haifa, modeled simply after the Health Bureau of New York City."[34]

Over the years, Hadassah was able to turn to Straus repeatedly to fund their health care projects and he obliged, giving him a distinct role as Hadassah's greatest benefactor. The establishment of the Straus Health Centers in Jerusalem and Tel Aviv in the 1920s were the culmination of Straus's dream of establishing the institutional basis for a centralized, modern system of preventive medicine and public health in the Jewish homeland. It is estimated that Straus gave about two million dollars to Zionist causes by the time of his death in 1931.[35]

If much of Hadassah's money was American, so too was its model of social activism. Among the Progressive movement's achievements was the development of child welfare programs. "Child-saving" was the term used by Progressive reformers for their efforts to rescue children from poverty, disease, and mistreatment. Writers like John Spargo and photojournalists like Jacob Riis and Lewis Hine all raised public awareness through documenting, in writing and photographs, the terrible working and living conditions of many slum children. Other activists, notably many of the women associated with the Settlement House movement, pushed for government to intervene on behalf of the weakest members of society—women and children. Growing public awareness and concern about neglected, underprivileged, and dependent children led to new policies and legislation laying out society's obligations toward children. Out of these reform efforts emerged a wealth of new laws covering child labor, compulsory school attendance, juvenile courts to keep young offenders out of the criminal justice system for adults, and pensions for widowed mothers.

Some American reformers lobbying for new protective legislation charged that the government demonstrated more interest in collecting information about the boll weevil (a pest that attacked cotton crops) than about the nation's children. There was an irony in this charge given that it was not unusual in this period for reformers to argue on behalf of child welfare as though children were, like cotton, one more crop or natural resource; as a 1914 handbook called *Health Work in the Schools* put it: "The children of to-day must be viewed as the raw material of a new State; the schools as the nursery of the Nation. To conserve this raw material is as logical a function of the State as to conserve the natural resources of coal, iron, and water power."[36]

In 1912, reformers succeeded in establishing a new federal government office—the Children's Bureau—to oversee youth work. Ladd-Taylor describes this as the moment when the "maternalists entered government." Reformers like Wald and Florence Kelley pressed the Children's Bureau to serve as a clearinghouse for the collection of data on preventable diseases, infant mortality, juvenile delinquency, and the like. The Children's Bureau also published and distributed child care guides for parents; these pamphlets "railed against 'superstition' and asserted the authority of modern science over tradition."[37]

Concurrent with the child-saving movement was also a gradual professionalization of social work. As volunteer charity workers embraced "scientific" techniques, they also sought to organize the provision of charity along more efficient and scientific lines. This included casework as a means of keeping track of charity recipients and ensuring that assistance was tailored to individual—or an individual family's—needs. There was also a drive to coordinate and systematize the work of different welfare organizations. As welfare work became better organized, welfare workers sought the "professional" training that would provide them with recognized credentials and expertise.[38] And if social workers needed professional training, all agreed, so women and mothers also needed training in the new scientific techniques of child raising.[39]

Changing ideas about the causes of poverty paralleled this rise of the professional social worker. Poverty was previously seen by many as a personal failing. The poor were held responsible for their own misfortune; they were seen as paupers whose poverty was hereditary or arose from character flaws and whose dependence was reinforced, if not created, by charity. Now the poor increasingly came to be regarded as victims of larger social problems deserving government assistance and protection. All these new ideas and methods were adopted by Hadassah and exported to Palestine, where the organization launched a succession of Progressive-style social programs aimed at ameliorating child poverty and related social ills. Like their colleagues working in the United States, Hadassah's reformers in Palestine hoped to organize and run programs for which the Zionist government of a new state would eventually assume both financial and administrative responsibility.

Because settlement house workers in the United States dealt mostly with inner-city immigrant women and their children, they believed it was their role to push women to Americanize their child-raising practices. Maternal education was seen as the key to improved health for families and a necessary element of the modernization and Americanization of immigrants. As historian Richard A. Meckel explains: "Convinced that immigrant life would improve significantly with the adoption of the scientific management of the home, [social workers] sought to instruct immigrant mothers in nutritious cooking, domestic sanitation, proper ventilation, and the hygienic care and feeding of infants and children."[40] Thus did health education and Americanization become intertwined.

Similarly, Hadassah also saw itself as an agent of modernization and West-ernization that brought uplift and civilization to immigrants. The nonimmi-grant population of the Yishuv—Arabs and Jews alike—were also regarded as in need of educating and civilizing. For Hadassah, "Western" and "Ameri-can" were synonymous. Even without the rhetoric of "Americanization," Hadassah's nurses and other workers, as Americans, delivered American ideas and practices to the people of the Yishuv. American standards were pro-claimed, by Hadassah, to be the highest standards, and reaching them was a laudable goal: "We have brought American ideals of efficiency into the land," wrote Jessie Sampter in 1922; the following year, Rose Jacobs wrote, "Hadassah has gradually introduced into Palestine the highest ideals of nurs-ing . . . acquired by us through our American experience."[41]

American experts in medicine and education were brought to Palestine by Hadassah to offer advice; similarly, with whatever funds were available, Hadassah sent locally trained Palestinians and others to the United States where, it was assumed, they would get the most advanced training in their field. For Szold and her organization, the highest praise was to hear that their trainees were well prepared. Thus, in 1923, after a Palestinian nurse was sent to New York City to learn public health nursing, Szold wrote that

> Miss Shatz of the Henry Street Settlement . . . gave me the greatest comfort anyone could have given me. She told me of the success that had been achieved by our graduate nurse, the product of our Nurses' Training School in Jerusalem, who had been associated with the Henry Street Settlement for sev-eral months, and who had given complete satisfaction there as though she had been trained in one of the old institutions of New York City.[42]

Hadassah's infant welfare services, like its medical services in general, were available not only to Jewish but also to Arab women, both Muslim and Christian. This was a matter of principle for Hadassah, which "followed a policy of active friendliness towards the Arabs," explained Irma Lindheim. "It is our duty to convince the Arabs that Zionism is not the old National-ism but the new brotherhood." Szold was very concerned about Arab-Jewish relations and, reported the *New York Times*, she

> refuses to believe that there is no way for a true neighborly understanding be-tween the two peoples. She thinks that it is imperative for the Zionist leaders to find a modus vivendi with their Arab colleagues. The peoples, too, she says, must be educated in a spirit of friendship. With emphasis, she declares: "The acid test of the Jewish nation and the Zionist movement will be the degree of their ability to find a way of conciliation with the Arabs."[43]

With additional funding from Nathan Straus, Hadassah hired an Arabic-speaking nurse in August 1923. Hadassah got political mileage from these efforts at inclusion, claiming a measurable improvement in relations between Jews and Arabs. Rose Jacobs, for example, wrote that Hadassah's medical work had exerted "a great influence in overcoming the prejudices of our Semitic neighbors in Palestine."[44] Similarly, a reception held in New York City in 1923 in honor of the medical unit's Dr. Rubinow featured a guest speaker who gushed:

> I had understood that the work of the Zionist Medical Unit was exclusive, but I was surprised and gratified to learn that this is not so. How splendid, and how characteristic of an organization nurtured in America! It is comparatively easy to be kind to people we like, but to be kind to people, regardless of personal prejudice, to be just as ready to love persons, unlovable and disliked, that is hard. And that is what the Zionist Medical Organization is doing.[45]

Ultimately, Hadassah judged the public health campaign a success on both practical and moral grounds:

> The department has done more than the tangible work of improving the health conditions under which children are born and bred in Palestine. It has accomplished the moral task of elevating an outlook, of bringing about an acceptance of scientific methods in treatment and prevention and clean physical surroundings as absolute essentials in the rearing of children.[46]

Hadassah's interest in maternity care burgeoned into a concern for child welfare. If Zionist women were responsible for Jewish children in general, they must bear a particular responsibility for parentless children. As early as 1917, Hadassah's Alice Seligsberg began raising the issue of the large numbers of Jewish war orphans in Europe and the obligation of American Jews to take responsibility for their care, arguing that "we must assume the largest part of the burden of providing for our own people."[47] This was an issue of special interest to Seligsberg, a child welfare worker who founded and ran Fellowship House, a social and placement center for orphans in New York City.[48]

Seligsberg discussed the options at length, dwelling particularly on the merits of orphan asylums compared to placement of children in private foster homes. This debate would be taken up later with more vigor once Hadassah, through its support for Youth Aliyah, was confronted with the need to look after large numbers of children and youth. An editorial in *The Maccabaean* took up the issue, which it described as "an urgent national problem," and proclaimed: "The pitiable little war orphans are the wards of the nation, of the whole Jewish people."[49]

In April 1918, a Zionist Commission sent by the American and English Jewish communities went to Palestine to investigate the situation of war widows and orphaned children. In 1919, the American Jewish Joint Distribution Committee asked Seligsberg to be executive director of the newly formed Palestine Orphan Committee.[50] Seligsberg directed the work of this committee for its first year. The committee was responsible for just over four thousand children and tried to provide either foster placements or subsidies to allow the children to remain with relatives.[51]

In 1921, a brief article in *The New Palestine* reported that along with their support for medical work, Hadassah chapters were also "actively devoting themselves to . . . the orphans of Palestine." City by city, individual Hadassah chapters raised funds to support children: "Detroit raised enough money to adopt four orphans, Newark adopted an orphan as a result of a talk by Miss Alice L. Seligsberg, and St. Louis adopted two orphans already and is raising money for more."[52] Jessie Sampter, from her home in Palestine, published an open letter in the *Hadassah News Letter* pleading with Hadassah members to make "personal contacts with Palestinian orphans" and describing how she adopted a little girl rescued by the Hadassah nurses.[53]

For Seligsberg, the orphan project also provided an opportunity to address the question of whether Hadassah was willing to take on other large-scale child care projects. Indeed, she suggested: "Perhaps our present financial adoption of orphans may carry us on to projects of child-care in Palestine long dreamed of by some Hadassah members."[54] As usual, Hadassah felt obliged to defend its expanding social service mandate against detractors within the male-dominated American Zionist leadership: "Can there be a question that child-caring is of the essence of Zionist work in Palestine?" Szold wrote in a 1921 "Letter from Palestine" printed in *The New Palestine*. "Let us devote ourselves to motherhood work. Our first aim was 'The Healing of the Daughter of Our People,' let our second aim be to make our land 'A Joyful Mother of Children.'"[55] These "Letters from Palestine" were a regular feature in the Hadassah newsletters. Presented as letters from Szold to Hadassah members at large, Szold used them as a forum to discuss at length some aspect of the social, political, or economic situation of the Yishuv.

At Hadassah's ninth annual convention, in Baltimore in 1923, the organization listed among contributions by its members the many items of clothing produced by 445 sewing circles under the auspices of the Palestine Supplies Department (also known as the Palestine Supplies Bureau) and sent to 2,800 orphans and needy Jewish institutions. With the motto "Palestine

Must Be Built on a Sanitary Foundation," the Palestine Supplies Department offered Jewish women a chance to "serve Palestine with the labor of your hands," and brochures explained that the sewing groups "afford to Jewish women participation in the upbuilding of the National Homeland by actual, personal service, as valuable as money."[56] As part of Hadassah's commitment to self-education, one woman at each sewing circle was appointed to read aloud from Zionist texts while the others sewed. Along with the gratification at providing necessities to those who had so little, sewing work was also felt to offer a beneficial, even transformative, effect on the women involved: "Through the Sewing Circles, Jewish women are brought into direct and immediate contact with the Builders of Zion. Through their work in the Sewing Circles they become transported to the Land of Our Hope, and for the time being, they are themselves transformed into Chalutzoth [sic]." By 1939, Hadassah claimed that ten thousand volunteers across the United States working for the department sent sixty-five thousand articles, many of them hand sewn, to Palestine each year.[57]

In 1922, Hadassah was approached by an American recently returned from a visit to the Yishuv, Dr. Maurice Harris. He was shocked by the extent of malnutrition he saw among Jewish schoolchildren there, and Hadassah accepted his offer to organize the Palestine Penny Luncheons Fund Committee to solicit penny donations from American Jewish schoolchildren to fund school lunches for children in the Yishuv. The Penny Luncheons scheme was introduced by Hadassah as "an educational project for American children," and, indeed, Harris claimed that his primary interest was in "urging a closer fraternal bond" between American Jewish children and Palestinian Jewish children. Ideally, American children would subsidize the entire budget of this venture. A committee was set up in the United States to organize and administer fundraising and "to stimulate American Jewish children to be interested in Palestine, by appealing to them two or three times during the year for contributions to the Palestine School Luncheon Fund. In return for their contribution (usually five or ten cents), the children receive stories written in Palestine about the land and its inhabitants."[58]

Articles about the fund in the *Hadassah News Letter* stressed that it should not be regarded as a simple philanthropic venture. Rather, it should be seen as an educational exchange: "The children of Palestine have something to tell American children about themselves and their land. The children of America are serving the children of Palestine by helping them to raise the health and aesthetic standards of living."[59] As American Jewish women were spiritually enriched by their connection to Palestine through their participation in Hadassah, so too "the child who gives to Palestine receives as much as he gives—for he is establishing a new contact with the Jewish people and is broadening his spiritual experience."[60]

In 1928 Hadassah reported that nine schools were serving hot midday meals to their students but that this meant that only fifteen hundred schoolchildren were being fed out of an estimated total of twenty-five thousand children in need. Ever conscious of possible criticism, Hadassah emphasized that the program was educational and "involves no pauperization." Those children who could afford to pay for their meals did so, and others paid only a token amount or were subsidized. One Hadassah writer explained that "no matter how poor the child is, he pays something, even one cent, so that he isn't made to feel he is receiving charity." In case readers did not understand the full import of this point, she added: "The history of pauperism in Palestine is as unpleasant as it is long. All our efforts in our social welfare work must be directed towards counteracting this tendency, which has almost become a habit in Palestine." Similarly, it was also deemed necessary to explain how serving lunch to schoolchildren was a productive part of the national upbuilding program: "Undernourished children cannot grow into a sturdy generation of builders of the new Palestine. Hadassah's health work must be not only reparative, it must be preventive and constructive."[61]

The first penny lunches served in American schools were provided by women's voluntary social organizations in the early 1900s. They were inspired in part by Spargo's research into the effects of malnourishment on children. In 1920, the New York Board of Education took over the responsibility for lunch programs in its schools. In many ways the School Luncheons program was regarded as the linchpin of Hadassah's public health campaign. The program provided not only a daily nutritious meal but also a community lesson in nutrition ("food values") and food preparation. Although children were the primary recipients of the program, they were expected to convey this new information to their parents: "It is through the tiny children that Hadassah is carrying the knowledge of nutrition and dietetics into the homes of men and women, many of whom would still call down the 'evil eye' on any one who broached the subject of vitamins!"[62] Publicity materials stressed that healthy infants and children would grow up to be healthy adults and that "the entire work of reconstruction in Palestine depends first upon the health of the people living and working in the country."[63] An article for the *Hadassah News Letter* claimed the expansion of the lunch program as a victory for American-style scientific efficiency:

> Dietetics always seemed a natural part of efficient America. But to see that it has taken root even in the remote parts of the Old City of Jerusalem was a sur-

prise even to those who knew vaguely that the school systems are taking gigantic strides in Palestine. The fact becomes less surprising when it is remembered that it was an American institution, after all, that introduced dietetics into Palestine—Hadassah, whose efforts for School Luncheons have made possible the transition from haphazard eating to scientific food planning.[64]

Sephardic and Oriental Jewish children were especially singled out as being in need. One Hadassah pamphlet offers "a teacher's first-hand account" of the School Luncheons system. The teacher, who worked in the Sephardic Talmud Torah (religious school) in the Old City of Jerusalem, wrote that most of the Oriental pupils had no choice but to leave school "in the very lowest grades, forced by necessity to earn their own bread." In general, "most of the children are hungry" and malnourished, "underweight, often backward in physical and moral development."[65] Hadassah's School Luncheons program provided the fortunate few recipients with their only full and balanced meal of the day.

In fact, for these children, the School Luncheons program soon expanded beyond the simple provision of midday meals to a full-fledged "domestic science" program. The children who participated learned how to shop for locally grown produce, how to choose a nutritionally balanced menu, how to prepare and cook the food, and then served the meals to their schoolmates. The principal of a school in Haifa wrote to Hadassah's Sophia Berger that through the School Luncheons program, "scores of girls—perhaps for the first time in their lives—saw a clean and dainty Jewish kitchen, food tasty and nourishing because it was prepared according to the rules of dietetics, and a table prettily set, all prepared at low cost."[66]

Yaffa Schlesinger, a sociology professor at Hunter College in New York City, grew up in Jerusalem and attended a girls' school there in the 1930s. She has vivid memories of Hadassah's School Luncheons program: "We had a teacher and her helper. There were huge pots. We had to have our hair covered, we had to make sure our hands were clean. More than once a little girl would drop a huge bowl of soup—we had to learn to cope with that." The girls ate while sitting at long tables "like the Puritans," Schlesinger recalls, from dishes emblazoned with "Daughter of my people," part of Hadassah's motto. Schlesinger recalls this and other Hadassah programs in which she participated with gratitude: "They gave us more than hygiene and nutrition, they gave us a standard of living . . . They didn't just talk about it, but we participated in it, there was an air of festivity about it."[67]

Hadassah articles and publicity pamphlets mentioned that many children, particularly those of Oriental background, had never used knives and forks before. Hadassah's Lotta Levensohn explained that some of the children also had to overcome their aversion to vegetables (which they disdainfully referred to as "grass") as well as learn to recognize the nutritive value of many locally grown but often unfamiliar fruits and vegetables.[68] In a "Letter from Palestine," Szold reported that among the girls eating their midday meal at one school,

> there is a large percentage that had never before sat down on a chair before a table to eat meals. It is an undertaking, thus, that has educational features over above the mere teaching of cooking—good habits and manner, and eventually it will be the means of teaching the food values of the rich variety of cereals and vegetables obtainable in Palestine, which are largely disregarded now, particularly by the new arrivals.[69]

The problem did not start with the children, however. It began with adult ignorance of the basic principles of nutrition. Hadassah worried about the widespread health problems in the Yishuv that resulted. American readers of *The New Palestine*, for example, were warned that "thousands are suffering from malnutrition or ill chosen diet, because they do not realize that the choice of food and the methods of its preparation which may have been more or less suited to life in the Ukraine, Poland, Roumania and Galicia, are not suited to the fundamentally different physical conditions of life in Palestine."[70] Many of the European immigrant women of the Yishuv held fast to their own homestyle foods and food preparation methods. They did not understand the nutritional value of local fruits and vegetables, and they did not know how to prepare these foods. Gerda Arlosoroff-Goldberg explained:

> In household management one almost universally finds a stiff-necked adherence to habits and customs acquired in the former country of residence. . . . There are still many thousands of people in this country who eat, sleep and live in the same way as they used to in Chicago or Warsaw. It is quite clear that such a state of affairs is bound to produce many evils.[71]

Arlosoroff-Goldberg complained about women's "ignorance as to how to prepare and utilize local products" and the prevailing sense "of helplessness in the face of new, unknown and special local conditions." Among the Eastern European *halutzim*, the problem was compounded by a pioneering ideology that prized austerity and toughness. Hortense Levy noted:

> There have been tragic times when the patients who came to Hadassah's doors could not provide themselves with a balanced diet, but all too often it is discovered that they do not understand the relation of food to health. Many of the brave men and women who came in the early days to build up Palestine

wanted to show how they could rise above material things like food. They scoffed at what they called daintiness. They lived on anything that was handy. But their vitality was reduced. Other people came to Palestine not knowing what the eastern countries provide in the way of food.[72]

Clearly, Hadassah had to intervene. Rose Zeitlin argued that "many practices in cooking, both native to the country and imported, have to be discarded or corrected, and new dishes introduced."[73] Hadassah's health center in Jerusalem (officially called the Nathan and Lina Straus Health Center for all Races and Creeds) opened a "model Palestinian kitchen" that was intended to develop into "a practical laboratory for solving the complicated feeding problems of a population not yet adjusted to its new environment."[74]

In addition, Hadassah sent a Miss Bawley from Palestine to America for a year of "intensive training" in dietetics. Bawley returned to Palestine "armed with the most approved American practices" and ready to build a department of dietetics. Bawley taught schoolteachers the principles of nutrition and how to build a classroom lesson around food shopping and preparation. Bawley also worked out of the Straus Health Center training other "native dieticians" who were then sent to rural districts to teach women "scientific kitchen management."[75]

It was difficult to convince adults to change their habits, but schoolchildren were virtually a captive audience. Hadassah's nurses and dieticians fanned out into Palestine's schools teaching children to spread the twin messages of nutrition and sanitation to adults. The School Luncheons program was part of the campaign to change food practices at home, said Hadassah. "One effect of the school luncheons has been to make the children aware of the deficiencies of their home surroundings. Having acquired a knowledge of food values . . . they realize the shortcomings of the meals they receive at home." Under the heading "Teaching Mother How to Cook," Hadassah explained that

> there are many cases where a child has insisted on his mother's coming to school to learn how the cooking teacher prepares the meals which have made her child so critical of the food she herself prepares. And when such a mother comes to school, sees the kitchen and the dining room, she is amazed at the orderliness and cleanliness, and begins to understand why her child is not satisfied with what he gets at home.[76]

Similarly, a 1937 Hadassah pamphlet said:

> Because of what he [the schoolchild] has learned through these lunches, he becomes dissatisfied with badly prepared home meals and insists that his parents

come to school to learn how the teacher has prepared various dishes. This contact with a clean, orderly kitchen is mother's first lesson in household management and often the beginning of a new understanding.[77]

It is not clear whether driving a wedge between parent and child, although welcome from Hadassah's perspective, was intended or not. But as these publicity materials indicate, Hadassah encouraged children to promulgate their health education messages among adults. As Lotta Levensohn explained: "Even the mothers are being educated through the little ones. . . . The child usually wins out, and the entering wedge has been inserted into the household."[78] This strategy was also employed by Hadassah's counterparts in the United States. Historian Elizabeth Ewen, in her account of immigrant women in New York during this period, describes how settlement house workers encouraged children to try "to force American customs on their parents." Ewen quotes a social worker who said: "Parents are being criticized as to their mode of cooking and eating, until one desperate mother sent word to me to please tell her where to buy an American cookbook."[79]

Like diet and food preparation, instruction in hygiene and sanitation were important elements of the School Luncheons program and gradually evolved into a broad public health education campaign among schoolchildren. Hadassah nurses took special courses in public welfare work that emphasized prevention and education. They were then sent to inspect school facilities, examine and treat students for illness, and teach students about hygiene. Health clubs were organized for older students, and the nurses also started a "Health Scouts" movement for high school students. The Health Scouts were required to pass a first aid course, ensure that sanitary conditions were maintained in their schools and communities, and give instruction in sanitary methods to younger children. If all these conditions were met, they were entitled to wear the official Health Scout uniform and the "Health Pin," described as "a 'seeing eye' typifying Hygeia keeping an ever-watchful lookout."[80]

An article in the *Hadassah News Letter* explained that through the Health Scouts program, "the child becomes an instrument of bringing health and sanitation into the home." The Health Scouts were also required to take responsibility for inspecting shops, factories, and other facilities beyond the school, helping them to "develop a strong sense of communal responsibility so necessary in a pioneer country."[81] Another Hadassah writer described the "missionary task" of the Health Scouts and explained: "Many an overworked mother at home, and many a bewildered . . . sister has been worried into a realization of personal and communal cleanliness by one of these scouts in the family."[82]

By 1923, through Junior Hadassah, the section for young American Jewish women established in 1920, the organization contributed over thirteen thousand dollars "for the financial adoption of Palestinian orphans" and was "the second largest contributor toward the maintenance of orphans in Palestine" after the Joint Distribution Committee.[83] The newly launched Palestine School Luncheon Fund was able to send over seven hundred dollars to Palestine. In 1926, Szold sent a message to be read to the delegates assembled at the Twelfth Annual Hadassah Convention in Buffalo, New York: "Your commitments to Palestine are now so many and so important," Szold wrote, "that in a moral sense you are yourselves actually in the land."

Given that American Zionists were often criticized by Palestinian and European Zionists for their preference for donating funds rather than promoting *aliyah* (immigration) to the Yishuv, Szold, a rare example of an American who did live in the Yishuv, offered Hadassah supporters pride in their achievements by suggesting that one could also be a *halutz* (pioneer) through philanthropic commitments.[84] By 1926, there were 244 Hadassah chapters in the United States with a total membership of 29,495 doing just that.

But the fact of her being "in the land" was an important point for Szold, as it was for the Zionist movement in general. There was certainly some resentment among Palestinian Jews against American Zionists for their lack of interest in *aliyah*, checkbook Zionism, and absentee control of Palestinian organizations. As Hadassah got increasingly more involved in creating and administering social welfare projects in the Yishuv, Szold became even more determined to ensure that these endeavors would be put under local control and management as soon as possible. If Szold resisted control from New York, she was not above trying to control decision making by the Hadassah administration in New York, where her views carried more weight. On the Palestinian side, in 1931, Szold was able to create the Palestine Council, made up of the small number of Hadassah members who lived in Palestine and could act as a liaison and buffer between the Yishuv and Hadassah in the United States.[85]

There was a lot to administer. Six years after it began, the Palestine School Luncheon Fund had a twelve-thousand-dollar annual budget and served a hot midday meal daily to at least fifteen hundred schoolchildren.[86] As hoped, the budget was met from the children in the Jewish schools of the United States, "thus bringing our American boys and girls close to Palestine."[87] This inaugurated a new phase in Hadassah's "propaganda" work at home—namely, a drive to persuade American Jewish youngsters to bolster the Zionist cause through philanthropy. The idea that American children, by this youthful commitment to help pay for school lunches for Palestinian children, would become "closer" to Palestine, a closeness that might last a lifetime, echoes Szold's assertion to convention delegates that Hadassah supporters were, "in a moral sense . . . actually in the land."

In her 1926 message to Hadassah convention delegates, Szold argued: "Though Hadassah is coming into its own in Palestine, its true character is not yet known. It is not yet thought of as an organization with educational aims." Nevertheless, she suggested: "The Welfare Centers are educational institutions in the most modern popular sense." Szold pointed also to the Hadassah-run Nurses' Training School as evidence that "we are slowly penetrating to another educational field. Through the Penny School Luncheons which are being prepared by the guests themselves, under the supervision of cooking teachers, we are approximating a domestic science course in the public schools of Palestine."[88]

Although Hadassah was still raising money and in other ways supporting the development of a modern medical system in Palestine, Szold, aware that administration and funding of medical work must eventually be transferred to the Yishuv, was already looking to extend the organization's mandate into another, related field. By asserting that some of the projects begun under the rubric of health education and preventive medicine were, in fact, educational undertakings, Szold implied that Hadassah had already, in effect, entered the educational field.

Public education was, of course, a crucial part of preventive medicine. As Hadassah's emphasis on preventive medicine grew, so did its effort to find innovative ways to educate adults and children about health. The establishment of the Straus Health Center in Palestine in 1927 was an important advance in this area. The health center was supposed "to become the center from which propaganda will radiate to all sections of the country."[89] Along with the usual medical facilities, the center included a "propaganda center" with exhibits, a museum, and a library; a gym in which young people might perform "corrective exercises prescribed by the Center physicians" and "club rooms" (one for boys, one for girls) where the youngsters would be taught "health standards, personal and social hygiene"; a model kitchen and living room; a soup kitchen (also used for teaching cooking and dietetics); and more. Dr. Ephraim Bluestone, director of the Hadassah Medical Organization (HMO), explained: "What we want is to teach the people how to keep themselves in health, and to provide them with the opportunity for detecting disease at the time when the chances for checking it are best,—in the beginning. We have to teach them, also, to think in terms of health, and not of sickness, when they turn to the Health Center."[90] In 1933, after visiting Hadassah's health welfare centers, American nurse Amy Perry wrote: "These buildings are the last word in improvements and really combined the features of a health center and a settlement house."[91]

From the American settlement houses, Hadassah adopted another innovative American educational strategy: the "model flat" method for teaching housekeeping and sanitation. Mabel Hyde Kittredge, who established the first model flat in a New York City tenement in 1902, looked forward to "an up-to-date, scientific way to live" and declared:

> If household administration is to take its place in the front rank with the other professions of the day, educators as well as women must wake up and realize that the whole housekeeping question is dependent upon scientific management, efficiency, skilled labor, and effective tools. . . . We must establish an adequate twentieth century theory of household economics and then we must put this within the reach of every girl in our public schools.[92]

Kittredge was active with the Henry Street Settlement and advised Lillian Wald.[93] Like the early Hadassah nurses, Kittredge was shocked by the unsanitary and chaotic conditions of many of the immigrant households she visited. She was especially disturbed by what she regarded as dangerously misguided child-rearing techniques. "The internal anarchy and disorder of too many a tenement home is its curse," she wrote in 1905.[94] Kittredge observed that in these households there were no regular meals or bedtimes and no understanding of germs or food preservation. Infants were nursed irregularly and young children were fed strong tea, coffee, alcohol, and the same heavy foods eaten by adults; there was often no fresh air or ventilation in the flats; children played unsupervised in the streets late at night; and there was general ignorance about both personal and household hygiene as well as elementary treatment of ailments and injuries.

The use of the model flat as both an example of "right living" and a teaching center was Kittredge's educational attack on these problems. A model flat was a rented apartment, usually in a tenement, staffed by a woman who also lived in the apartment. Two early model flats Kittredge set up were simply furnished "along scientific lines" so that tenement dwellers might realistically afford to copy what they saw. Children took classes in housekeeping; cooking, including lessons in marketing and food values; and home nursing. Adults were exposed to a scientifically managed household in which unnecessary labor was eliminated and household tasks were scheduled and dealt with methodically on the most efficient basis possible.

A variation on the "model flat" strategy proved to be a very popular educational tool for Hadassah. As part of a 1924 Palestine Health Week program run by Hadassah, an exhibit in Jerusalem showing the rooms of "Mrs. Do

Care" and "Mrs. Don't Care" attracted thirty thousand visitors over a two-week period. The two "rooms" were made of packing crates. In Mrs. Don't Care's room, dust and flies settled on uncovered food and a baby (represented by a doll) languished unattended on the floor. A nurse staffed Mrs. Do Care's room, and she "demonstrated the use of appliances for the baby and for the household in general." Other exhibits were designed to explain school hygiene, municipal hygiene, and maternity and infant hygiene. Over six thousand people attended the many lectures offered as part of Health Week, including six hundred women who attended talks "for women only" given by women physicians.

The *Hadassah News Letter* explained that "a day was set aside for Moslem women when they could come without fear of meeting men . . . many Moslem women came at other times, too, and, in their eagerness to see all there was to be seen, unveiled themselves in the presence of strangers." Other parts of the program were directed at children, included an essay contest with prizes for the best essays on the topic "What Did I Learn from Health Week?"[95]

Evidently such exhibits still had drawing power more than a decade later. In 1935, Hadassah erected an exhibit in its health center in the Old City of Jerusalem consisting of two miniature houses; one labeled "Do Care House" and the other, "Don't Care House."[96] The model houses, of course, were arranged so as to contrast clean and orderly versus dirty and disorganized housekeeping styles. According to Hadassah, these methods of reaching Yishuv women were having an impact. "Exit Magic, Enter Science" is a subheading in one pamphlet, which explains:

> The women are eager to learn and to know. But in some there is still evidence of resistance, of some inner conflict. To these the words of the nurse sound strange, even blasphemous. In 1921 Hadassah . . . began to teach modern scientific care of mother and child. From then on the Eastern women have wavered between allegiance to tribal custom and acceptance of new ideas. The first Hadassah nurses met with skepticism, outright laughter and even derision. But slowly, very slowly, as they observed the beneficial effects of Hadassah's teaching . . . the Eastern women became more hospitable to new ideas.[97]

Hadassah's promotion of science as applied to domestic life grew out of the turn-of-the-century American domestic science movement.[98] In the early 1900s, buoyed by optimism about science's potential to point the way to social improvements, a legion of newly minted "experts," most of whom were women, attempted to apply scientific principles to household management and parenting. This meant applying industrial standards of efficiency to housekeeping and treating housekeeping as a serious occupation.[99] Armed with the latest scientific ideas about how disease was spread through bacteria and contagion, early home economists endeavored to teach poor and immigrant women the rudiments of "sanitary science" with a focus on how to preserve, handle, and prepare food and how to ensure personal and household hygiene in order to prevent disease.[100]

Hadassah's representatives in Palestine shared Kittredge's passion for making women efficient managers of orderly households and used many of her pedagogic techniques, including role modeling and even child's play, to advance this goal. The housekeeping centers and model flats, Kittredge explained, "find their motive power and are successful by means of the universal love in every little girl to play at keeping house." In common with Hadassah workers, Kittredge saw value in using children as a conduit for educating immigrant parents, even if this sometimes meant sowing conflict between the generations and fomenting discontent:

> Train a girl to know a home of order from one of unrest. Teach a woman to be miserable at the thought of a close room or an unaired bed for her baby, and the social worker can go off and do something else. . . . We must have restlessness and dissatisfaction first. This comes from a realization of the right way and a disgust with the wrong way, and then will come the push from the homemaker herself, not from a few outside reformers.[101]

This strategy was endorsed by Szold, who wrote that "the chief thing that the settlement worker should do is rouse a noble discontent. . . . The women are too patient! If they had only risen up and demanded better sanitation and living conditions."[102]

Children's playgrounds were another hallmark of American Progressivism that Hadassah imported to Palestine. Irma Lindheim's aunt, Bertha Guggenheimer, had a long-standing interest in the playground movement in America and, after a trip to Palestine, told her niece: "I am going to make it possible to begin establishing playgrounds in the Old City where Arab and Jewish children can learn to play together. . . . If they can begin early to get along together, they can go on that way when they are older."[103]

Organized playgrounds were designed to help slum children overcome a host of urban ills including poverty, congested living conditions, filth, disease, and inadequate parental supervision. According to advocates, these playgrounds, where children's play was carefully supervised by experts, "would insulate youngsters from pervasive city vices, act as a deterrent against juvenile crime, and provide adolescents with the supervision and moral purpose missing from their lives." Reformers also "believed supervised play, especially team games, to be an effective agent of Americanization" for immigrant children.[104] Settlement house activists were among the first to support the playground movement. Indeed, Lillian Wald, along with Felix Adler and Jacob Riis, started the Outdoor Recreation League, which opened New York City's first outdoor playground in 1898. In Chicago, Jane Addams built a small playground at Hull House in the 1890s and became a leader in the children's play movement.

Wald and Addams joined with other reformers in 1906 to start a new organization, the Playground Association of America, which lobbied for the creation of playgrounds in urban slum areas. The association portrayed playgrounds as educational rather than merely recreational tools that served to advance a number of social goals: they helped to socialize children through building character, encouraged interethnic harmony and acculturation, taught cooperation and consensus as part of an education in democratic values, and promoted physical and moral health. This was best achieved by staffing the playgrounds with professionals who would guide and supervise the children's activities.[105] "In short," says Dominick Cavallo, "they felt that children's play was too important to be left to children." Ultimately, as with most projects launched by Progressive reformers, the goal was to convince the government to assume responsibility for building and administering such playgrounds and, by 1920, "reformers had succeeded in making organized play a concern of public policymakers."[106]

Hadassah was no less ambitious for its playgrounds in Palestine, asking: "Was it possible to transplant the spirit of non-caste and nonsectarianism, prevailing in the American playground, to Palestine? . . . Particularly Jerusalem needs something to breed good fellowship."[107] Guggenheimer paid for the establishment of the first organized playground in Palestine in 1925. A year later, the *New York Times* reported that Guggenheimer set up a fifty-thousand-dollar trust fund for the establishment of more playgrounds, which would

> be operated along the lines of American playgrounds. The American Playground Association is cooperating in the work and is giving special training to American workers to take charge of the Palestine play centers. . . . The playgrounds are expected to prove of invaluable service in promoting good feeling between the children of different races who, mingling together in play, will break through the prejudices that now often keep them apart.[108]

The Mount Zion playground in the Old City of Jerusalem was free and open to children of all backgrounds between the ages of three and fifteen. Hadassah nurses on site regularly checked the children for any contagious diseases, and it was hoped that the children's fear of being excluded from the playground would prompt them to look after their own health. The playground offered supervised activities including "handwork" like weaving, drawing, and paper cutting; team sports; a stage where the children could present plays; a "small meteorological station"; a little museum for archeological and natural objects found by the children; and, during the summer, classes in carpentry, embroidery, and other vocational subjects. The playground was "thoroughly equipped with apparatus which has been sent from America . . . such as are found on all well equipped American playgrounds." As was the case in American playgrounds, this one in Jerusalem was heavily staffed with an athletics instructor, two play leaders, and a nurse. The playground also offered "a sanitary water system and showers" so that during the hot weather the children could take a shower both before and after playing.[109]

"At first," the playground organizers admitted, when parents of the Arab children in the neighborhood saw the ground being prepared for the playground, "there was a little stone throwing but as they watched the development and saw the fine arrangement and opportunities that could benefit their children, they became enthusiastic." As children from the different communities became regular visitors to the playground, the goal of cross-cultural harmony seemed to have been achieved: "Although the playground caters to the different races, there has never been an instance of racial unpleasantness at any time. A sense of fine fellowship was established right from the start during team work, when a conscious effort was made always to mix the groups and never to have a group of children of one race play by themselves."[110]

The second Guggenheimer playground was opened in the Mahane Yehuda area of Jerusalem—also a poor neighborhood crowded with Jewish immigrants from the Middle East. The average daily attendance at this playground was five hundred children. Facilities included a garden where children planted flowers, a building with a small library, a piano, and woodworking tools. Local teenagers were recruited to volunteer as play leaders and "the day's last hour is devoted to group work, conversations and discussions."[111] Leaving social utility aside, Hadassah's playground organizers stressed the simple value of providing a safe, clean space for children to enjoy themselves:

> A good many of the boys and girls, although some of them are only nine and ten years of age, already work and have the burden of household responsibilities

and it is indeed delightful to meet the same boys and girls, mere children, some of them working in the markets as little errand boys or helping in the care of the home, on the playground in the afternoons, forgetting all in the abandonment of play.[112]

As far as Hadassah was concerned, their Palestine playgrounds were meeting objectives. The director of the Guggenheimer playgrounds, Rachel Schwarz, wrote glowingly about "the educational value of the playground and its influence on character development through its emphasis on fair play, energy, group solidarity." Schwarz was especially pleased about "the influence of the playground on the relations between children of different communities. Instead of fighting and throwing stones, as they did before playground days, they now play together on terms of cordiality and friendship."[113] A block of money was set aside in Bertha Guggenheimer's will to continue the playground program. By 1950, Hadassah had built close to fifty playgrounds, and in that year the project was turned over to the Israeli government.[114]

By the 1930s, with a full panoply of child welfare services and programs underway, certain themes emerged in Hadassah fundraising materials and publications directed at its American Jewish membership. One recurring theme was that the Oriental Jews were in particular need of Hadassah's social welfare services. Among the problems thought to afflict this group were child labor, child marriages, illiteracy, superstition, and poor hygiene and nutrition. The Yemenites were described by Sampter as "a bit of Oriental medievalism in a modern community."[115]

Another theme was Hadassah's public health work directed at mothers and children. Hadassah told its members that there was hardly a mother in Palestine who could not benefit from instruction in modern techniques of child rearing. Hadassah nurses taught women how best to bathe, clothe, and feed their babies. Publicity pamphlets repeatedly described strange customs that Hadassah workers confronted, like the use of amulets and the belief in taboos: "They have been taught to pin dogs' teeth and birds' beaks on the clothes of their newborn infants to safeguard them against the evil eye. . . . They have been taught to wear amulets on throat and arms."[116]

The shock value of such exotic habits made for compelling reading. As late as 1940 an *American Journal of Nursing* article on Hadassah's work in Palestine opened dramatically: "Can you imagine putting mascara on a baby's eyes to enhance his beauty or branding him with a hot iron to drive out his fever?"[117] The challenge for Hadassah was to convince women to abandon these folk traditions once and for all: "Hadassah must continually fight the superstitions and taboos that hamper its work; where it has succeeded in eliminating them in one corner, they crop up in another. . . . It takes patience, perseverance, alertness and understanding to clear away the rubbish of medievalism that still prevails in Eastern countries."[118]

Patience and hard work were rewarded. By 1935, said the organization, twenty-five thousand children and mothers were registered at Hadassah's infant welfare stations, and over 80 percent of Palestine's Jewish population received some direct health services from Hadassah.[119] In the pages of the *Hadassah News Letter*, the Hadassah Medical Organization's director, Dr. Ephraim Bluestone, explained that public health lay at the heart of Hadassah's vision of the Jewish state-in-the-making:

> The right of every individual to health is the foundation of all our efforts in the field of preventive medicine. The right of the State to a healthy community is the foundation of public health idealism. . . . No country may now be considered truly modern that has not taken advantage of the teachings of hygiene which the last few generations have so painstakingly developed.[120]

But the long-term survival of these public health projects depended on Hadassah's skillful use of propaganda to solicit donations. Taking the long view, Hadassah members thought that if children's compassion could be cultivated early, they might begin a habit of lifelong giving to Jewish causes. Thus, while Hadassah promoted its maternity and infant work with propaganda aimed at women and designed to solicit their maternal sympathies, it also sought to interest American Jewish schoolchildren in the cause of their Palestinian brethren. While the organization could not realistically hope to raise large sums of money from young people, it tried to inculcate a sense of Zionist fellowship in American Jewish children.

Given Hadassah's ongoing commitment to Zionist education among American Jewish women, this foray into educating American children was not unexpected. Hadassah members had already given some thought to the issue. In an early essay on the subject, Henrietta Szold's sister, Bertha Szold Levin, asked: "What relation shall a child have, not to a concrete state, but to a movement, a hope?" She discussed means by which an American Jewish child might be encouraged to feel the "nationalistic spirit" of Zionism even while living in the Diaspora. She concluded that along with "a good, thorough Jewish education" the child must contribute to the homeland through service to the cause. Ultimately, Levin claimed, "The youth whose sense of loyalty has been quickened by proper educational methods and by wholesome group life, whose sympathies and vision have been broadened by glimpses of his kinship with the community and all mankind, will, when he comes to shoulder the obligations of adult life, not fail his people in service."[121]

But this would not happen automatically. It took investment. To this end, Hadassah directed some of its fundraising and publicity campaigns in the United States at schoolchildren. During World War I, for example, Hadassah distributed small illustrated booklets written in simple language describing the lives of Palestinian children and how they were bettered by Hadassah's child welfare programs. The stress was on shared experience and hopes: "We are so glad to meet you! We have been told about the children in America. Do you know anything about us? We are the children of Palestine. Like you, we go to school, study, do our lessons, and play out in the sunshine." American children were also asked to share their good fortune with children of the Yishuv. Like fundraising appeals to adults, these materials emphasized that donating money makes everybody feel good: "Come with us to visit the children of Palestine. . . . Then you will know why contributing to Hadassah's Child Welfare Fund is a double joy. It brings health and high spirits to the boys and girls of America who *give*, and to their pals in Palestine, who *receive*."[122]

American children were asked to put their donated pennies and nickels in specially designed little envelopes that were passed around their Sunday schools. On the cover of each was inscribed a picture and a short poem:

Dear American Children

THANK YOU for the money you have put in this bag. It helps the children of Palestine to become as healthy and happy as the children of America. It brings them good food, good playgrounds, and good medical care.

> For the Brave Children of Palestine
> Around the land of Palestine
> Where Allied armies fight today
> The children, too, help "hold our line"
> By keeping fit in every way.
> Hadassah feeds them healthy food.
> It gives them playgrounds, camps and care.
> Drop in your coins! They can do good
> If you will send our youth your share!

> For the Youngest Citizens of Israel
> To perfect the skill and train the hand
> Of children who will build the land,
> For food to make them strong and sound

For summer camps, or a new playground,
For teachers trained in household art,
Equipped to guide both mind and heart,
Give your gift and give TODAY!
Help the democratic way![123]

These poems reprise some of the main themes of Hadassah's fundraising appeals to adults: the idea that American Jews are duty bound to help Palestinian children achieve the same levels of health, education, and recreation as their American counterparts; the argument that Hadassah's child welfare work is part of the war effort and that Americans must also contribute their "share"; the claim that child welfare is critical to the Zionist nation-building enterprise and that donating money is the "democratic way" to contribute to this goal.

When war again broke out in Europe, Hadassah appealed to both adults and children for donations to support Hadassah's child welfare work in Palestine. Publicity materials from this period also tied child welfare work to the larger war effort. A 1941 brochure, for example, asserts: "During this time of crisis, Hadassah's child welfare work must be viewed as an indispensable part of the total defense program of the Jewish National Home."[124] Written in 1943, a pamphlet titled *Does it Matter?* claims that "Hadassah is helping the pioneers of the Jewish National Home to contribute their maximum to the war and to assure that democratic victory for which we are all fighting!" and asks: "Help us make sure that Palestine . . . will continue to be an oasis of democracy. Help us to prepare those boys and girls to be fit protectors of the rights of man for which all Allied nations are fighting today, and fit co-citizens of that democratic world which we are building."[125]

We see that Hadassah's wartime fundraising materials, while still requesting donations for child welfare work, now took on a new political dimension. The materials stressed that Palestinian Jews were fighting under the banner of the British Army and on the side of the Allies; that Palestinian Jews, the personification of Zionism, lived the democratic values and goals of the Allied cause; and that the care taken to help children during the war would pay dividends after the war ended. As always, parallels were continually drawn between American and Palestinian children: "Hadassah is training Palestine's young citizens to be fit to solve, in their part of the world, the same problems which our children, here in the United States, will have to face after the fighting has ceased!"[126]

An emergent theme in the Hadassah fundraising material of this period was that by donating money, Americans, including children, could participate in nation building. "Are you a helper?" is the refrain of one such pamphlet for children. If so, the proper course of action was clear: "Begin putting coins in your envelope today."[127] And each coin, children were assured, would be gratefully received. In Hadassah's pamphlets for young people, the children of Palestine were always portrayed as thankful to the children of America for helping them. Hadassah reassured their child donors, as they did their adult donors, that the money went directly to support those who needed it: "Many American children contribute to the Hadassah child welfare fund. The pictures will show how this money has helped to bring health and happiness to the boys and girls of Palestine."[128]

While many of Hadassah's fundraising materials for adults played to the maternal instincts of women, in child-oriented appeals there was little reference to Hadassah as a women's organization, although one pamphlet reminds the child reader that his mother is well-acquainted with Hadassah: "These playgrounds were given to Palestine by an American woman and are supported and supervised by Hadassah. Your mother can tell you about Hadassah, explain why it is interested in the children of Palestine, and why it has put such stress on their having playgrounds on the 'American style.'"[129] Surprisingly, there are almost no direct references either to Zionism or to the character of Palestine as a Jewish state-in-the-making. At most, Palestine is described as "the Jewish homeland." In a rare exception, a 1941 booklet offers:

Palestine is called THE JEWISH NATIONAL HOME because Jews originally came from there and because some have never left the country. Many of our people returned to Palestine recently as part of the Zionist upbuilding movement so that they could make it once again into a modern, progressive land where great masses of our people might live a normal life.[130]

In the end, Hadassah's fundraising appeals to American children were designed not only to raise money but also to raise awareness of Zionist goals and make American Jewish children active participants in the cause. While Hadassah always encouraged the Zionist education of women, fundraising campaigns for its child welfare projects allowed the organization to reach out to a new constituency among the young. Hadassah tried both to ensure that American Jewish youngsters forged a lifelong connection to the Jewish homeland and to strengthen their sense of Jewish identity and culture in the face of the assimilatory pressures of American life.

By the 1930s Hadassah had a loyal constituency among American Jewish women and children for its maternity and child welfare programs in the Yishuv. The organization could take the credit for creating a Palestine-wide network of child welfare programs and services as part of its comprehensive health services. Through the educational spin-offs of all these programs, Palestinian Jewish children learned about the basic principles of health and nutrition. Thousands of children received medical checkups and care in school and through Hadassah-run health centers. Thousands were fed through the School Luncheons program and benefited from the recreational activities offered at the Guggenheimer Playgrounds. Hadassah's experience in establishing and administering child welfare programs stood it in good stead when it assumed responsibility for Youth Aliyah in 1935 and shifted its attention to the deadly crisis facing European children.

Notes

1. Seth Koven and Sonya Michel, eds., *Mothers of a New World: Maternalist Politics and the Origins of Welfare States* (New York and London: Routledge, 1993), 4; Seth Koven and Sonya Michel, "Womanly Duties: Maternalist Politics and the Origins of Welfare States in France, Germany, Great Britain, and the United States, 1880–1920," *American Historical Review* 95, no. 4 (October 1990): 1079.

2. Figures for the Jewish population of Palestine in this period vary widely and are contentious. Justin McCarthy has tried to balance and correct the demographic figures for Palestine from conflicting sources including Ottoman, British Mandate, and Zionist authorities. Justin McCarthy, *The Population of Palestine: Population History and Statistics of the Late Ottoman Period and the Mandate* (New York: Columbia University Press, 1990), 24, 26.

3. McCarthy, *The Population of Palestine*, 219, 37. McCarthy calculates that as a result of Jewish immigration in the 1930s, the Jewish population of Palestine increased from 17 percent of the total in 1931 to 31 percent in 1946.

4. For a portrait of the health and sanitation conditions of Mandatory Palestine, see Naomi Shepherd, "Patching up Palestine," in *Ploughing Sand: British Rule in Palestine, 1917–1948* (London: John Murray, 1999), 126–78. For a contemporary and detailed description of the problem, see also M. J. Rosenau and Charles F. Wilinsky, "A Sanitary Survey of Palestine," in Elwood Mead, ed., *Reports of the Experts Submitted to the Joint Palestine Survey Commission* (Boston, Mass.: Daniels Printing, 1928), 537–741.

5. Shepherd, *Ploughing Sand*, 15–16.

6. Maxa Nordau, "Pioneer Types: The Women Workers of Palestine," *The New Palestine*, 15 October 1926, 203.

7. Hadassah, the Women's Zionist Organization of America, *What is Hadassah?* 1926/7, RG 17/B 3, HWZOA.

8. See Rosenau and Wilinsky, "A Sanitary Survey of Palestine," 671. The Zionist Executive was the executive arm of the World Zionist Organization.

9. Molly Ladd-Taylor, *Mother-Work: Women, Child Welfare and the State, 1890–1930* (Urbana and Chicago: University of Illinois Press, 1994), 43.

10. Irma Lindheim, *Parallel Quest: A Search of a Person and a People* (New York: Thomas Yoseloff, 1962), 169, 170. Lindheim succeeded Henrietta Szold as national president of Hadassah and held the post from 1926 to 1928.

11. Editorial, *The New Palestine*, 14 March 1924, 203.

12. For a discussion of maternalist politics in the United States, see Ladd-Taylor, *Mother-Work*.

13. Jessie E. Sampter, "Babies in Palestine," *The New Palestine*, 3 August 1923, 122.

14. Editorial, "Our Wards," *The Maccabaean*, February 1918, 25.

15. Irma Lindheim, "The Fifteenth Anniversary," *Hadassah News Letter*, March 1927, 3.

16. The first is the title of an undated Hadassah publicity pamphlet, *Hadassah Mothers the Children of Erez-Israel*, RG 17/B 1, HWZOA. The photo on the cover shows an Oriental Jewish mother with two young children. The second is the caption accompanying the photo of Hadassah nurses holding infants on the cover of the March 1923 *Hadassah News Letter*.

17. *Hadassah Bulletin* 33, June 1917, 14.

18. *Hadassah Bulletin* 23, July–August 1916, 9.

19. "From Report of Infant Welfare Work in Jerusalem," *Hadassah News Letter*, August 1923, unpaginated.

20. "From Report of Infant Welfare Work in Jerusalem."

21. There are no firm figures on infant mortality rates in Palestine until the 1920s. According to the *American Journal of Nursing*, the death rate of Jewish infants under one year, per 1000 live births, fell from 131.25 in 1925 to 58.20 in 1938—a decrease of nearly 56 percent. Among the Arab population of Palestine, the decline for the same period was from 200.49 to 127.61 per 1000 live births. See Julietta K. Arthur, "Child Welfare in the Holy Land," *American Journal of Nursing* 40, no. 4 (April 1940), unpaginated, Hadassah reprint, RG 17/B 1, HWZOA. Arthur perhaps took her figures from the "A Sanitary Survey of Palestine" section in Mead, ed., *Reports of the Experts Submitted to the Joint Palestine Survey Commission*. This survey attributed the declining infant mortality rate to the work done by Hadassah.

22. Hadassah, the Women's Zionist Organization of America, *Infant Welfare Work Under the Hadassah Medical Organization in Palestine*, 1923, 1, RG 17/B 1, HWZOA.

23. "Hadassah Convention Summary Report," *The New Palestine*, July 13–20, 1928, 53; Marlin Levin, *It Takes a Dream: The Story of Hadassah* (Jerusalem: Gefen, 1997), 116–19.

24. Mina Carson, *Settlement Folk: Social Thought and the American Settlement Movement, 1885–1930* (Chicago: University of Chicago Press, 1990), 74.

25. Hadassah, the Women's Zionist Organization of America, *Out of the Cradle Endlessly Rocking*, 1936, RG 17/B 1, HWZOA. This pamphlet takes its title from Walt Whitman's poem of the same name about childhood.

26. "Hadassah's Baby Insurance Through Education," *Hadassah News Letter*, February 1928, 5.

27. "Hadassah's Baby Insurance Through Education," 5.

28. Rachel Pesah, "What a Nurse Sees," *Hadassah News Letter*, October 1928, 7.

29. Photo caption, *Hadassah News Letter*, September–October 1930, 2.

30. Irma Kraft, "Mother O' Mine in Jerusalem," *Hadassah News Letter*, March 1924, unpaginated.

31. Jessie E. Sampter, "Babies in Palestine," *The New Palestine*, 3 August 1923, 123.

32. Hadassah, *Infant Welfare Work Under the Hadassah Medical Organization in Palestine*, unpaginated.

33. Richard A. Meckel, *Save the Babies: American Public Health Reform and the Prevention of Infant Mortality, 1850–1929* (Baltimore: Johns Hopkins University Press, 1990), 78. See also Lina Gutherz Straus, *Disease in Milk, the Remedy Pasteurization: The Life Work of Nathan Straus* (New York: Arno, 1977).

34. "Nathan Straus Plans Big Work for Holy Land," *New York Times*, 21 December 1913, sec. 5, 8.

35. Melvin I. Urofsky and David W. Levy, eds., *Letters of Louis D. Brandeis*, vol. 3 (Albany: State University of New York Press, 1978), 299.

36. Ernest Bryant Hoag and Lewis M. Terman, *Health Work in the Schools* (Boston: Houghton Mifflin, 1914), 4. The boll weevil anecdote is repeated in many sources; see, for example, Florence Kelley, "The Children's Epoch," *Charities and the Commons* 15, no. 14 (6 January 1906): 433–34. The motto of the Children's Bureau was "Better mothers, better babies, and better homes." See also Sheila M. Rothman, "The Ideology of Educated Motherhood," in *Woman's Proper Place: A History of Changing Ideals and Practices, 1870 to the Present* (New York: Basic Books, 1978), 125.

37. Ladd-Taylor, *Mother-Work*, 74, 81ff.

38. For a historical look at how charity workers became professional social workers, see Kathleen Woodroofe, *From Charity to Social Work in England and the United States* (Toronto: University of Toronto Press, 1968).

39. For a discussion of the ideas underlying this effort to educate women about child rearing in the United States, see Julia Grant, "Modernizing Mothers: Home Economics and the Parent Education Movement, 1920–1945," in *Rethinking Home Economics: Women and the History of a Profession*, ed. Sarah Stage and Virginia B. Vincenti (Ithaca, N.Y.: Cornell University Press, 1997), 55–74.

40. Meckel, *Save the Babies*, 121. Although some women did breast-feed, many were undernourished, in poor health, working long hours, or otherwise forced to rely on buying milk.

41. Jessie Sampter, "Constructive Healing," *The New Palestine*, 10 March 1922, 149; Rose Jacobs, "Hadassah: Its Greater Significance," *The New Palestine*, 9 March 1923, 177.

42. Henrietta Szold, *Hadassah News Letter*, December 1923, 2.

43. Irma Lindheim, "Messages to the Convention," *Hadassah News Letter*, December 1929, 14; Joseph M. Levy, "Honors for Miss Szold," *New York Times*, 15 December

1935, sec. 10, 11. For more on American Zionist interest in binational options in Palestine, see Rafael Medoff, *Zionism and the Arabs: An American Jewish Dilemma, 1898–1948* (Westport, Conn.: Praeger, 1997).

44. Jacobs, "Hadassah: Its Greater Significance," 177.

45. Dr. S. S. Goldwater, "Dr. Rubinow's Achievement," *Hadassah News Letter*, March 1923, 9.

46. Editorial, *Hadassah News Letter*, March 1927, 6.

47. Alice L. Seligsberg, "Jewish War Orphans," *The Maccabaean*, February, 1918, 52. This article came from a speech that Seligsberg delivered before the Baltimore Federation of Jewish Women's Clubs, 27 November 1917.

48. Rose Jacobs, "Alice L. Seligsberg," *American Jewish Year Book* 43 (1941–1942): 432.

49. Editorial, "Our Wards," *The Maccabaean*, February 1918, 25.

50. The American Jewish Joint Distribution Committee (JDC or "Joint") was established in 1914 to provide rescue and relief overseas to Jewish victims of war and persecution.

51. Eliezer David Jaffe, *Child Welfare in Israel* (New York: Praeger, 1982), 13; Jacobs, "Alice L. Seligsberg," 434.

52. "Hadassah Chapters Active in All Parts of Country, Collect Funds for Activities in Palestine and Sew Garments for Supplies Department," *The New Palestine*, 25 February 1921, 2.

53. Jessie Sampter, "A Plea for Personal Contacts with Palestinian Orphans," *Hadassah News Letter*, March 1924, unpaginated.

54. Alice L. Seligsberg, "Hadassah: 1912–1922, A Review of Its Aims and Achievements," *The New Palestine*, 10 March 1922, 149.

55. Henrietta Szold, "Palestine Realities: A Letter from Palestine to Hadassah," *The New Palestine*, 10 March 1922, 147.

56. Ruth B. Fromenson, "The Palestine Supplies Bureau," *Hadassah News Letter*, March 1928, 11.

57. Hadassah, the Women's Zionist Organization of America, *Serve Palestine with the Labor of Your Hands*, 1934, RG 17, HWZOA; *A Stitch in Time*, 1938, RG 17, HWZOA; *A Stitch in Time*, 1939, RG 17, HWZOA; Rose Halpern, "Hadassah's Sixteenth Anniversary," *The New Palestine*, 16 March 1928, 321.

58. Dr. Maurice Harris, "The Genesis of School Luncheons," *Hadassah News Letter*, March 1929, 7; "Educational Project for American Children," *Hadassah News Letter*, December 1924, 6.

59. "Educational Project for American Children," 6.

60. "Editorial Note: Palestine Penny Luncheons," *Hadassah News Letter*, December 1925, 2.

61. David de Sola Pool, "School Luncheons," *Hadassah News Letter*, March 1928, 8; Lotta Levensohn, "The Entering Wedge," *Hadassah News Letter*, November 1928, 5, 7; Ethel S. Cohen, "School Luncheons—A Review," *Hadassah News Letter*, March 1927, 2.

62. Arthur, "Child Welfare in the Holy Land."

63. Hadassah, *Out of the Cradle Endlessly Rocking.*

64. Dorothy Kahn, "Meet the Chefs," *Hadassah News Letter,* October 1936, 8. See also Gordon W. Gunderson, "History of the National School Lunch Program," in *The National School Lunch Program Background and Development, Administrator's Manual* (New York: Nova Science Publishers, 2003).

65. M. Simchonith, *Eating a Hadassah Lunch,* Hadassah, the Women's Zionist Organization of America, n.d., RG 17/B 1, HWZOA.

66. Z. Carmi, "Penny Luncheons in Palestine: Letter Sent to Miss Sophia Berger by Z. Carmi of the Public Schools of Haifa," *Hadassah News Letter,* November–December 1927, 9.

67. Yaffa Schlesinger, New York, telephone interview by author, 2 January 2002.

68. Lotta Levensohn, "The Entering Wedge," *Hadassah News Letter,* November 1928, 5.

69. Henrietta Szold, "Miss Szold's Seventh Letter," *Hadassah News Letter,* June 1924, 8.

70. David de Sola Pool, "Without Regard to Race or Creed: The Straus Soup Kitchens and Health Centers in Palestine," *The New Palestine,* 3 February 1928, 150.

71. Gerda Arlosoroff-Goldberg, "The Woman in Palestine: Problems of Household Economy," *The New Palestine,* 4–11 January 1929, 9.

72. Hortense Levy, "Dietetics in Hadassah," *Hadassah News Letter,* March–April 1931, 3.

73. Rose Zeitlin, "A Palestinian Kindergarten at Lunch," *Hadassah News Letter,* May–June 1930, 5.

74. De Sola Pool, "Without Regard to Race or Creed," 150.

75. Levy, "Dietetics in Hadassah," 3.

76. Simchonith, *Eating a Hadassah Lunch.*

77. Hadassah, the Women's Zionist Organization of America, *Hadassah Child Welfare in Palestine,* 1937, RG 17/B 1, HWZOA.

78. Lotta Levensohn, "The Entering Wedge," *Hadassah News Letter,* November 1928, 5.

79. Elizabeth Ewen, *Immigrant Women in the Land of Dollars: Life and Culture on the Lower East Side, 1890–1925* (New York: Monthly Review Press, 1985), 89.

80. Beracha Habas, "'Health Scouts' Champion Cleanliness," *Hadassah News Letter,* September–October 1930, 5–6.

81. Rebecca Shulman, "A Child Welfare Program," *Hadassah News Letter,* May–June 1933, 14.

82. Rose L. Halprin, "Child Welfare," *Hadassah News Letter,* December 1936, 6.

83. "The Hadassah Convention: Summary Report," *The New Palestine,* 29 June 1923, 28; "Palestine Orphans," *Hadassah News Letter,* June 1923, 9; Rose K. Malmud, "The Story of Hadassah," *Hadassah News Letter,* March 1927, 5–6.

84. "The Hadassah Convention: Summary Report," *The New Palestine,* 29 June 1923, 28.

85. Mrs. Moses P. Epstein, "Hadassah Report to the ZOA Annual Convention," *The New Palestine*, 6 November 1931, 51. For a discussion of why some American Hadassah members chose to put down roots in Palestine, see Naomi Ann Lichtenberg, "Hadassah's Founders and Palestine, 1912–1925: A Quest for Meaning and the Creation of Women's Zionism" (Ph.D. diss., Indiana University, 1996).

86. "Hadassah Convention, Summary Report," *The New Palestine*, 13–20 July 1928, 53.

87. Rose Halpern, "Hadassah's Sixteenth Anniversary: Women's Zionist Organization Reviews Work of Past Sixteen Years and Outlines Program," *The New Palestine*, 16 March 1928, 321.

88. "Greetings from Miss Szold, Twelfth Annual Hadassah Convention," *The New Palestine*, 9 July 1926, 39.

89. Lina Straus, "The Work of Nathan and Lina Straus," *Hadassah News Letter*, January 1928, 5.

90. Lotta Levensohn, "Bet Ha-Briut, Straus Health Center for Palestine," *The New Palestine*, 5 November 1926, 273–75. Bluestone arrived in Palestine to take up the post of HMO director in March 1926 and left two years later.

91. Amy Perry, "An American Nurse Visits Hadassah Health Welfare Centers," *Hadassah News Letter*, November–December 1933, 10.

92. Mabel Hyde Kittredge, "Housekeeping Centers in Settlements and Public Schools," *The Survey* 30, no. 5 (3 May 1913): 189.

93. Mina Carson, *Settlement Folk*, 93–94. According to Carson, Kittredge "was a Park Avenue society woman . . . who found her way to Henry Street around 1900." Her model flat work led to the establishment of the Association of Practical Housekeeping.

94. Mabel Kittredge, "Home-making in a Model Flat: The Next Step in Public School Extension," *Charities and the Commons* 15, no. 5 (4 November 1905): 176.

95. "Health Week in Palestine," *Hadassah News Letter*, January 1925, 1–2, 7.

96. Lillian Wald suggested that there be such a "model flat" at the Henry Street Settlement in New York City. See Carson, *Settlement Folk*, 93.

97. Hadassah, *Out of the Cradle Endlessly Rocking*.

98. See Sarah Stage, "Ellen Richards and the Social Significance of the Home Economics Movement," in Stage and Vincenti, eds., *Rethinking Home Economics*, 17–33.

99. For scientific housekeeping see, for example, Barbara Ehrenreich and Deirdre English, "Microbes and the Manufacture of Housework," in *For Her Own Good: 150 Years of the Experts' Advice to Women* (New York: Anchor, 1978), 127–64; for scientific motherhood, see Rothman, "The Ideology of Educated Motherhood." For the ideas of scientific management where they originated, in industry, see Samuel Haber, *Efficiency and Uplift: Scientific Management in the Progressive Era, 1890–1920* (Chicago: University of Chicago Press, 1964).

100. See Nancy Tomes, "Spreading the Germ Theory: Sanitary Science and Home Economics, 1880–1930," in Stage and Vincenti, eds., *Rethinking Home Economics*, 34–54; Nancy Tomes, "The Private Side of Public Health: Sanitary Science,

Domestic Hygiene, and the Germ Theory," *Bulletin of the History of Medicine* 64, no. 4 (Winter 1990): 509–39; John Duffy, "Bacteriology Revolutionizes Public Health," in *The Sanitarians: A History of American Public Health* (Urbana and Chicago: University of Illinois Press, 1990), 193–204.

101. Kittredge, "Housekeeping Centers in Settlements and Public Schools," 188–92, 192.

102. Irving Fineman, *Woman of Valor: The Life of Henrietta Szold, 1860–1945* (New York: Simon & Schuster, 1961), 254.

103. Lindheim, *Parallel Quest*, 221.

104. Dominick Cavallo, *Muscles and Morals: Organized Playgrounds and Urban Reform, 1880–1920* (Philadelphia: University of Pennsylvania Press, 1981), 17.

105. The proceedings of the first convention of the Playground Association of America were published in the form of a series of articles in *Charities and the Commons* (3 August 1909), and their titles are indicative of the optimism of the playground advocates: Luther Halsey Gulick, "Play and Democracy," 481–86; Joseph Lee, "Play as a School of the Citizen," 486–91; Elmer Elsworth Brown, "Health, Morality and the Playground," 500–501; Henry Baird Favill, "Playgrounds in the Prevention of Tuberculosis," 501–6.

106. Cavallo, *Muscles and Morals*, 25, 48.

107. Leah Klepper, "Zion Hill Playground—A Model," *Hadassah News Letter*, March 1929, 15.

108. "Palestine Receives Playground Fund," *New York Times*, 23 May 1926, sec. 2, 20.

109. Eva Dushkin, "Zion Hill Playground, Jerusalem," *Hadassah News Letter*, 29 June 1928, 3, 5.

110. Dushkin, "Zion Hill Playground, Jerusalem," 3.

111. Rachel Schwarz, "A Day at a Palestine Playground," *Hadassah News Letter*, March–April 1931, 7.

112. Dushkin, "Zion Hill Playground, Jerusalem," 5.

113. Rachel Schwarz, "Children's Playground—Mt. Zion," *Hadassah News Letter*, December 1928, 5.

114. Levin, *It Takes a Dream*, 119.

115. Jessie Sampter, "The Children's House," *Hadassah News Letter*, January–February 1931, 6.

116. Sampter, "The Children's House," 6.

117. Arthur, "Child Welfare in the Holy Land." For an explanation of Yemenite Jewish folk medicine and folklore, including ideas about the evil eye, and the use of amulets and branding among Yemenite Jews in Israel, see Michael Weingarten, *Changing Health and Changing Culture: The Yemenite Jews in Israel* (Westport, Conn.: Praeger, 1992). Weingarten is a medical doctor who practices in the predominantly Yemenite community of Rosh Ha'ayin in Israel. He also discusses traditional Yemenite infant care.

118. Arthur, "Child Welfare in the Holy Land."

119. Hadassah, *Out of the Cradle Endlessly Rocking*. Palestine's Jewish population in 1935 is estimated to be about 353,959 out of a total population of 1.3 million. See McCarthy, *The Population of Palestine*, 36.

120. E. M. Bluestone, M.D., "Health, Homeland and Hadassah," *Hadassah News Letter*, March–April 1930, 7.

121. Bertha Szold Levin, "A Point of View on Junior Zionist Education," *The Maccabaean*, February 1917, 158–59.

122. Hadassah, the Women's Zionist Organization of America, *Join the Circle of Palestine's Children*, 1938, RG 17/B 1, HWZOA.

123. Hadassah, the Women's Zionist Organization of America, *Dear American Children*, 1940, RG 17/B 1, HWZOA; *For the Brave Children of Palestine*, 1943, RG 17/B 1, HWZOA; *For the Youngest Citizens of Israel*, n.d., RG 17/B 1, HWZOA.

124. Hadassah, the Women's Zionist Organization of America, *For Palestine's Children*, 1941, RG 17/B 1, HWZOA.

125. Hadassah, the Women's Zionist Organization of America, *Does It Matter?* 1943, RG 17/B 1, HWZOA.

126. Hadassah, *Does It Matter?*

127. Hadassah, the Women's Zionist Organization of America, *A Palestine News Reel*, 1937, RG 17/B 1, HWZOA.

128. Hadassah, the Women's Zionist Organization of America, *Meet the Children of Palestine*, 1937, RG 17/B 1, HWZOA.

129. Hadassah, the Women's Zionist Organization of America, *This Is a Story about David and His Sister, Miriam*, 1941, RG 17/B 1, HWZOA.

130. Hadassah, *This Is a Story about David and His Sister, Miriam*.

CHAPTER FOUR

~

"A New Type of Woman": The Struggle for Women's Equality in the Yishuv

Hadassah's ongoing battles for respect and acceptance within the American Zionist movement made the organization an advocate of women's place in organized Zionism. But what was that place? Before Hadassah began, most Zionist organizations, like most Jewish organizations in general, expected women to limit themselves to a lesser, supporting role.

While women attended the First Zionist Congress in 1897, they were denied voting rights. Twelve women at the Congress issued a proclamation that set forth an educational role for women in the Zionist movement. The group also declared that they would take responsibility "for creating Zionist women's associations wherever there are Jewish communities." Even at this early stage, Zionist women not only clearly felt that they had a particular, perhaps maternal, sphere of interest and influence but also opted to organize separate women's groups.[1]

At the Second Zionist Congress in Basle in 1898, women were allowed to attend as elected delegates and to participate in decision making through voting. American Zionist Emma Gottheil (who was later involved in starting Hadassah and whose husband Richard Gottheil was the head of the Federation of American Zionists) was elected to a cultural committee at the Second Zionist Congress. But reflecting continued uncertainty about the appropriate role of women in the Zionist movement, in 1900 Gottheil informed the Fourth Zionist Congress that "it is not up to us women to solve the great problems, we leave this to our husbands and brothers, but as long as we maintain the . . . religious atmosphere, that cannot be sepa-rated from our nationality, our duty is perhaps no less important than that of men."[2]

Theodor Herzl, echoing the notion that women dominated a separate Zionist estate, described women's educational role and their maternal re-sponsibility to promote Zionism for their children's sake:

> The forms of life that assert themselves with Zionism at their centre . . . would be a much finer occupation for leisure hours and even for occupied hours to be-come acquainted with the Jewish idea and to act for it than to tattle at after-noon teas or lose one's household allowance at cards or kill time in all sorts of useless ways. This would be a form of self-education and self-development which, widely different from empty pleasures, would be of use to the children, for a woman who is a good Zionist must also be an attentive and farsighted mother. . . . A mother must understand that Zionism, if it is a great and im-portant movement, is so particularly for the children, because they are the cit-izens of the future. . . . Every woman is the centre of a circle, small or large. In her limited circle she can do much. She can educate disciples, agitators who, according to such a snowball system, will in turn become the centres of circles in society. They will develop new circles and educate new disciples, the disci-ples becoming mistresses of the Zionist idea.[3]

Hadassah's original incarnation as a women's study group reflects the early Zionist movement's narrowly conceived ideas of how women should participate in the movement. But American Zionist women were also in-fluenced by broader social currents and the advances of women in the American Progressive movement. A dozen years after the First Zionist Congress, in keeping with early-twentieth-century notions of women's ex-panding maternal responsibilities in the social realm, Hadassah focused on bringing health and social welfare services to the women and children of the Yishuv.

Even as Hadassah proved its ability to set up and administer such services, however, the organization was repeatedly forced, in the forums of the Amer-ican Zionist movement, to defend its identity, autonomy, and fundraising pri-orities as a separate women's organization and fight for control of its own re-sources and projects. Throughout, the Hadassah organization cultivated an image of itself as a nonpartisan, nonpolitical, nonsectarian organization de-voted to health care, children, and related "motherhood" issues. Based on previous experience, Hadassah's leaders believed that the organization's suc-cess, if not its very survival, depended on avoiding the political infighting that afflicted other Zionist bodies.

As a women's Zionist organization Hadassah was, naturally, particularly interested in the situation of Jewish women in the Yishuv. And their situation was often difficult. An influx of young, single women immigrants arrived in the Yishuv during the 1920s. They were motivated by Zionist convictions and prepared to live and work as pioneers. But most of them had no agricultural training and few other skills. Moreover, the Yishuv had few job opportunities even for skilled workers. Together with a handful of other women's organizations, Hadassah looked for practical ways to help these and other working women—providing assistance when they first arrived, helping them in accessing work, or offering vocational training.

Although Henrietta Szold was involved, often through sitting on the executive, with some of these other organizations, relations between women's groups were strained. Disagreements about fundraising strategies, operating principles, and choice of projects, along with rivalry for scarce funds and political support, fueled tensions between groups whose activities, membership, and clientele often overlapped. In most disputes, however, due not only to her personal clout but also to the support she commanded from Hadassah in the United States, Szold prevailed.

At the same time, as Jewish women in the Yishuv began to organize to fight for their political and social rights, Hadassah supported their cause. As Alice Seligsberg pointed out, Hadassah women had learned not only from their experiences in the American Zionist movement but also from the American political scene overall:

I believe it is only through the suffrage movement that women have discovered how indispensable organization is, for the attainment not only of rights, but also of influence in the community. Generation after generation, the finest women have failed to exercise influence outside their homes, have failed to help in the solving of social problems, because all women stood separate and alone as links not welded into a chain. It is only the chain that is strong enough to hold its place against mass pressure. If women wish to contribute to the Zionist movement those talents that are peculiar to women, they must unite as women. One of the explanations of Hadassah's persistence may lie in . . . the realization by the Zionist women of America that unless well organized they will not count at all in the formation of opinion and the control of policies in those matters in which, as women, they have the deepest concern; namely, the protection of the weak, the healing of the afflicted, the safeguarding of the present and future generations.[4]

Thus, while Hadassah usually tried to avoid the appearance of political partisanship, its members were willing to take a public stand in support of efforts to advance women's equality in the Yishuv. Hadassah's Lotta Levensohn, for example, announced:

> All forward-looking Palestinian women are solidly behind the effort of the Women's Equal Rights League to secure social, legal, and political equality. Witnessing the struggles of women for their natural human rights in Palestine, the seasoned Zionist cannot but be a bit complacent in remembering that women have had full and equal rights in the Zionist movement ever since the first Congress in 1897.

Levensohn also argued that Hadassah programs and projects exemplified this commitment to women's equality. Levensohn pointed out that in the Hadassah Medical Organization, for example, "the principle of equal rights prevails: equal pay for equal work is the rule for all classes of workers from highest to lowest."[5] Others said that Hadassah's efforts to create a nurses' training school were a way to expand women's role in society even as they served society as a whole: "In training native Jewish girls as nurses, they were not only supplying aids for the moment, but were educating the entire community to the importance of sanitation and to a modern attitude towards women's work."[6]

Many Jewish women in the Yishuv were unhappy with the legal restrictions imposed on them by the Ottoman "millet" system that persisted under the British Mandate. Under this confessional system, each religious group in Palestine was allowed autonomy in matters of religious practice, personal law, and education. As a result, while the British Mandatory government had legal authority overall, in the areas of marriage, divorce, and parental rights, Jewish women in the Yishuv were forced to abide by narrowly defined Jewish religious law as defined by traditionalist rabbis whether or not the women themselves were religious believers.[7]

Although the World Zionist Organization recognized women's suffrage in 1899, discussions in 1918 about enshrining women's right to vote as law were torpedoed when ultraorthodox Jewish groups threatened to boycott the planned elections. In response, some Russian immigrant women founded a group called the Women's Equal Rights League in 1919 with the slogan "One constitution and the same law for men and women." The group lobbied to eliminate discrimination against women in the British Mandatory and religious judicial systems. In an effort to force women's legal rights onto the political agenda, the group later entered candidates in elections to the National Assembly.[8] The National Assembly (*Asefat Ha-Nivharim*—also called the Elected Assembly or the Representative Assembly) was the authoritative and representative body of the Jewish community of Palestine under the British Mandate.

Ultimately, women were both voters and candidates in the elections held for the National Assembly on April 19, 1920. Four of the twenty parties running in the elections included women candidates on their lists; fourteen of these women (five of them from the Women's Equal Rights League list) were elected.[9] Orthodox groups contested the election results and continued to protest against women's suffrage, which was not yet enshrined in the electoral constitution.[10] In 1923, the Orthodox proposed a referendum to decide the issue. Women's organizations, along with their allies, campaigned against the idea and solicited the support of Diaspora women's organizations including Hadassah. The *Hadassah News Letter* noted: "The vexatious feature of the opposition to women's voting rights was that, if the adversaries succeeded with their policies, for the first time it would have happened that, once political rights had been gained by women, they were to be deprived of them."[11]

Szold spoke out in support of women's suffrage at a public meeting in Jerusalem, and in 1925 Hadassah responded to the league's appeal for letters of protest by cabling the National Assembly:

> National Board of Hadassah, the Women's Zionist Organization of America representing twenty-five thousand women with suffrage rights organized in two hundred eleven cities of the United States, urges that election law to be adopted by national assembly recognize the right of women to vote and to hold office as befits Jewish community in the Homeland which Jews of whole world are building. They want it built up on foundations of justice laid in Jewish law and in prophetic literature.[12]

Ultimately, the withdrawal of some Orthodox groups from the debate undermined support for a referendum and women kept their right to vote and to hold elected office. In elections held on December 5, 1925, twenty-five women were elected to the Assembly (representing 12 percent of the total membership). On January 15, 1926, the Second National Assembly announced that it "declares equal rights for women in the civil, political and economic life of the Hebrew settlement and demands of the Mandatory Government that it secure this equality in all the laws of the land." Despite this victory at the National Assembly level, women continued to battle for the right to vote at the local level for many years. Only in 1940 were women finally able to vote in the local elections in Petach Tikvah.[13]

Szold herself regarded women's rights as crucial to the political development of the Jewish community and publicly supported the goals of the

Women's Equal Rights League. She identified the equality of women as a necessary step toward the goal of integrating the different Jewish social and ethnic groups of the Yishuv. In a speech given before an audience of three thousand supporters at the Hotel Pennsylvania, she said:

> You may have heard that there is a movement among the women of Palestine to secure equal rights for women before the law. It is not only a political, but also and primarily a legal movement. The Jewish women of Palestine are petitioning the Rabbis to begin at once with the task which must eventually be undertaken of modifying the ancient Jewish law in such ways that the Jewish woman may not stand behind her Mohammedan and her Christian sisters. Today a Jewish woman in Palestine cannot be the guardian of her children in accordance with the Jewish law, and under certain circumstances she cannot inherit the fortune which she may have helped her husband to accumulate. That is the line of adjustment to modern conditions along which the women who have formed an organization for that purpose have been working. Their efforts, whether crowned immediately with success or not, will lead to the consolidation of the Jewish community in Palestine.[14]

Gratifyingly for the Hadassah organization, Szold's appointment as a member of the Palestine Zionist Executive in 1927 was hailed as a triumph for all women in the Zionist movement: "Miss Szold has attained a position in Jewish life which no other woman in modern times has achieved," trumpeted an editorial in *The New Palestine*, which concluded that she was "the spiritual and intellectual leader not only of American Jewish womanhood, but of Jewish womanhood the world over."[15] Meanwhile, Szold declared her intention to help organize Palestinian women to assert their own interests.

Buoyed by Zionist idealism, activist women and women's organizations in the Yishuv operated in high hopes of the eventual achievement of social and political equality for women.[16] This optimism was reflected in the American Zionist press. In 1918, an editorial in *The Maccabaean* had prophesied:

> There will be no need for "Votes-for-Women" campaigns in the new Jewish State that is to be established in Palestine. Equal suffrage is being accepted as a matter of course by the pioneers, who are engaged in the task of reorganizing Jewish communal life. It is noteworthy that equal suffrage is characteristic of the Zionist organizations throughout the world. Women are so prominently identified with the movement that their right to vote at the International Congresses and at the national conventions is taken as a matter of course.[17]

Similarly, articles appeared suggesting that the Zionist collective settlements were the nucleus of a radically new society complete with a new role for women. Maxa Nordau wrote in *The New Palestine* that the position of women there [Palestine] is exactly the same as that of man. She has the same freedom in her work, in her life and in her opinions . . . there is social equality. A new type of woman is emerging there, energetic, independent without provocation, and still not masculine, not at all. Just as feminine as a drawing-room doll, only better. . . . It's probably the only place in the world where such a thing exists . . . the result is a new woman, strong and open-minded and hearted.[18]

In the same vein, *The New Palestine* published an interview with Sophie Loeb, an American journalist and welfare worker who had just returned from a trip to Palestine. Loeb, according to the article,

spoke with particular admiration of the co-operative women's colonies where groups of women support themselves independently by agricultural labor. As a woman, she viewed the complete spiritual and physical equality of the sexes prevalent in Palestine with especial interest. "Nowhere in the world," said Miss Loeb, "do women enjoy the complete moral enfranchisement that they do in Palestine. The women's colonies, where the entire physical and mental burden is shouldered by women only, are the best evidence of this."[19]

But Loeb was mistaken. In fact, the women's agricultural colonies or farms she admired were not a sign of women's empowerment but of marginalization. They were a desperate effort to solve the problem of women's exclusion from agricultural work in the communal settlements. These women-only farming operations were designed to provide them the agricultural training that most would-be *halutzot* (women pioneers) lacked and, as a result, kept them distant from the economic core of the regular agricultural settlements.

While many young women had arrived eager to take up the pioneering life and work alongside men in agriculture, they soon found themselves, despite their protests, relegated to kitchen or nursery work. And even women with agricultural experience were not always welcome. "We girls were met with indifference and scorn everywhere," wrote one young woman. "Wanting to work together with our male comrades, we were immediately insulted and ridiculed. . . . They found it altogether impossible to understand why women would want to work in the fields and they viewed us with suspicion."[20]

Being relegated to the economic margins left many women disappointed if not angry. These *halutzot* were ardent followers of Zionist thinkers like Ahad Ha'am and A. D. Gordon, who stressed the importance of "self-labor" (doing one's own work rather than hiring others), collective living, and the return to the soil as the essence of Zionism and the pinnacle of heroic pioneering.[21] If they could not work as farmers on the land, women felt they would miss out on the true pioneering experience:

> In the thick of that passionate movement toward the land the women workers suddenly found themselves thrust aside and relegated once more to the ancient tradition of the house and the kitchen. They were amazed and disappointed to see how the cleavage was opening, the men comrades really uniting themselves with the land, but they, though on it, not becoming part of it.[22]

Women's social and political aspirations in the Yishuv resulted, in part, from their reading of Zionist ideology. Zionism was not only a political movement but one that promised a sociocultural revolution aimed at creating an egalitarian society. Zionism would produce a new type of person—in the parlance of the time, the "New Hebrew Man." He would be a physically robust pioneer who would achieve "self-realization" through "the conquest of the soil." Through the establishment of collective settlements the pioneers would labor to "redeem the land." The New Hebrew Man was always described in masculine terms and was the antithesis of the stereotype of the weak, ineffectual, intellectual, neurotic Diaspora Jew. European Zionist leader Max Nordau was especially vocal in calling for the physical improvement of the Jews as a vital part of Zionist regeneration and argued for the development of *muskeljudentum* (muscular Jews), meaning that Jews must develop their physical strength rather than their intellectual abilities. This would be achieved, of course, through work on the land.[23]

But for all the masculine rhetoric and imagery, Zionist notions of social equality included, at least on a theoretical level, and as far as many women were concerned, the implicit promise of equality between men and women. This encouraged many women to hope that the emerging Zionist society would offer them a chance to break free from traditional gender roles. The pioneer expectations of women were also shaped by overly romantic notions of the Russian revolutionary movement, in which women like themselves were said to have transcended many gender barriers. But Russian revolutionary stories and Zionist ideals of gender equality clashed with social realities. One woman pioneer wrote that she was "astonished to find in Palestine separate women workers' institutions." She explained:

> We . . . women pioneers of the third immigration stream of 1919 to 1923, found it hard to understand the women workers' movement of Palestine. We had been brought up in and by the Russian revolution, at a time when women were occupying important economic and cultural positions. We believed that the wall which divided man's work from woman's had fallen forever. . . . But

before long the realities of Palestinian life taught me to approach the woman question in quite another way.[24]

Women who had witnessed, if not been part of, Russia's revolutionary movement were especially disturbed by what they regarded as a backslide in relations between men and women once they arrived in Palestine: "Over there, in the Russian exile, men and women had been equal comrades in the movement," wrote one woman. "We worked together, suffered together in the prisons and in the remote communities to which we were expelled; the moment the first pioneer certificates reached us, admitting us into Palestine, we were divided into the two classes: men comrades and women comrades."[25]

Women's training farms were intended to solve this problem by providing young women with agricultural training and hands-on experience in running a farm. The first such farm was started by activist Hanna Meisel in 1911. Meisel was born in Belorussia and studied agriculture and natural sciences in Switzerland and France before graduating with a doctorate in science. She arrived in Palestine in 1909. After joining the collective farm at Sejera, where women worked only in the kitchen, a disappointed Meisel came up with the idea of setting up a farm where women could learn about growing vegetables, raising poultry, dairy farming, cooking, and household management.

The Jewish National Fund leased the land for the farm, and the Berlin-based Women's Organization for Cultural Work in Palestine paid Meisel's salary, the rent on the land, and various other expenses. As a training institution, the farm was not expected to be self-supporting. Approximately twenty young women lived on the farm; in total, about seventy were trained there. Meisel also wanted to provide cooking courses and instruction in home management to the trainees, but apparently most were opposed to the idea. The young women involved in such ventures were often quite radical in their thinking—Margalit Shilo says that they "did not aspire to be farmer's wives" but "they did have a strong desire to shatter all the accepted norms." In her memoirs, one of the trainees later explained the young women's objections to studying home economics: "What sort of subject is that? All their lives women have worked in the kitchen. 'Kitchen and children' has been the slogan throughout the generations. What did a woman see in her life? She never left the children's room or the kitchen . . . the kitchen is a bitter necessity, but to make a goal of it?"[26] After funding ran out, the farm closed in 1917. With financial support from the Canadian Hadassah-WIZO organization, Meisel went on to establish a girls' agricultural school in Nahalal in 1923. She was principal of the school until 1960.[27]

Meisel's campaign to prove that with sufficient training young women could gain acceptance as agriculturalists was not entirely successful. Even when the idea of training girls and women for agricultural work was accepted, many still considered women's primary role to be a domestic one, that is, homemaking and child rearing as a knowledgeable but junior partner. An article in *The New Palestine*, for example, praised the Nahalal farm school as a place where girls "are taught the principles of domestic science and trained in the conduct of an orderly household," thus equipping them to become "interested and efficient partners in the development and conduct of farm homes."[28]

Among women's organizations active in the Yishuv, the Women's International Zionist Organization (WIZO) was a significant force helping to develop programs for girls and women. Founded in London in 1920, WIZO was designed as a federation that would unite women's Zionist organizations around the world. Although by virtue of the type of its programs and scope of its interests, WIZO was seen as the international counterpart of Hadassah, the two organizations kept their distance from one another and even regarded one another with some unease. Nonetheless, except for its geographic base and Hadassah's responsibility for medical care in Palestine, WIZO's agenda was similar to that of Hadassah. By mutual agreement, Hadassah limited its Diaspora activities to North America while WIZO was free to recruit members from all other countries.

Henrietta Szold acted as liaison between the two groups. In 1922, WIZO elected a five-member Palestine Executive that included Szold.[29] Founding member Dr. Vera Weizmann told an interviewer that many of the women who joined WIZO had previously "believed quite sincerely that the part taken by their husbands in the active work was sufficient and that there was no special duty for them to perform" but that the Balfour Declaration encouraged them to make a distinct contribution and so WIZO "sought an opportunity to help women in their own sphere." After examining the status of women in the Yishuv, WIZO concluded that

> domestic science, which was urgently needed in a country like Palestine was, for the most part, neglected. Young women who went to Palestine from Eastern lands found themselves untrained and totally unequipped to meet the needs of the new life. It was clearly the duty of Jewish women to come to their assistance, to help them secure the essential training which would enable them to take their positions either as land workers, farmers, or colonists' wives.[30]

After setting up a Palestine committee of WIZO to investigate local conditions, the organization decided to focus on helping women pioneers. A member of WIZO's executive explained that "thousands of untrained women and girls have entered Palestine. To turn these elements from a burden to a productive factor" the organization devised special "methods for training women in various urban trades and industrial occupations." With the slogan "Preparation of Women for Life in Palestine," WIZO took on a series of vocational projects: a girls' agricultural school, a hostel for girls in Tel Aviv, several infant welfare stations, and several girls' farms.[31]

Despite Szold's involvement in WIZO, and a shared vision with Hadassah, the relationship between WIZO and Hadassah was often uneasy if not cool. Hadassah rejected a WIZO offer to affiliate the two organizations, fearing that it might compromise Hadassah's independence of action. Szold criticized WIZO's organizational structure for its dependence on orders from a head office in London. Still, Szold did make several attempts, over the course of several years, to coordinate the two organizations' activities and responsibilities in Palestine, but she did not succeed. Szold even suggested that the two organizations try to formalize their communication and cooperate on joint projects. This too went nowhere. Ultimately, Hadassah and WIZO were only able to agree "that neither would invade the field of work chosen by the other in Palestine."[32]

Szold, obviously disappointed that WIZO and Hadassah could not combine their resources, was dismayed to learn that WIZO was prepared to affiliate with some local Palestinian women's organizations. But Hanna Meisel, a member of WIZO's World Executive in 1920, argued that both Szold and Hadassah should support WIZO's efforts to bring women's organizations together. Indeed, it was WIZO's mandate to solidify women's Zionist activities worldwide—except in North America, which was Hadassah's territory. As Meisel put it, Hadassah in particular

> should know the value of a strong and united Zionist women's organization, as Hadassah has been for the Zionist movement of America; WIZO should be the same for the world women. . . . The importance of the tasks undertaken by the WIZO cannot be overestimated; firstly, it educates women of the Galut [exile] for Zionism and makes them share in the building up of Palestine; it prepares women for life in the country and looks after children. There is no other body that is sufficiently interested and able to cope with these tasks. We must, therefore, protect it from everything that might weaken or destroy it.

Like Hadassah, WIZO's founders were frequently forced to defend the necessity of a separate Zionist women's organization. Using language strikingly reminiscent of Szold's own defense of Hadassah in clashes with the American

Zionist movement, Meisel made the case for WIZO's special "women's" mandate:

> Women are more active and have more initiative in separate organizations than in joint organization with men, where they leave the main work to the men or they are pushed aside against their will by the men who wish to hold the reins in their own hands. In joint organization, women lose their independent standing and their confidence in themselves. They are always in the minority. . . . The special needs of women are better understood by women than by men. Only women understand these needs, only they feel them and try to find solutions. It is, therefore, no accident that institutions for women were established only by women's organizations. Therefore, certain branches of work concerning women, which are not considered sufficiently by those men who are directing affairs of the Yishub [sic] and the building up of Palestine, as it is not given to them to feel the needs of women; neither can they value sufficiently the influence of women on life generally and on the building up of the land particularly. These special needs of women demanded expression and found it in the WIZO.[33]

But WIZO did not have the ground to themselves. Even as WIZO and Hadassah agreed to stay out of one another's way, both had a smaller but still tough competitor nipping at their heels from the left. A third Diaspora women's organization, Pioneer Women, was also actively involved in helping the Yishuv's women pioneers. Founded in 1925 in the United States, Pioneer Women was created as an organization of working-class Jewish women sympathetic to Labor Zionism and allied with the Palestinian women workers' movement (*Moezet Ha-Poalot*). The following year, at its first convention, the organization joined the Socialist International and the World Zionist Organization. In keeping with its Socialist Zionist roots, Pioneer Women focused, in the beginning, on supporting women's cooperatives in Palestine.[34]

Perhaps frustrated by the inability of Hadassah and WIZO to mesh their Palestine activities and concerned that other women's organizations could further fracture the women's movement (and undermine her power as the major spokesperson for women in the Yishuv), Szold announced in 1924 that "the women's organizations of Palestine have developed to such an extent that . . . plans were made for a general inclusive women's organization, to deal not only with problems involving the welfare of mothers and children, but all questions interesting the women of the land."[35] This new organization launched by Szold was called the *Histadrut Nashim Ivriot* (HNI) or Federation of Hebrew Women. The HNI's mandate was to both facilitate Hadassah's social welfare work and create its own related projects. Szold intended the HNI to be an organizational umbrella that could coordinate all women's activities in Palestine and also "serve as a bureau of information on the needs of Palestine to Jewish women abroad." Any woman's organization in Palestine with more than fifteen members could become a constituent group of the HNI.[36]

By 1929 the HNI had fourteen local branches and, as Szold described it, "functions as an agent of Hadassah" delivering Hadassah-funded services and supplies. Like Hadassah, the HNI founded kindergartens, provided school lunches, ran a summer camp, and organized Hebrew language classes for women.[37]

Although the HNI was on paper an autonomous, indigenous organization, it was in reality tightly controlled by Szold and the Hadassah organization. Hadassah provided some funding and, with Szold's advice, dictated how the money should be spent. Although the members of the HNI hoped Hadassah would fund projects decided on by the HNI members, Hadassah insisted that the HNI would have to raise money locally for any new projects and that rather than expect more Hadassah money, the HNI should aim to gradually become financially self-sufficient. Given the scarce resources of Palestinian Jewish women, the organization was essentially hamstrung unless it did fundraising of its own abroad. This, of course, would bring the HNI into a collision course with either Hadassah or WIZO or both.[38]

Indeed, Szold repeatedly warned that the HNI's efforts to raise funds abroad for its projects "produce confusion in the minds of women interested in Palestine and its development" and might undermine fundraising drives by established organizations like Hadassah and WIZO. Szold complained that there were already too many Palestinian organizations competing for attention as they solicited funds in the United States and that they "resort to the publicity methods first developed and applied by the large central funds. They have as it were stolen their thunder." For these reasons, Hadassah also took steps to stop the HNI from approaching potential donors in the United States. Then, the HNI raised the ire of WIZO when it attempted to fundraise for its own projects in Europe.[39]

The launch of a monthly Hebrew-language women's journal called *Ha-Isha* (The Woman) in 1927 marked a rare occasion of cooperation between Hadassah, WIZO, and the HNI. Subtitled "A Monthly Journal Devoted to the Life and Activities of Women in Palestine," the journal had as its primary purpose, Szold explained, "to become the organ through which the women of Palestine could become thoroughly well organized, while at the same time Zionist women all over the world would be put in touch with Jewish women's work in Palestine."

The ulterior motive for starting the journal was, Szold admitted, "to secure a common undertaking in which the organized Zionist women of the world . . . might cooperate." Editorial control rested with the women of the HNI in

Palestine; production costs were the shared responsibility of Hadassah and WIZO. Lotta Levensohn, a former Hadassah president who now lived in Jerusalem, accepted the position of Hadassah representative on the journal's editorial board. English-language and German-language supplements were planned for the benefit of would-be subscribers unable to read Hebrew.[40]

Early issues of the journal dealt with weighty social, political, and legal topics including women's legal status, the working women's movement, women lawyers, and child marriages. The following year the journal included a discussion of "the difficulties encountered by European women in adapting themselves to rural life in Palestine and gives as a solution a systematic and scientific study of household management." The journal recommended the establishment of "a course in home economics for women in Palestine, modeled after such courses given in America."[41]

The journal was ambitious, but the readership was small. In 1927, the editors acknowledged that with only four hundred subscribers in Palestine, "it is still somewhat too early to judge if the aim of 'Ha-Isha' to create a bond between Palestinian women of all parties can be achieved within the near future." In addition, they noted that "various criticisms have been received from Palestinian readers, recording their own and their husbands' complaints that 'Ha-Isha' furnished no practical hints on household problems, care of children and invalids, etc." In response, the editors promised to provide readers with a special supplement containing practical advice.[42]

Not all *Ha-Isha* staff were pleased. One editor, Sarah Thon, resigned, saying that she was "unable to make the paper less 'high-brow.'"[43] But the other editors did their best to oblige their readers without sacrificing quality. In a subsequent issue *Ha-Isha* suggested that for those "engrossed in the immediate practical problems of child education and household management, the special articles on Puerperal Fever and its Prevention, The Timid Child, and The Nutritive Values of Fruits and Vegetables are of special interest."[44]

Ha-Isha may have lacked mass market appeal, but it did show Hadassah and WIZO's commitment to educating Palestinian women. It was this commitment, backed up by a strong Hadassah presence on the ground in Palestine, that Szold felt was so important. And it was this presence, Szold argued, that ensured Hadassah would avoid the pitfalls that resulted from the arms-length involvement so typical of other American Zionist organizations. She urged Hadassah to send someone to Palestine as a liaison between American and Palestinian women:

> You must have your own representative in Palestine. You must have someone
> . . . who will always keep you informed of what is happening to your work and

to Palestine. That person must be a Zionist, must know Hebrew well, and must know all departments of Zionist work. . . . She must participate in the organization of the womanhood of Palestine. She must know how to cooperate with the 400 working women who have already organized themselves. She must be able to reach the hand of fellowship to the WIZO which has made a valiant beginning in Palestine. She must know how to go to the women whose ancestors have lived in Palestine for generations. She must be a Palestinian from the moment she sets her foot on Palestinian soil.[45]

In this way Szold hoped that Hadassah might link American and Palestinian women together and build bridges to women's organizations already active in the Yishuv.

The plan to create a Palestine Women's Council was another effort to co-ordinate and consolidate the Zionist women's organizations working in the Diaspora with those in Palestine. The idea was first raised by the HNI at a meeting of Palestinian women's organizations in Jerusalem in 1924 and was supported by Szold. The council was to "act as a bureau of information and advice to women all over the world interested in the development of Palestine" and was to include representatives of Zionist women's organizations in the Diaspora as well as in Palestine. A detailed plan was dispatched to the National Board of Hadassah in New York and advanced by a delegation of Palestinian women attending the Biennial Conference of WIZO, held in conjunction with the Zionist Congress in Vienna in August 1925.

Hadassah agreed to the plan, but WIZO rejected it. Without WIZO support, the idea crumbled. Szold, however, remained optimistic that the council would eventually be established and was encouraged by the 1924 meeting: "I felt justified in indulging in the dream of a future when these women, augmented many-fold, would create the center towards which Jewish women all over the world would look for guidance and unification."[46]

The creation of and support for new women's organizations in the Yishuv were just one part of Hadassah's larger agenda of guiding Palestinian women toward modernization and Westernization. If former Eastern European women pioneers would benefit from exposure to these areas, it was the Oriental Jewish women, seen as prisoners of backward cultures, who were thought most in need of assistance. From the moment of their arrival in Palestine, members of the Hadassah organization were particularly interested in "uplifting" the women and children of the Yishuv's Oriental Jewish population. A Hadassah doctor described

these communities . . . with standards foreign to present day civilization, and an oriental point of view looking askance at hygienic rules of our day. Many of them, unable to read or write, live without any higher needs. Every man in this group marries several women, raising families averaging ten in number. The women must work and provide for the house while the husband either wastes his time or goes almost begging from door to door. It is hard to find among them even one woman who is not covered with charm stones and other kinds of "remedies."[47]

Although the Yemenites and other Orientals were occasionally romanticized for their authentic "Easternness" and preservation of Jewish traditions, they were more often discussed with some condescension and portrayed as the subjects of concern. A 1926 article in *The New Palestine* portrayed Oriental Jewish women living behind a veil of ignorance and poverty:

> Their almond-shaped black eyes have the dreamy, submissive expression of the ever restrained, ever dominated woman of the Orient. I must confess, they do not seem unhappy, they have no desire for any other lot than theirs. Their mother, their grandmother has had the same life—why should it change? Married at 14, they look up to their man as a master who may be kind, and distribute them work and babies—and if he is not kind they have to take him just the same—they don't wish for anything better, anymore than a dog believes he could live his own life, and they are not sadder or unhappier than he is.[48]

Hadassah feared for the future of girls among these communities. A Hadassah nurse working in a poor neighborhood of Jerusalem described the lot of a typical girl:

> When she reaches the age of five or six she is already mature and must help her mother in the housework, and must help with the younger children, or she is sent to serve in other households. Blows, curses, scoldings, constitute the educational system under which she is brought up, until she reaches the age of 13 or 14, the period for the gathering of her dowry and her marriage. And so the young generation grows up broken in body and spirit, a degenerate generation which carries on its tradition of filth and ignorance.[49]

The American women were especially troubled by polygamy, the low status of women, and the phenomena of child labor and child marriage among the Oriental Jews they encountered. But their efforts to intervene were often resented. As Jessie Sampter acknowledged in a 1926 article for the *Hadassah News Letter*:

It is difficult because the Yemenite men hate us. That sounds terrible. The women among the Yemenites are in a very low position; we are trying to help them and their husbands are not pleased, especially as the Yemenite Jews believe in the ancient Jewish law—they are allowed several wives and . . . some still practice it. There are cases where we have been instrumental in freeing a woman from the difficulties which arise. So you will understand why we are not popular with the men and why we don't want to be.[50]

Sampter, a Hadassah member who moved to Palestine permanently in 1919, lived in Rehovot—then a village of two thousand people including one hundred Yemenite families living on the outskirts. She was fascinated by Yemenite Jews, and wrote many articles for the American Zionist press describing the difficulties faced by Yemenite girls and women. "Yemenite Girls: Types Among the New Immigrants," published in *The New Palestine* in 1927, is typical of her writing on this topic. The article profiles the lives of three young girls who all worked long hours as domestic servants. Without hectoring, Sampter depicts the privations and hardships of daily life for these children.

Sampter wrote that one of the girls was fortunate to have "forward-looking, cultured" employers who were willing to let her attend the evening classes organized "for the little working girls but her father would not permit her to attend. And he would not be moved. To all arguments he answered: 'It is against our tradition to educate girls. It would only spoil her.'"[51] That is not to say Oriental women did not try to better their own lot. Other articles by Sampter detail the efforts made by Yemenite women to prevent their husbands from marrying additional wives and to ensure that their daughters, as well as their sons, received an education.

By 1930, Sampter's perspective had broadened. She was no longer concerned just about cultural lag among Yemenites. She was just as enraged by what she regarded as the Yishuv's systemically poor treatment of Oriental Jews: "They are treated as inferiors, almost as a servant class, by their fellow immigrants. . . . We treat them like stepchildren, half-breeds." Sampter also decried the poor health of Yemenite children, "most of them dangerously undernourished . . . and perpetually hungry." Efforts to encourage Yemenite girls to get an education were thus stymied on two sides: "We have to fight on the one hand the employing woman who keeps her 'servant girl' working until late at night, and on the other hand the Yemenite father who believes it is a sin for a woman to read."[52]

Even as Palestinian pioneers continued to struggle, new immigrants poured into the country faster than any organization could design programs to help

them. At the end of 1926, the *Hadassah News Letter* reported that nearly eight
thousand single women, aged sixteen and up, had arrived in Palestine over the
previous two years:

> The total number of working women in the country is about 8000, of whom
> some 2000 are engaged in agricultural work. Some 700 women are employed
> as seamstresses, dressmakers, and embroiderers, at a very low daily wage. . . .
> Some 500 women are employed in factories, 150 in building trades. . . . In of-
> fice work and the professions about 800 women are employed. The number of
> unemployed women is about 1000.[53]

Because they lacked education and skills appropriate to the Palestinian
situation, most of the young women immigrants were ill equipped for any but
the most menial work. A memorandum from the secretary for women's work
of the Palestine Zionist Executive listed options available to newly arrived
immigrant women: joining an agricultural settlement or a wage worker's
group in the colonies; entering the women's agricultural school at Nahalal or
the Domestic Science school in Tel Aviv (both funded by WIZO); joining a
women's farming group for two years of preparatory training in order to become a member of an agricultural settlement; joining a women's collective to
learn various types of wage work as well as poultry farming and gardening on
the small household farm belonging to the group; or, finally, seeking "urban
occupations" as dressmakers, household help, or factory workers. But even
these options required women to have guidance and additional training. The
memorandum recommended the creation of hostels to shelter immigrant
girls and women immediately upon arrival in the country and to offer "some
training in rational cooking and household management."[54]

A proposal by a group called the Women's League for Palestine to create
such a hostel for the reception of young immigrant girls was endorsed, in substance although not in its particulars, by Szold, who hoped the hostels would
allow the young immigrant girl to "remain under wise guidance and supervision until she finds herself and determines what she wants to do and can do
in the conditions prevailing in Palestine with which, since they are strange
to her, she must have the opportunity of getting acquainted." However, Szold
was concerned that the league lacked sufficient funds to pay for both the proposed vocational training and the employment placement services to be offered through the hostels. Given the league's limited budget, Szold argued
that the hostels should at first limit themselves to offering short-term accommodation and help the girls to find jobs so that they could "be gotten out
as quickly as possible."[55]

Along with the street-level work of developing programs to help women adapt to life in the Yishuv, both Szold and Hadassah gave priority to backing the struggle for women's suffrage, political rights, and social equality in the Yishuv. Szold stressed that the recognition of women's rights was a crucial step in developing a modern Jewish society on a par with developed Western countries. For Szold, the achievement of women's rights was not so much a goal in itself as a vital building block of the creation of a new Jewish society based on principles of social equality. As she explained to Hadassah's National Board:

> Here in Palestine an organic life is being developed. You and I may not like some of its manifestations. As a matter of fact I confess to you that some of its manifestations have aroused my indignation and destroyed my nerves. But for better or for worse, that is the organic life that is being developed by Zionists here who are bone of the bone and flesh of the flesh of our ideal, the ideal we pursue in common with them. If we don't like some of the manifestations of their organized living, we can't withdraw to an island and draw up our skirts, and refuse to participate in their deliberations. We've got to get into their deliberations and influence their course and character.[56]

To spread the message of women's rights required organizational cooperation. Szold herself consistently worked to bring Zionist women's organizations together, to coordinate their efforts, and to develop lines of communication between women in the Diaspora and women in the Yishuv.

Involvement in the campaign for women's rights in Palestine, Hadassah leaders believed, had a reciprocal, beneficial effect on American Jewish women: "Not only is Palestine strengthened," argued Rose Halprin in the *Hadassah News Letter*, "but Jewish life in America becomes more vital as we succeed in interesting large numbers of American Jewish women in our program."[57] Similarly, Rose Jacobs wrote of "the education in politics which the Zionist woman is achieving by virtue of her contact with the internal structure of the Palestinian community, as well as with the place of Palestine in the international scene." As a result of their work for Hadassah, Jacobs concluded, American Jewish women got an "almost professional preparation."[58]

And if women's rights might at first seem like a Western import—the imposition of yet more American ways on the Yishuv—for Szold and Hadassah, the priority was to ensure that Palestinian women's organizations, like Palestinian society overall, would at some point become independent and self-sufficient rather than continuing to depend on assistance from the Diaspora.

Helping women to learn the basics of running an organization was a first step. In 1926, Jessie Sampter recalled the first meeting of the newly formed HNI:

> Miss Szold called a meeting . . . of all classes of Jewish women in Jerusalem— women, many of whom had never attended any kind of meeting, who didn't know how to speak in order. About forty came. There were educated women and illiterate women, European women, Yemenites, Sephardim. There was every strange and Oriental costume represented. We conducted the meeting in Hebrew, but had to translate it into four languages. It was hard to persuade the women to speak in order. Slowly the organization developed. A year or two later we had two or three hundred members. We had Hebrew classes; the meetings were orderly; the addresses didn't have to be translated.[59]

Clearly, just as American Jewish women gained both organizational experience and confidence in themselves as political actors through their participation in Hadassah, Palestinian Jewish women were receiving a similar political education through their participation in the Hadassah-supported HNI.

The drive to bring Hadassah closer to the Palestinian scene while at the same time encouraging local control was advanced in 1924 with the appointment of Nellie Straus Mochenson as Hadassah's representative in Palestine. According to the *Hadassah News Letter*, this "marked our coming of age. . . . It has made us citizens of Palestine." Mochenson's role was to keep Hadassah "in close touch with developments in Palestine, particularly in the world of women's work and organization." Along with sitting on various committees as Hadassah's representative, Mochenson was also credited with the successful organization of the Health Week events.[60]

Mochenson's role was superseded by the creation of the Palestine Council of Hadassah in 1930. Levensohn explained that the council would "take advantage of the presence in Palestine of several American women bred in the Hadassah tradition and familiar with Hadassah methods, in order to bring Hadassah closer to the Yishuv and the Yishuv closer to Hadassah."[61] More precisely, the council "would serve as a sounding board through which the Hadassah in America could hear more clearly the voice of Palestinian womanhood, and through which it could make its own aims in the field of women's work better understood in Palestine."[62]

To begin with, the council took over the administration of three non-medical projects: the school luncheons, the Guggenheimer Playgrounds, and clothing distribution (administered jointly with the HNI). But the goal was larger. "The interest of the Yishuv was to be stimulated" by the council "with a view to enlisting its moral and financial support, at first with a view to expansion and eventually to integration in the Yishuv's own services."

The Yishuv, a state in waiting, would operate a national infrastructure in waiting.

Ultimately, in 1936, the Palestine Council of Hadassah joined with the Mizrachi Women's Organization, the Working Women's Council, and the Women's Equal Rights League to form a new Council of Jewish Women's Organizations. The purpose of this council was to be "an agency which would be authorized to speak for the Jewish women of Palestine in matters of common national interest." In 1937, Hadassah reported that the new council "has already done some useful work as the mouthpiece of the Palestine Jewish women vis-à-vis non-Jewish circles" and was consulted by the Va'ad Leumi.[63]

The struggle for women's voice and rights was a struggle of small steps and many hard-fought victories. In 1935, a short article in the *New York Times* announced that Hadassah helped to win such a victory for women's rights in Palestine:

> After a long struggle for equal property rights, Jewish women in Palestine will be recognized henceforth as co-lessees with their husbands in the rental of land from the Jewish National Fund. . . . The united efforts of the Jewish women of Palestine and this country brought about a change in the legal formula for lease contracts, permitting a double signature for man and wife, with equal rights for both.[64]

This was the struggle for the kind of practical legal rights that Szold had described to three thousand American Hadassah supporters in her speech at the Hotel Pennsylvania over a decade earlier—a development that she hoped would lead to the "internal consolidation" of the Yishuv.

In her constant struggle to rally support for women's programs and facilities in Palestine, Szold was even willing to appeal to non-Zionist Jewish organizations. While on a visit to the United States in 1935, for instance, Szold tried to convince the members of the National Council of Jewish Women (NCJW), a non-Zionist group, to extend their interest in immigrant girls from the United States to Palestine:

> An immigrant girl is stranded in the large cities, Tel-Aviv or Haifa. Our industrial system is not yet so great that such girls can find their place easily. What a wonderful thing it would be if the National Council of Jewish Women were to say to itself, "We have an obligation to the immigrant girl." The immigrant girl of years ago had her face set to America. The face of the immigrant girl today cannot be set toward America. America is no longer the goal of the immigrant. The country of immigration today is Palestine. . . . It is that

I would like you to say to yourself. It is the duty of the Council of Jewish Women to take care of the immigrant girl who turns to Palestine.[65]

Although some measure of cooperation and coordination among women's organizations was, of necessity, eventually achieved, Szold never realized her dream of a single, politically inclusive, strong women's organization in Palestine that would operate as the nerve center of an international Zionist women's movement and, one suspects, in which she would play a leading role. Nevertheless, Hadassah's successes in helping to organize Jewish women in the Yishuv as well as the United States gave the organization new confidence:

We live in the twentieth century. Women do men's work in the community, efficiently and with full realization of their responsibility. To be womanly, in twentieth century America, is to be comrade and partner. To be womanly in Zionism, means nothing less; to participate freely and completely in all that concerns the upbuilding of Palestine, to share the responsibility as well as the labor, to be fearless and resolute where the welfare of the Land of Israel is concerned.[66]

For Hadassah, advancing the equality of women in the Zionist movement and in the Yishuv, like its commitment to building social welfare services, was now an inextricable part of the organization's mandate.

Notes

1. Priska Gmur, "'It Is Not Up to Us Women to Solve Great Problems': The Duty of the Zionist Woman in the Context of the First Ten Zionist Congresses," in *The First Zionist Congress in 1897—Causes, Significance, Topicality*, ed. Heiko Haumann (Basel: Karger, 1997), 294.

2. Gmur, "It Is Not Up to Us Women," 293.

3. Theodor Herzl, "Women and Zionism," *The Maccabaean*, February 1917, 156.

4. Alice L. Seligsberg, "The Woman's Way: A Brief Analysis of Methods," *The New Palestine*, 23 June 1922, 432.

5. Lotta Levensohn, "Women of Palestine," *Hadassah News Letter*, May–June 1930, 2, 8. (In 1927 Levensohn was appointed to serve as a "liaison officer" between Palestine and America as part of her work on the Advisory Council set up by the Hadassah Medical Organization to serve as its administration.)

6. Hortense Levy, "Hadassah and Other Women's Organizations," in *Modern Palestine: A Symposium*, ed. Jessie Sampter (New York: Hadassah, the Women's Zionist Organization of America, 1933), 286.

7. Naomi Shepherd, *Ploughing Sand: British Rule in Palestine, 1917–1948* (London: John Murray, 1999), 245.

8. Hanna Herzog, "The Fringes of the Margin: Women's Organizations in the Civic Sector of the Yishuv," in *Pioneers and Homemakers: Jewish Women in Pre-State Israel*, ed. Deborah Bernstein (Albany: State University of New York Press, 1992), 287; see also Sarah Azaryahu, *The Union of Hebrew Women for Equal Rights in Eretz Ysrael: Chapters in the History of the Women's Movement of Eretz Ysrael*, trans. Marcia Freedman (Jerusalem: Union of Hebrew Women for Equal Rights in Israel, 1948; reprint: Haifa: Women's Aid Fund, n.d.). The organization referred to here as the Women's Equal Rights League is sometimes also called the Union of Hebrew Women for Equal Rights.

9. Elections to the National Assembly were based on proportional representation, and political parties ran via lists of their candidates as they do in elections to the Israeli Knesset today. There were four such elections in the pre-state period: 1920, 1925, 1931, and 1944. The assembly set up the Va'ad Leumi (National Council) to draft a constitution for the autonomous Jewish community and to secure British approval. The assembly was abolished shortly after statehood. The Women's Equal Rights League ran candidates on Women's Lists in five national elections.

10. For an explanation of Orthodox religious attitudes toward women's suffrage, see Zvi Zohar, "Traditional Flexibility and Modern Strictness: Two Halakhic Positions on Women's Suffrage," in *Sephardi and Middle Eastern Jewries: History and Culture in the Modern Era*, ed. Harvey E. Goldberg (Bloomington: Indiana University Press, 1996), 119–33. Zohar points out that when the suffrage question was first raised in Palestine (as part of the effort to establish a representative body in 1917), women could vote in only five countries in Europe. By 1921, however, ten more countries in Europe had granted the vote to women. But "the line separating suffrage from nonsuffrage states divided the continent north and south: the entire south of Europe . . . did not allow women to vote" (120). The battle for women's suffrage in the United States began in the 1860s and was finally won with the passage of the Nineteenth Amendment in 1920.

11. "Women's Votes in Palestine," *Hadassah News Letter*, December 1925, 7.

12. "Women's Suffrage Rights," *Hadassah News Letter*, August 1925, 14.

13. Sylvie Fogiel-Bijaoui, "On the Way to Equality? The Struggle for Women's Suffrage in the Jewish Yishuv, 1917–1926," in Bernstein, ed., *Pioneers and Homemakers*, 270; Azaryahu, *The Union of Hebrew Women*, 27.

14. Szold, "Jewish Palestine in the Making," in Aaron S. Klieman and Adrian L. Klieman, eds., *American Zionism: A Documentary History*, vol. 5, *My Brother's Keeper: Fostering Projects in the Jewish National Home* (New York: Garland, 1990), 4. This speech was also reported in the mainstream American press: "3,000 Greet Woman Palestine Leader: Miss Henrietta Szold Describes Work and Problems in the Holy Land," *New York Times*, 1 May 1923, 4.

15. Editorial, *The New Palestine*, 16 September 1927, 203.

16. Very little has been written about women in the Yishuv. The best primers—covering the status of women and some of the major women's organizations—are Bernstein, ed., *Pioneers and Homemakers*, and Deborah Bernstein, *The Struggle for*

Equality: Urban Women Workers in Prestate Israeli Society (New York: Praeger, 1987). Ada Maimon was a pioneer and political activist who fought for women's rights in pre-state Israel. She wrote a thorough guide to women's organizations, activities, and status in the Yishuv: *Women Build a Land*, trans. Shulamith Schwarz-Nardi (New York: Herzl Press, 1962). A useful essay by Hortense Levy, "Hadassah and Other Women's Organizations," also surveys the development and work of various women's organizations in the Yishuv and may be found in Sampter, ed., *Modern Palestine: A Symposium.*

17. Editorial, "Woman Suffrage in Jewish Palestine," *The Maccabaean*, June 1918, 160. See also Fogiel-Bijaoui, "On the Way to Equality?" in Bernstein, ed., *Pioneers and Homemakers.*

18. Maxa Nordau, "Pioneer Types: The Women Workers of Palestine," *The New Palestine*, 15 October 1926, 204.

19. Marie Syrkin, "Palestine, Hope of Jewry: Interview with Sophie Irene Loeb," *The New Palestine*, 30 October 1925, 340. Loeb (1874–1929) was a social worker and journalist. In 1926 she chaired the first International Child Congress.

20. Sarah Malchin, "The Woman Worker in Kinneret," *Hapoel Hatzair* 11–13, 1913, quoted in Maimon, *Women Build a Land*, 23. Malchin was the only woman among the sixteen members of the collective that established the first independent workers' farm in 1911 in Degania.

21. For a discussion of the ideas of Ha'am, Gordon, and other major Zionist thinkers, see Shlomo Avineri, *The Making of Modern Zionism: The Intellectual Origins of the Jewish State* (New York: Basic Books, 1981).

22. Rachel Janaith, "At Work," in *The Plough Woman: Memoirs of the Pioneer Women of Palestine*, ed. Rachel Katznelson-Rubashow, trans. Maurice Samuel (Westport, Conn.: Hyperion, 1976), 138.

23. For *muskeljudentum*, see George L. Mosse, "Max Nordau: Liberalism and the New Jew," in *Confronting the Nation: Jewish and Western Nationalism* (Hanover, N.H.: Brandeis University Press, 1993), 161–75. See also Oz Almog, *The Sabra: The Creation of the New Jew*, trans. Haim Watzman (Berkeley: University of California Press, 2000); Michael Berkowitz, *The Jewish Self-Image in the West* (New York: New York University Press, 2000); Michael Berkowitz, "Zionist Heroes and New Men," in *Zionist Culture and West European Jewry Before the First World War* (Chapel Hill: University of North Carolina Press, 1993), 99–118.

24. Miriam Schlimowitch, "The Women's Farm in Nachlath Jehudah," in Katznelson-Rubashow, ed., *The Plough Woman*, 159.

25. Zipporah Bar-Droma, "Comrade So-and-So's Wife," in Katznelson-Rubashow, ed., *The Plough Woman*, 182.

26. Margalit Shilo, "The Women's Farm at Kinneret, 1911–1917: A Solution to the Problem of the Working Woman in the Second Aliya," in *The Jerusalem Cathedra*, ed. Lee I. Levine (Jerusalem: Yad Izhak Ben Zvi Institute, 1981), 271. See also Margalit Shilo, "The Women's Farm at Kinneret, 1911–1917," in Bernstein, ed., *Pioneers and Homemakers*; Gerald M. Berg, "Zionism's Gender: Hannah Meisel and the

Founding of the Agricultural Schools for Young Women," *Israel Studies* 6, no. 3 (Fall 2001): 135–65. Note: Meisel's name appears with various spellings including Maisel and Maisl, and sometimes as her married name, Meisel-Shohat.

27. Maimon, *Women Build a Land*, 29. For Canadian support, see the section on WIZO in Hortense Levy, "Hadassah and Other Women's Organizations," in Sampter, ed., *Modern Palestine: A Symposium*, 292–93.

28. Elwood Mead, "Farming in Palestine: Preparing Young Women for It," *The New Palestine*, 23 May 1924, 416.

29. Raphael Patai, ed., *Encyclopedia of Zionism and Israel* (New York: Herzl Press, 1971), s.v. "WIZO" by R. Jaglom and R. Gassman. There are now WIZO affiliates in over fifty countries, including Canada.

30. Meir Zev, "Women in Zionism: An Interview with Dr. Vera Weizmann," *The New Palestine*, 21 March 1924, 225.

31. Henrietta Szold, "Memorandum I: On Women's Organizations in Palestine," Jerusalem, May 1929, RG 7/HS/B 31/F 356, HWZOA; Seraphina Polak, "WIZO—Educator of Palestine's Women," *Hadassah Newsletter*, April 1942, 20–21. For a history of WIZO and a thorough description of its activities, see Hanna Herzog and Ofra Greenberg, *A Voluntary Women's Organization in a Society in the Making: WIZO's Contribution to Israeli Society* (Tel Aviv: Tel Aviv University Institute of Social Research, 1978).

32. Henrietta Szold, "Letter to the National Board of Hadassah," 21 December 1929, 2, RG 7/B 13/F 130, HWZOA. See also Hanna Herzog, "The Fringes of the Margin: Women's Organizations in the Civic Sector of the Yishuv," in Bernstein, ed., *Pioneers and Homemakers*, 283–303.

33. Hanna Maisl-Shohat, "Memorandum: Affiliation," n.d., F 49/1443/3, CZA.

34. Paula Hyman and Deborah Dash Moore, eds., *Jewish Women in America: An Historical Encyclopedia* (New York: Routledge, 1997), s.v. "Pioneer Women" by Mark Raider; Rebekah Kohut, "Jewish Women's Organizations in the United States," *American Jewish Year Book* 33 (1931): 187–89.

35. "Revisiting Palestine: The Country's Remarkable Progress; An Interview with Henrietta Szold," *The New Palestine*, 23 May 1924, 417.

36. "Women's Organizations," *Hadassah News Letter*, July 1924, 13.

37. Henrietta Szold, "Memorandum I: On Women's Organization in Palestine," 2.

38. Herzog, "The Fringes of the Margin," in Bernstein, ed., *Pioneers and Homemakers*, 290.

39. Henrietta Szold to Rose Vitales, 12 February 1931, RG 7/HS/B 12/F 127, HWZOA; Henrietta Szold, "Memorandum II: On the Plan Submitted by the Women's League for Palestine," Jerusalem, May 1929, RG 7/HS/B 31/F 356, HWZOA. See also Herzog and Greenberg, *A Voluntary Women's Organization*, 29–30.

40. Henrietta Szold, "Miss Szold's Seventh Letter," *Hadassah News Letter*, June 1924, 8–9; Henrietta Szold, "Ha-Isha: First Woman's Journal in Palestine," *Hadassah News Letter*, June 1926, 2.

41. "Ha-Isha," *Hadassah News Letter*, April 1927, 6.

42. "Six Months of Ha-Isha," *Hadassah News Letter*, February 1927, 6.

43. Henrietta Szold, Jerusalem, to the National Board of Hadassah, New York City, 14 October 1928, RG 7/HS/B 13/F 138, HWZOA.

44. "Ha-Isha," *Hadassah News Letter*, December 1928, 6.

45. Henrietta Szold, "Jewish Palestine in the Making," 1923, RG 7/HS/B 18/F 179, HWZOA.

46. Henrietta Szold, "Palestine: Two Conferences," *Hadassah News Letter*, October 1926, 2.

47. Dr. Emanuel Cohen, "Obstetric and Infant Welfare in Palestine by Hadassah," *Hadassah News Letter*, November 1926, 3.

48. Maxa Nordau, "Pioneer Types: The Women Workers of Palestine," *The New Palestine*, 15 October 1926, 204.

49. Rachel Pesach, "What a Nurse Sees," *Hadassah News Letter*, October 1928, 7–8.

50. Jessie Sampter, "Histadrut Nashim in Rehoboth," *Hadassah News Letter*, January 1926, 6. For more on this issue, see Nitza Druyan, "Yemenite Jewish Women—Between Tradition and Change," in Bernstein, ed., *Pioneers and Homemakers*, 75–93; Nitza Druyan, "Yemenite Jews on the Zionist Altar," in *Review Essays in Israel Studies*, ed. Laura Zittrain Eisenberg and Neil Caplan (Albany: State University of New York Press, 2000), 153–72.

51. Jessie E. Sampter, "Yemenite Girls: Types Among the New Immigrants," *The New Palestine*, 6 May 1927, 424.

52. Jessie E. Sampter, "Errors in Utopia: Critical Comments on Palestine's Attitude to the Oriental Jew," *The New Palestine*, 16 May 1930, 306–7.

53. "8000 Working Women in Palestine," *Hadassah News Letter*, December 1926, 2.

54. "Memorandum on Hostel Prepared by the Secretary for Women's Work of the P.Z.E. and Representative of the W.I.Z.O.," n.d., F 49/1443/3, CZA.

55. Szold, "Memorandum II: On the Plan Submitted by the Women's League for Palestine."

56. Henrietta Szold, Jerusalem, to the National Board of Hadassah, 23 March 1929, RG 17/HS/B 17/F 168b, HWZOA.

57. Rose L. Halprin, "Dear Hadassah Members," *Hadassah News Letter*, September–October 1932.

58. Rose Jacobs, "Hadassah and the American Woman," *Hadassah News Letter*, March 1941, 16.

59. Sampter, "Histadrut Nashim in Rehoboth," 6.

60. "The Palestinian Representative of Hadassah, the Women's Zionist Organization," *Hadassah News Letter*, August 1925, 5.

61. Lotta Levensohn, "Palestine Council of Hadassah," *Hadassah News Letter*, February 1937, 6.

62. Lotta Levensohn, "The Palestine Council of Hadassah," *Hadassah News Letter*, January–February 1933, 6.

63. Lotta Levensohn, "Palestine Council of Hadassah," *Hadassah News Letter*, February 1937, 20–21.

64. "Wins Fight in Palestine: Hadassah Reports Equal Rights Gained for Women on Leases," *New York Times*, 20 July 1935, 11.

65. Henrietta Szold, "Speech at the Dinner Given by Executive Committee, National Council of Jewish Women," 26 December 1935, RG 7/HS/B 18/F 202, HW-ZOA. The NCJW was a non-Zionist but not anti-Zionist organization. Members who were Zionists were free to join Hadassah as well; some did so. See Faith Rogow, *Gone to Another Meeting: The National Council of Jewish Women, 1893–1993* (Tuscaloosa: University of Alabama Press, 1993).

66. "If This Be Politics—!" *Hadassah News Letter*, 11 May 1928.

CREATION OF HADASSAH (1890s–1910s)

Henrietta Szold, 1899. Courtesy of Hadassah, the Women's Zionist Organization of America, Inc.

The first two Hadassah nurses, Rose Kaplan (left) and Rachel Landy (right), with Hadassah's Eva Leon (middle) in Jerusalem, 1913. Leon, along with the Strauses, accompanied the nurses on their voyage to Palestine. Courtesy of Hadassah, the Women's Zionist Organization of America, Inc.

On the eve of sailing for Palestine, American Zionist Medical Unit nurses with members of Hadassah's Central Committee in New York, 1918. Bottom row, from right to left: Henrietta Szold, Alice L. Seligsberg, Dora Lefkowitz, Ruth Fromenson, Emma Gottheil, Bertha Wenheim, Ida Danziger, Libby Oppenheimer. Courtesy of Hadassah, the Women's Zionist Organization of America, Inc.

CHILD WELFARE (1920s–1930s)

This donkey was used to deliver pasteurized milk from the first Mother and Infant Welfare Station in the Old City of Jerusalem, early 1920s. The milk was distributed to the needy at minimal cost. Courtesy of Hadassah, the Women's Zionist Organization of America, Inc.

Mothers and children waiting to be seen by a nurse at a Health Welfare Center, Jerusalem, c. 1920s–1930s. Courtesy of Hadassah, the Women's Zionist Organization of America, Inc.

Infant welfare nurse instructs mother on proper food for baby, c. 1920s–1930s. Courtesy of Hadassah, the Women's Zionist Organization of America, Inc.

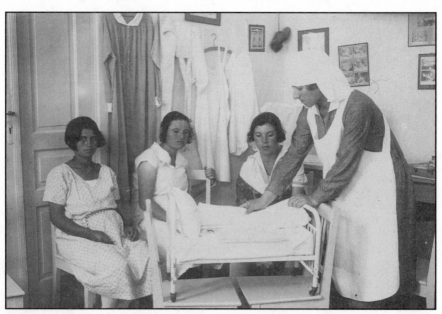

Bedmaking demonstration at an Infant Welfare Station, Tel Aviv, 1924. Courtesy of Hadassah, the Women's Zionist Organization of America, Inc.

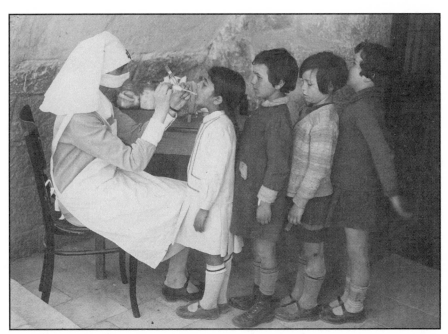

School nurse examines children as part of Hadassah's School Hygiene Program, Jerusalem, 1929. Courtesy of Hadassah, the Women's Zionist Organization of America, Inc.

Classes in corrective exercises at the Nathan and Lina Straus Health Center, Jerusalem, 1929. Courtesy of Hadassah, the Women's Zionist Organization of America, Inc.

SCHOOL LUNCHES

Children carrying the dishes to set the dining room table for the School Luncheons program, 1929. Courtesy of Hadassah, the Women's Zionist Organization of America, Inc.

Children in a Sephardic Talmud Torah (religious school) in the Old City of Jerusalem set the tables as part of the School Luncheons program, 1936. Courtesy of Hadassah, the Women's Zionist Organization of America, Inc.

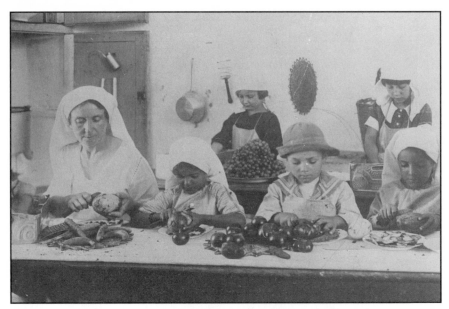

Learning to prepare locally grown foods was part of the School Luncheons program. Courtesy of Hadassah, the Women's Zionist Organization of America, Inc.

PLAYGROUNDS

Arab and Jewish children play together at Hadassah's playground in Jerusalem, in the shadow of an ancient Roman wall, 1929. Courtesy of Hadassah, the Women's Zionist Organization of America, Inc.

A Hadassah fundraising pamphlet, c. 1928–1936. Courtesy of Hadassah, the Women's Zionist Organization of America, Inc.

WOMEN IN THE YISHUV (1930s)

Many women in the Yishuv wanted to work alongside men. Here, a woman drives a truck in 1943. Courtesy of Hadassah, the Women's Zionist Organization of America, Inc.

Henrietta Szold surrounded by one of the first graduating classes of nurses from Hadassah's Nurses' Training School, c. 1921–1922. Courtesy of Hadassah, the Women's Zionist Organization of America, Inc.

YOUTH ALIYAH: EUROPE (1940s)

Henrietta Szold (right) with her personal secretary Emma Ehrlich (left), in Szold's office on Rambam Street in Jerusalem, 1942. Courtesy of Hadassah, the Women's Zionist Organization of America, Inc.

Youth Aliyah girls from Europe at Kfar Glickson–Alonei Yitzhak in 1949. Photograph by Hazel Greenwald, courtesy of Hadassah, the Women's Zionist Organization of America, Inc.

YOUTH ALIYAH: ORIENTAL (1950s)

Yemenites in a ma'abara (tent camp) near Tiberias, 1951. Photograph by Hazel Greenwald, courtesy of Hadassah, the Women's Zionist Organization of America, Inc.

Eleanor Roosevelt with some Youth Aliyah boys at Ramat Hadassah Szold youth village before her portrait in the Eleanor Roosevelt Music Room there, 1955. Photo by the Jewish Agency for Israel, Jerusalem, courtesy of Hadassah, the Women's Zionist Organization of America, Inc.

YOUTH ALIYAH: (1990s)

Youth Aliyah still educates the children of new immigrants to Israel. Youngsters from Ethiopia in class, 1993. Courtesy of Hadassah, the Women's Zionist Organization of America, Inc.

~

CHAPTER FIVE

"Persecuted, Uprooted": Youth Aliyah and the Rescue of European Jewish Children

By 1930, the enforcement of restrictive immigration laws in the United States meant that European Jews were not going to find refuge there. Zionist leaders hoped that, in reaction, American Jews might take a renewed interest in Palestine and Zionism. Louis Brandeis, for example, believed that American Jews had an obligation to help European Jews resettle in Palestine: "The closing of the doors of the United States . . . has increased the need of keeping Palestine open—and the duty of American Jews to labor to that end," he wrote to the head of the Jewish National Fund.[1] By the end of 1933, with the Nazis in power, many American Jews did realize that Palestine was the only possible refuge for European Jews, and, as a result, membership in Zionist organizations like the Zionist Organization of America (ZOA) and Hadassah shot up steadily over the next few years.[2]

With its two decades' worth of work in Palestine, Hadassah had, by the 1930s, cemented its reputation for both organizational integrity and effective action. The organization succeeded in establishing and maintaining an extensive network of health and social welfare services in the Yishuv. Hadassah's national president, Rose Jacobs, noted with satisfaction in 1935 that "Palestine is in a happy prosperous state. . . . Palestine's health program of today . . . has been built on the basis of Hadassah's work serving a generation of Palestinians." With Hadassah's full cooperation, the devolutionary program by which the Va'ad Leumi would gradually take over such services and programs as it was able to administer and fund was well under way. As Jacobs put it, "Hadassah conceives it as its duty always to turn over to the Yishub [*sic*] the activities that rightfully belong to it—for administration and financial support." Given that Hadassah was, piece by piece, handing over control of its projects, the organization needed to find a new focus. Jacobs argued that "the saving of European Jewish youth is the crying need of the hour. Hadassah is that channel through which can be made effective the appeal for the rescue of our youth. . . . We can help convert the Youth Aliyah project into a great movement."[3]

The idea of Youth Aliyah first came up in 1932 while Szold was working for the Va'ad Leumi, traveling the country to investigate conditions and trying to develop her social welfare plan. She received a letter from a German Zionist activist named Recha Freier. The letter described Freier's scheme, which she called "youth aliyah," to help Jewish youngsters get out of Germany. In a climate of growing anti-Semitism and a deteriorating economy, these young people were no longer allowed to attend school and were similarly excluded from employment. Freier asked Szold for help in getting immigration certificates for a group of such youngsters to enter Palestine, where they could lead productive lives free from anti-Semitic discrimination.

Freier had been encouraged to contact Szold by Dr. Georg Landauer, a member of the executive of the World Zionist Organization (WZO). He told Freier that the organization might support Freier's plan provided that she first secure agreement from the Va'ad Leumi that it would not only assume financial responsibility for the arrangements but would also supervise the youth once they had arrived in Palestine.[4] Thus Freier appealed to Szold, as the director of the social welfare department of the Va'ad Leumi, for assistance. But Szold was at this point preoccupied with a staggering array of local social problems and was frustrated by the lack of funds available to the Va'ad Leumi. With so much domestic Palestinian need unaddressed, Szold showed little interest in, or sympathy for, Freier's scheme on behalf of bourgeois German youth. Szold kept to her principled and firm commitment not to encourage any new projects that the Yishuv could not support financially. Citing the Yishuv's inability to provide for the many neglected and impoverished local youth, Szold refused to get involved.[5]

The British Mandatory government set quotas or "schedules" for the numbers and categories (e.g., workers, capitalists, students) of Jewish immigrants permitted to enter Palestine. Jews who wanted to enter Palestine had to qualify for an immigration certificate first. These quotas were linked to Palestine's supposed "economic absorptive capacity" and were normally set every six months. The Colonial Office in London distributed some of these immigration certificates to its consular and passport offices in Europe and to the Jewish Agency. Some businesses and institutions in Palestine, including some schools, were allowed to apply for certificates, which they could then distribute.

Because Szold had relative ease of access to these immigration certificates directly from the Mandatory government, her refusal frustrated hopes that these German youth would enter Palestine. Moreover, as Freier explained, Szold took steps to prevent Freier from seeking help from other sources:

> I wrote to Miss Szold presenting the problem of Jewish youth in Germany and my plans for solution. The reply was in the negative after a long lapse of time because of the unsolved problem of the children in Israel, the lack of funds for delinquents and defective [sic] that she had to acquire. Upon my threat to go to America and to collect funds there, Miss Szold informed me that she would take steps to hinder my getting help. There was no echo of a National chance to have an Aliyah of youth. Miss Szold's letter was not sent only to me, a copy went to the Union of Zionists for Germany in Berlin. A message from it went to all groups of Zionists that it should not be supported.[6]

Rebuffed by Szold, Freier contacted Enzo Sereni, an Italian-born Zionist who lived in Palestine but who was at that time in Germany as an emissary (*shaliach*) of the *Ha-Kibbutz Ha-Meuchad* kibbutz movement. Sereni was enthusiastic and arranged for Freier to contact the *Histadrut* (General Federation of Labor) in Tel Aviv to find agricultural placements for some German boys.[7] The *Histadrut*'s Jacob Sandbank wrote to Freier in the spring that several agricultural settlements in Palestine were prepared to accept the group.[8] Freier then met with members of the German Jewish community and its organizations in order to promote her scheme but found that they were reluctant to endorse her plan. There were concerns about separating children from parents and sending the children to an unknown situation; fears that religiously Orthodox children would be sent to secular or even antireligious settlements in Palestine; and questions about the quality of care and education the children would receive in Palestine.[9]

In June 1932, however, Freier was contacted by Dr. Siegfried Lehman, the director of the Ben Shemen children's village in Palestine. (Ben Shemen had been established by Lehman in 1927 to house and educate Eastern European orphans and was funded by a Berlin Jewish organization.)[10] Lehman, also with access to immigration certificates, offered Freier places in Ben Shemen for twelve German boys.[11] Although Freier preferred to send the youth to kibbutzim, she accepted Lehman's offer. On October 12, 1932, the first group of boys set out from Berlin to Palestine. Freier regarded this as the first Youth Aliyah group, although the term "youth aliyah" was not yet widely used.[12]

Despite repeated setbacks, Freier continued organizing to send German youth to kibbutzim. She later wrote that, even in the face of community apathy and opposition in Germany, she remained fully convinced of the necessity for "the formation of a great and permanent movement for the transfer of Jewish youth from the Diaspora to the Palestinian colonies, to enable them to live and to take root in the soil of their fatherland."[13]

Although Freier secured agreement from several kibbutzim in Palestine to take German youngsters, Szold still refused to obtain immigration certificates, this time arguing that the Palestinian kibbutzim were unable to provide proper educational facilities. Freier attempted to sidestep Szold by setting up an organization that could lobby the Mandatory government directly for immigration certificates to send German youth to Palestine. The *Jüdische Jugendhilfe* (Aid to Jewish Youth) organization was established the same day as the Nazis assumed power: January 30, 1933. The German-born Giora Josephthal, a volunteer social worker and *Hechalutz* (Zionist pioneering youth movement) activist, took on the role of director of the youth settlement organization.[14]

In May 1933, Freier traveled to Palestine, where she visited Ein Harod, Nahalal, and other agricultural settlements and met with their members. During these meetings, a plan to place youth groups in *moshavim* (agricultural cooperatives) was drawn up. A public meeting was held in Tel Aviv to discuss the Youth Aliyah scheme in general and lay out some of the operating details. But there was no avoiding Szold, and in Jerusalem, Freier met her for the first time face to face. Freier repeated her request for immigration certificates for German youth and Szold, once again, refused.

There were a number of reasons for Szold's resistance. The kibbutzim, she again claimed, lacked houses and school buildings, making living conditions there unsanitary and primitive. Szold's priority was the thousands of Palestinian Jewish youth unable to attend school because they had to earn money to support their families. Moreover, Szold doubted that either American or German Jewry would be willing to provide sufficient funds to support Freier's project or that German parents would be willing to send their children to live in substandard conditions. Finally, Szold believed that any funds available for education should go to support the education of local youth.[15]

Upon her return to an increasingly beleaguered Jewish community in Germany, fearful for the future of its youth, Freier discovered that opinion in the community had shifted in favor of her idea. In her absence, the German Zionist Organization had established a Department for Children and Youth Aliyah and joined the *Jüdische Jugendhilfe* organization. In June 1933, several organizations united to form a coordinating committee, the *Arbeitsgemeinschaft für Kinder und Jugendaliyah* (Joint Movement for Children and Youth

Aliyah) based in Berlin.[16] Another agency that was to play an important role in the development of the Youth Aliyah movement was established by the Eighteenth World Zionist Congress (August 21–September 4, 1933) in Prague: the Central Bureau for the Settlement of German Jews in Palestine, with Dr. Chaim Weizmann in London and Dr. Arthur Ruppin in Jerusalem as its cochairmen. As part of the Jewish Agency, the Bureau for the Settlement of German Jews was authorized to negotiate with the British Mandatory government for immigration certificates for German Jews.[17]

In October 1933, Szold represented the Va'ad Leumi at a conference held in London to discuss relief measures for Jews in Germany. At this meeting, the British branch of the Women's International Zionist Organization (WIZO) lent their support to Freier's Youth Aliyah scheme and persuaded Szold to visit Berlin (November 7–10, 1933) and meet with organizers. Szold wrote that she went to Berlin "unexpectedly" and there "became initiated in the methods of organization of the transfer of children and juveniles to Palestine." She described it as "a deep-cutting experience for me." Even as she was converted to the idea of Youth Aliyah, Szold also noted that in Berlin "I found much confused organization, no understanding of Palestinian conditions, and much talk at cross-purposes."[18]

Without including Freier, who was away in Denmark during Szold's visit, Szold visited the office of the *Jüdische Jugendhilfe* in Berlin and, according to her biographer, Joan Dash, Youth Aliyah's basic "educational scheme was composed by Miss Szold and the Jugendhilfe together during that week in Berlin." On her return to Palestine, Szold was contacted by Ruppin, who asked her to take on the responsibility for the youth section of the Central Bureau for the Settlement of German Jews in Palestine. On November 27, 1933, Szold agreed "to concentrate in her hands all the matters relating to the transfer of children from Germany and their education in Palestine." Dr. Georg Landauer agreed to serve as treasurer. Szold wrote: "The children's undertaking is, of course, added to my social organization work."[19]

But even without Szold's involvement, by 1933 German children and youth were already arriving in Palestine, many without their parents. They were among the estimated 164,000 immigrants, many from Germany, who fled the Nazi onslaught and arrived in Palestine from 1933 to 1936. By July 1934, about four thousand unaccompanied German children had applied for emigration to Palestine. "How we are going to provide places for 3000 to 4000 children passes my comprehension," Szold wrote. "And I am not thinking of funds. I am thinking of the forces of organization at our disposal."[20]

Despite her initial reluctance and continuing concerns, Szold began lobbying the British for immigration certificates for German youth who wished to enter Palestine. While cooperative British authorities at first required only the most basic information about each candidate (name, age, and address, along with a financial guarantee for their support from the Jewish Agency), Szold imposed her own requirements on the *Jugendhilfe*, asking for extensive information on each child's health, educational, and religious background and the parents' financial situation, among a slew of other questions.[21] The *Jugendhilfe*'s inability, in many cases, to meet Szold's exacting requirements meant that Szold requested, and received, fewer immigration certificates from the British authorities than might otherwise have been made available.

Young candidates for immigration via Youth Aliyah were subjected to a thorough process of selection before leaving Germany. Those who were judged too physically weak for hard manual labor, those with psychological or educational problems, and those who were not committed to the *halutzic* (pioneering) ideals of Zionism were weeded out. Many young people approved for certificates first moved to Berlin, and some of them attended the Youth Aliyah school established there by the *Jugendhilfe*. Freier explained:

> The aim of the school was to give the youths a full year's training for life in Palestine, more thorough than the training camps could give and with a longer probation period.
>
> Hebrew was in the centre of the curriculum. The main subjects were Jewish history, past and present, Zionism, the labour movement in Palestine, and science, as far as it was connected with agriculture in Palestine.[22]

A network of preparatory farm-based training camps (*hachsharot*) was also set up to provide the youngsters with experience in agricultural work and communal living. Such training camps were set up in many countries to prepare Diaspora Jewish youth for kibbutz life. Participants received training in agriculture as well as an education in the basic principles of communal living and Socialist-Zionist ideology. Graduates of a *hachshara* were expected to put this education into practice by moving to Palestine and living as pioneers on a communal agricultural settlement.

Freier, who remained deeply committed to the initiative she began, describes the setup of the *hachshara* thus: "It lay in agricultural surroundings and had as its basic idea the division of the day between study, agricultural and social activities in the same proportion as that practiced in youth groups at Palestinian kibbutzim." The *hachshara* also served as a kind of probation, explained Freier: "At the end of his stay in the training camp, the youth was either accepted for aliyah or rejected." A careful selection process was, in Freier's view, essential. "At the beginning," she later wrote, "the success of the movement was dependent on the proper selection of the youths. It was not aliyah alone, not rescue work, that mattered most, but the transfer of those who were needed to build up Palestine and who were able to become truly and firmly rooted there."[23]

In 1934, Giora Josephthal was appointed director of the *Jugendhilfe*.[24] In September 1934, he reported, "we had 3,500 *haverim* [comrades] on *hachshara*" in Germany and thirteen other countries. A survey of these youth conducted that same month showed that two thousand of them were engaged in agricultural training and seven hundred in trades. But Josephthal noted that although the movement emphasized agricultural training, "the mentality of the Jews in Germany has worked against us." Since most regarded agriculture as "unskilled labor," they preferred, naturally, to learn a trade.[25]

But along with the selection criteria imposed by Szold and the selection process of the *hachsharot*, there were other factors involved in deciding both who would be accepted by Youth Aliyah and where the successful candidates would be sent in Palestine. In a Zionist world wracked by political factionalism, once certificates were obtained for Youth Aliyah by the *Jugendhilfe*, they were distributed according to political criteria using a party key. Zionist youth movements were affiliated with a "parent" movement; hence immigration certificates were divided between various politically tied Zionist youth movements in proportion to the respective size of their membership. Once each received its share of immigration certificates, the Zionist youth movement usually sent its successful candidates for aliyah to live on a kibbutz belonging to its "parent" movement.

Much of the ideology and structure of Youth Aliyah, particularly the idea of the centrality of the *hevrat noar*, or self-governing youth group, derived from the precedents set by the Zionist youth movements in the Diaspora.[26] The first Zionist youth movement, the *Blau-Weiss* (Blue-White), began in Germany before World War I and was modeled on the non-Jewish German *Wandervogel* youth movement, which emphasized patriotism, the camaraderie of youth, physical fitness, and closeness to nature. After the war, Zionist youth movements soon spread throughout the Diaspora and members prepared for life on communal agricultural settlements in Palestine.

The ideological focus of such movements was on self-realization (*hagshama atzmit*) through immigration (*aliyah*) to Palestine and, for most, a commitment to a communal life based on some variant of Socialist-Zionist principles. Other non-Socialist streams of Zionism, like the Revisionists and religious Zionists, also had youth movements. But Youth Aliyah had trouble finding kibbutz placements for the religious youth in its care and often had to send them to secular settlements. For political reasons, Szold refused to send youngsters to settlements associated with the right-wing Revisionist movement. As Recha Freier explained:

> The Zionist youth organizations in the Diaspora were organic branch move-ments of the kibbutzim in Palestine with ideological differences, and they should be the starting point of Youth Aliyah, whilst kibbutzim and moshavim should take charge of the education of the young people who should be rooted in the soil and not fall prey to urbanization. Fathers and mothers should not be replaced by new fathers and mothers. The community at large should take the youngsters in and be their home.[27]

Now that Szold was committed to the Youth Aliyah scheme, what would Hadassah's role be? In the summer of 1935, Hadassah's National Board sent Rose Jacobs on a two-month investigatory trip. Her assignment was to survey social welfare projects in Palestine that might benefit from Hadassah funding and choose one particular project on which Hadassah might focus its atten-tion. Accompanied by Szold, Jacobs visited Youth Aliyah facilities and also looked at some vocational education projects.[28]

In late August, Jacobs and Szold headed to Lucerne, Switzerland, to at-tend the Nineteenth Zionist Congress. In Lucerne, the two women met up with Tamar de Sola Pool, president of the New York chapter of Hadassah. Ja-cobs and de Sola Pool told Szold that Hadassah might be willing to support Youth Aliyah financially. Fearing that American money would lead to Amer-ican control of the movement, Szold told the two women that Hadassah should continue to focus on funding medical services in Palestine and that she preferred to rely on European sources to fund Youth Aliyah. Szold said she would only agree to Hadassah funding if Hadassah refrained from inter-fering in Youth Aliyah policy and decision-making matters.[29]

Szold reported to the Nineteenth Zionist Congress on the first two years of Youth Aliyah's work: six hundred young people had been placed in eleven kibbutzim, four agricultural schools, and two vocational training centers. Meanwhile, in an effort to end conflicts over fundraising among American Zionist organizations, delegates at the Congress passed a resolution that pro-hibited Zionist organizations from independent fundraising for their own projects.[30] Nevertheless, barely had the resolution been passed when, on Au-gust 27, 1935, while attending the Congress, Georg Landauer, director of the Jerusalem office of the Central Bureau for the Settlement of German Jews in Palestine, and Jacobs drafted a confidential letter, in seeming violation of the resolution, stating that Hadassah would be the sole representative of, and fundraiser for, Youth Aliyah in the United States for a two-year probationary period.

With this contract, Hadassah guaranteed that it would subsidize the yearly expenses of one hundred German and Polish youth at a total cost of thirty thousand dollars a year. If Hadassah could maintain the one hundred children for those two years, then Hadassah could continue to be the sole agency representing Youth Aliyah in the United States during that period and any other person or organization wishing to assist Youth Aliyah would have to participate through Hadassah. If Hadassah failed to meet its commitment, then the *Arbeitsgemeinschaft für Kinder und Jugendaliyah* would initiate its own campaign in the United States.[31]

As soon as the congress in Lucerne ended, Szold and her assistant Emma Ehrlich set off to Amsterdam to attend the first Youth Aliyah Conference. The conference delegates agreed that Youth Aliyah should expand its scope outside Germany and accept young applicants from Poland and elsewhere in Europe.[32] From Amsterdam, Szold went to Berlin. There she met with Jewish organizations and the *Jugendhilfe*. Hundreds of German Jewish parents, panic-stricken in the aftermath of the declaration of the Nuremberg Laws, mobbed Szold at a Youth Aliyah meeting pleading for news of their children who had gone to Palestine with Youth Aliyah. Szold reassured them that their children were in good hands and said that she received many letters from these children begging for help to bring their parents to Palestine. She told the assembled crowd how she responded to the youngsters: "I am hardhearted and my answer is, it will be a long time before you can bring your parents here and I cannot let you go out into the city where you would learn nothing, earn a pittance and not be adjusted to the land to which we have brought you. . . . After two years you may begin to think of rescuing your parents."[33] Thus, even as she was confronted by German Jews frantic with the realization that their options for escape were narrowing, it appeared that Szold's priority was to ensure that Youth Aliyah's educational programs ran smoothly. Szold would maintain this characteristic rigidity despite the rapid deterioration of the situation of German Jews and in the face of criticism from Freier and others.

From Berlin, Szold returned to Palestine just as a tussle between Hadassah and the ZOA erupted over Hadassah's sole sponsorship of Youth Aliyah. Marian G. Greenberg, an American Hadassah member who served as the organization's first national Youth Aliyah chairman (1935–1941) and who wrote several in-house histories of Hadassah's involvement in Youth Aliyah, says that the Lucerne document "formalized Mrs. Jacobs' agreement to recommend the adoption of Youth Aliyah to the Hadassah Convention in November." After returning to New York, in September 1935 Jacobs presented the contract to a specially convened meeting of Hadassah's National Board.

The board accepted the contract and notified Landauer by mail. A Hadassah press release for general distribution to the mainstream American press described Youth Aliyah as "Hadassah's next step . . . a new chapter in its history" and asserted that "through the Youth Aliyah Hadassah now enters the great field of immigration and colonization."[34]

But one month later, American Zionist leaders, furious at the fundraising implications of the Hadassah project, protested, and in response the Jewish Agency Executive in Jerusalem cancelled the agreement.[35] As in the 1921 dispute between Hadassah and Keren Hayesod, one of the most vociferous opponents of Hadassah's go-it-alone fundraising efforts was Louis Lipsky, now chairman of the board of the American Palestine Campaign. As he had in 1921, Lipsky took the position that any separate fundraising campaign for a particular project (like Youth Aliyah) would jeopardize the annual fundraising efforts of the united Zionist organizations of America. Lipsky complained that if Hadassah independently raised funds for Youth Aliyah and only for Youth Aliyah, it would cause the "disintegration" of organized Zionism in the United States.[36]

Despite the opposition, Hadassah held firm and continued to plan its fundraising campaign. Jacobs sent a sharp note to ZOA president Morris Rothenberg: "It seems a great pity that many of your associates in the Zionist Organization are unappreciative of the value of an organization like Hadassah, which has been built up by Zionist idealism. It ought really to be cherished instead of being stunted."[37] The Zionist Executive appointed a mediator "with instructions to safeguard the interests of Hadassah, the American Palestine Campaign (Ampalc) and the integrity of the Zionist Organization."[38] Perhaps because of Hadassah's size, its track record, and its readiness to do battle for its fundraising independence, Hadassah's opponents conceded and allowed the Jacobs-Landauer agreement to stand. There was a small price to pay. As in 1921, Hadassah was forced to accept a formula whereby the United Palestine Appeal (UPA) counted funds raised by Hadassah as part of the money raised during its fundraising drive. At the twenty-first annual convention of Hadassah in November 1935, as the Nazis made life more and more difficult for German Jews, delegates voted unanimously to take on Youth Aliyah as their new project. This meant an enlarged financial responsibility for Hadassah, which was still committed to providing financial support for medical services in Palestine.[39] Mindful of its ongoing obligations, Hadassah created a National Youth Aliyah Committee to oversee Hadassah's Youth Aliyah work.[40]

While the dispute between Hadassah and the ZOA was still being ironed out, Szold worried that the attention lavished on Youth Aliyah would eclipse the plight of hard-pressed Palestinian Jewish youth. A letter sent from Palestine by Hadassah's Jessie Sampter to Hadassah's head office in New York describes in some detail the hardships faced by the "working youth from the cities of Palestine. . . . Many of them are of oriental parentage and have had very meagre schooling." The letter continued:

> We have two kinds of youth, with these differences: Those from Palestine work eight or nine hours a day, sleep in tents or leaky huts even in winter, have irregular and insufficient teaching, are not properly provided with clothing and blankets because most of them come from very poor homes. Those from Germany work five hours a day, live in well-built houses especially provided for them, have regular instruction by their own teachers two or three hours a day, have proper clothing and covering which they brought with them from home. At first they were given extra portions of nourishing food . . . but this has been stopped at their own protest. This situation creates inequality, jealousy, unrest and an atmosphere of division in which true social education is impossible, to say nothing at all of the physical suffering.
>
> Is there no one in America as much interested in the youth of Palestine as in the youth from Germany?[41]

But with Nazism and anti-Semitic nationalism running unchecked in Germany and anti-Semitism rising across Central and Eastern Europe, Hadassah was not yet ready to discuss these problems outside the circle of national leaders of the organization. The campaign to rescue Jewish children from Europe had to press ahead.

Hadassah's head office in New York asked Szold to travel to the United States to personally campaign on behalf of Youth Aliyah. Despite her many years living abroad, or perhaps because of them, she was still highly regarded in the United States, and Hadassah thought she would have the persuasive power to convince Americans to reach into their pockets in support of Youth Aliyah. As her friend and colleague Zena Harman put it: "Miss Szold's relationship with America was a particular one. America and the American countryside, American Jewry, were of her very being. She had been part of the process which forged and formed . . . the Jewish community. . . . She was the American Jewess par excellence." Szold set sail in December 1935, and her arrival in New York coincided with her seventy-fifth birthday. She was greeted with much fanfare and publicity. Harman wrote that "from every pulpit issued words of esteem and devotion for the woman who symbolised all that was majestic in womanhood and profound in Jewish spiritual values. She was acclaimed the outstanding Jewish woman of the century and among the great women of the world."[42]

Once again, Hadassah appealed for American support and, once again, did so by stressing the parallels between the American and the Zionist dreams. In a 1935 newsreel speech, Szold told Americans:

We have already brought out of Germany into Palestine one thousand boys and girls, between the ages of 15 and 17, from a land in which they could not attend school, to a land where they have fine educational opportunities; from a land in which they cannot pursue trades, into a land where they are taught trades; from a land in which they are repressed, into a land in which they are given opportunities of self-expression and full cooperation. Palestine is in that respect comparable to America, to the United States. As in the United States, our young people look forward to a life of usefulness. They arrive not knowing the language—they learn the language; . . . they devote themselves to . . . study. They go forward to a life of opportunity. . . . They are prepared to become good, useful citizens.[43]

Szold's visit and birthday celebrations received generous coverage in the *New York Times*. Articles pointed out the symmetry of Szold's own career: a half century earlier she waited at the Baltimore pier to meet the steamships carrying Jewish refugees fleeing Russian pogroms; now she was again dealing with refugees—this time, meeting German Jewish children arriving at the port of Haifa. "Miss Szold's life may be summed up in the word 'service,'" said the *Times*, which went on to describe her as a "pioneer in Americanization work."[44]

In the United States Hadassah continued to seek out new ways to win support from American Jewish women. A plan to use individual case histories (including photos) of children for publicity purposes was vetoed by Szold, however, who considered it too sentimental and was also concerned about making the children feel like charity cases. Harman adds that Szold "refused to allow Youth Aliyah to be dragged down to the level of a charitable, philanthropic enterprise. It was a positive, constructive movement of rehabilitation and education, an integral part of the Jewish renaissance."[45]

Given Szold's unwillingness to let Hadassah use photos and biographical profiles of individual children in its fundraising material, the organization needed other ways to give potential donors an immediate stake in the child rescue effort. The *Hadassah Newsletter* printed a poignant series of letters written by German children. It then reproduced these letters as a separate pamphlet titled *The Children Speak*. The letters were from "children in Germany who are looking forward to life in Palestine, and from young people in Palestine describing their experiences to their relatives and friends in Germany." Many of the young writers pleaded for help to get out of Germany.[46]

Just as Hadassah earlier sought endorsements from illustrious personalities to be used in its written propaganda, the organization now seized upon a new fundraising strategy of enrolling popular celebrities to boost public awareness of the cause. In February 1936, the American Jewish vaudeville, film, and radio star Eddie Cantor was enlisted to help Youth Aliyah by publicly appearing at fundraising events. He was very successful. Within a month, Cantor, who called himself "the ambassador of Hadassah," raised forty-four thousand dollars in the United States, and in 1938 he was able to raise another half a million dollars in England.[47] Hadassah members in the United States also recruited the wives of prominent Americans to support Youth Aliyah and met with Eleanor Roosevelt at the White House, where she agreed to accept an honorary post with Youth Aliyah.[48]

Marian Greenberg describes these first few years as "the halcyon days" of Youth Aliyah. German parents could afford to pay half the costs of their children's transportation and resettlement, and the children themselves, after passing through both a rigorous selection process and thorough preparatory training, were generally well-equipped to adjust to their new lives. While later arrivals, having experienced the trauma of war and dislocation, often suffered psychological problems, in this earlier period, "the chief concerns were practical: more [immigration] certificates, more places, more housing, more teachers, and more funds."[49]

The young prewar refugees arrived against a backdrop of a massive increase in Jewish immigration to Palestine overall. In 1934 there were forty thousand and in 1935 more than sixty thousand Jewish immigrants to Palestine, bringing the Jewish population to a total of 330,000. Their arrival was not universally celebrated. Concerned Arab leaders met with the British High Commissioner, Sir Arthur Wauchope, to protest both the increased numbers of Jewish immigrants and the expansion of Jewish landholdings. On April 19, 1936, Palestinian Arabs rioted. The British authorities, fearful of wider unrest, put a hold on immigration and appointed the Peel Commission, a royal commission of inquiry, to investigate the causes of the unrest. The moratorium on immigration was a blow to Youth Aliyah. Szold described her appearance before the commission:

There will be no certificates as long as the Royal Commission is sitting. They are here to hear grievances between Arabs and Jews. Because of Hadassah's insistence, I forced myself to begin to talk about Youth Aliyah. They cut me off saying, "We have heard all that before." Notwithstanding my rebuff, I tried it again and they cut me off again.[50]

As a result of the Arab revolt, the allotment of 1936 immigration certificates was delayed. Making the best of the situation, Szold, who was still concerned about the plight of Palestinian Jewish youth, used this as an opportunity to arrange to have local youngsters fill the vacant placements in the agricultural cooperatives. "The Lord knows how badly they need it," she wrote. "I ask myself if we think it most important to extend the blessings and privileges of Youth Aliyah to Poland and those other countries, why not reckon Palestine among those 'other' countries."[51] But Hadassah was left in a quandary, as Greenberg later recalled:

> Whenever the British Government withheld certificates, our apparatus went into a tailspin. The urgency of our appeal, particularly to non-Zionists, was geared to the need and possibility of bringing Jewish children out of Hitler's Germany into Palestine. We had to keep new children on the move. The contributors were not interested in providing for Palestinian children, nor were they so emotionally stirred by discrimination against Polish children before the war.[52]

The Peel Commission's 1937 report declared that Arab and Jewish interests in Palestine could not be reconciled and recommended the partition of the mandated area as a solution. Arab leaders rejected the plan, Zionist leaders were divided, and the British government gave up on the idea of partition.[53] Arab unrest persisted through 1938, and an alarmed British government considered restricting Jewish immigration. WZO president Chaim Weizmann, fearing for the future of Youth Aliyah, protested to Malcolm MacDonald at the Colonial Office:

> To save children from Germany . . . we have built up in Palestine a system of schools and training centres, and we have collected considerable sums of money, especially . . . in America, for their maintenance. But now we understand that the Palestine Administration is "worried" at the increase of our youth immigration, which may perhaps save 2,000 children from ruin and degradation. . . . We do not ask for certificates for more youths than we can place in these schools and centres. . . . I appeal to you, and ask you: how can one hope to justify it before the conscience of the world if these training centres founded in our National Home for the rescue of children stand half-empty, and the money accumulated for the purpose lies idle, while Jewish children perish in Nazi Germany?[54]

By 1938, cash-strapped German parents were no longer able to fund their children's resettlement. At the same time, Youth Aliyah was extended to other European countries including Austria, Czechoslovakia, Poland, and the Balkans. Since the Jewish communities in these countries had also become impoverished, Jewish new-world communities assumed more and more financial responsibility for Youth Aliyah. German exit restrictions on the amount of personal luggage meant that many children now arrived in Palestine with insufficient clothing. Hadassah's Palestine Supplies Department in New York City, and its nationwide system of volunteer sewing circles, were called upon to produce "mountains of garments" to send to Palestine.[55]

Along with its publicity and fundraising activities on behalf of Youth Aliyah, Hadassah also submitted a report to the Intergovernmental Committee on Refugees, which met in Evian, France, in the summer of 1938 at the behest of the American government. The report described the tragedy of a "stranded generation" of Jewish children in Europe and asked the committee both to help secure the "cooperation" of Great Britain for Youth Aliyah's work and "to help facilitate immediately the existent Youth Aliyah machinery and widen its potentialities for further transfer work," but no such assistance arrived.[56] Nothing came of the Evian conference. Doors to Jewish refugees were closing and the future of Youth Aliyah was increasingly uncertain.

As the Nazi oppression of Jews in Germany grew more severe, it became increasingly difficult for the Berlin office of the *Arbeitsgemeinschaft für Kinder und Jugendaliyah* to function. The organization was starved for funds, and it was also squeezed between the strict admission standards demanded by Szold and Youth Aliyah on the one side and the repressive legislation imposed by the Nazi government on the other. In November 1938, in the aftermath of Kristallnacht, some of the employees of the Berlin office were imprisoned. The following June, the central office of the *Arbeitsgemeinschaft für Kinder und Jugendaliyah* was transferred to London, far from those desperately seeking exit from Germany.[57]

In September 1939 the British government declared war on Germany. With this, the Yishuv also entered the war. With its attention focused on developments in Europe, Britain wanted to avoid any escalation of problems in Palestine. In May 1939, fearing large-scale Arab revolt, the British government issued a white paper restricting Jewish immigration and limiting land sales to the Jews in Palestine.[58] Many Zionists regarded the white paper as a repudiation of the promises made by the Balfour Declaration and the Mandate. They also feared for the fate of Jews in Europe. At its New York headquarters, Hadassah hosted a meeting of Jewish women's organizations who joined together to send a telegraph of protest to President Roosevelt asking him to condemn the new British policy.[59] At a 1939 meeting in Geneva, the World Zionist Congress endorsed the strategy of "Aliyah Bet," or illegal immigration.

For the Youth Aliyah children, Palestine's door was still open, if only slightly. They were entitled to go to Palestine under special provisions that allowed nearly unrestricted immigration certificates for students attending recognized educational institutions. As long as the Yishuv could provide institutional placements, such children could go to Palestine as legal immigrants. As a result, Youth Aliyah was able to rescue nearly five thousand children from European countries between 1934 and 1939.[60]

Even if Youth Aliyah's future was uncertain, it remained one of Hadassah's prize projects. But the organization's role was not entirely clear. Despite her close and constant contact with Hadassah's national board in New York, Szold was not always receptive to Hadassah's requests for a greater role in decision making and management. In the summer of 1939, Hadassah's national president, Judith Epstein, wrote to Szold requesting representation on the Palestine Committee of Youth Aliyah (consisting of Georg Landauer, Hans Beyth, and Szold), arguing that "Hadassah, which has been so deeply concerned with the success and carrying out of the Youth Aliyah movement [must] be given an opportunity for participation in the discussions and the decisions." The same request had been made to the London Committee of Youth Aliyah, Epstein said, and was "met very sympathetically." Such representation would "bring us into close contact," Epstein explained, "with the important decisions which are made on the spot."[61]

Hadassah's Youth Aliyah chair, Marian Greenberg, also pressed the issue, pointing out to Szold that Hadassah raised nearly eight hundred thousand dollars for Youth Aliyah during the previous year, was fully committed to continuing its support, and so had "a responsibility directly connected with the expenditure of these funds." Greenberg reassured Szold that "we do not, I repeat, desire administrative control, but rather administrative collaboration." Hadassah had, on its own initiative, she said, made valuable contacts in Europe, used its "good offices" to successfully intervene with government officials on behalf of children in Europe, enlisted other American organizations to support Youth Aliyah, and otherwise provided a great deal of concrete help beyond simple fundraising. Given all this, Greenberg suggested: "Surely we are justified in our feeling that we should receive the fullest measure of your confidence. We should like that confidence to be expressed in terms of sharing real responsibility in all matters in which we can be of assistance."[62]

Indeed, Hadassah was assuming an ever-greater share of the costs of Youth Aliyah. By the outbreak of the Second World War, Hadassah was shouldering 50 percent of the Youth Aliyah budget. By 1940, Hadassah, with sixty-six thousand senior members and fifteen thousand junior members, contributed nearly 80 percent of the budget. Indeed, in a confidential letter, Szold acknowledged that "due to world conditions, the Youth Aliyah became all but entirely dependent on the funds allocated to it by Hadassah."[63]

With Hadassah's help, Szold continued to organize new placements for the young war refugees arriving in Palestine without their families. While Szold continued to insist that Youth Aliyah offices in Europe select as candidates for immigration to Palestine only those youngsters who displayed good physical and mental health, her instructions were observed in the breach. It was no longer realistic to demand that proper paperwork be provided by parents, much less to expect that the youngsters might have any preparatory training. For Jewish leaders in Europe, it was a scramble just to get children out. Increasingly, those who could get out were sent if not to Palestine, then to Britain.

In London, the newly opened office of Youth Aliyah established training camps for young people in the various Western European countries where desperate Jews were given temporary refuge. By March 1, 1940, nearly two thousand refugee children were housed in these training centers where, under the tutelage of *madrichim* (youth group leaders), they learned about Zionist pioneering and prepared for a new life in Palestine under the care of Youth Aliyah.

Before long, Youth Aliyah officials in Palestine were also awash in refugee children who had been through no preselection process or training. If they did not fit Szold's preferred profile, at least they were alive, and Youth Aliyah would cope. Youth Aliyah's educational program was designed to transform bourgeois German urban youth into *halutzim*. As Hadassah's publicity explained to Americans:

> Children from all classes join Youth-Aliyah. The same fate, common to all, breaks down class distinctions. Boys and girls from every walk of German Jewish life throng to Youth-Aliyah. In these unhappy times they have learned that there will be no possibility for them to enter the professions of their fathers, and have begun to realize that the professional callings adopted by the former generation were unwise. . . . A common fate leads to one goal: as equal citizens— as Jewish farmers, to work on Jewish land and to help build up their new-old Homeland.[64]

The *New York Times* echoed Hadassah's rhetorical style in an editorial: "The account of the departure of a single group . . . from Berlin is a moving story. There gather to say good-bye to them parents belonging to many social classes, but at the moment there are no differences. The scene suggests the common fate that has befallen the Jewish community."[65]

Hadassah's assertion that young German Jews were prepared to gladly forgo their parents' choice of professions in favor of agricultural labor suggests that these youngsters willingly embraced Zionist ideology and its core tenet that Jews had to change their "unnatural" Diaspora-based occupational structure in order to build a new national society. In case readers did not grasp this point, one pamphlet elaborated:

> Town boys and girls return to the land! Sons and daughters of tradesmen are becoming farmers! High school children wish to become manual workers. Daughters of doctors and lawyers are learning domestic work, infant welfare and sick nursing. . . . There is no branch of work that is not undertaken with joy. . . . Manual work and healthy labour are creating a new type of Jew: purposeful, upright and full of trust.[66]

But it would seem that these claims that young German Jewish refugees were living exemplars of Zionist ideology had less to do with the Palestinian reality than with American marketing. As Hadassah gathered money, Youth Aliyah confronted unanticipated problems. In the rush to rescue German youth, Youth Aliyah officials in Palestine increasingly confronted arrivals who were not members of Zionist youth movements and did not necessarily share the movement's commitment to agricultural life. Their parents, most of them middle class, had encouraged them to study hard, attend university, and prepare for professions. Some youngsters resented Youth Aliyah's heavy-handed attempts at ideological indoctrination and protested being compelled to train for agricultural careers.[67]

Although Szold was not actively involved in implementing the educational curriculum of Youth Aliyah, after hearing a number of complaints from young people, she raised the question of whether it was a good idea to focus so exclusively on agricultural training. In 1940, as war in Europe made it ever more difficult to be selective in picking candidates for Youth Aliyah, Szold wrote that

> my experience with a considerable number of individual cases has aroused in me serious doubts as to the value of a system which pays no attention to individual ability and individual inclination. We should consider carefully whether pressing thousands of young minds into a single mold is a system that can be defended even as an emergency measure.[68]

As the outbreak of war in Europe forced more of the cost of Youth Aliyah onto Hadassah, the organization urged its members to form Youth Aliyah committees and to follow the "special Youth Aliyah fund-raising methods and procedure" outlined in the 1940 Hadassah manual. The manual explained that "the cost of maintaining and educating a young person in the cooperative colonies of Palestine is only $360 for the two year period of his training. For the children who are placed in special training schools . . . the costs are slightly higher." The manual evenhandedly pressed the "desperate need" of both native Palestinian Jewish youth and the young European refugees who arrived on their own, without Youth Aliyah's help, for the same "training and care" being provided to Youth Aliyah candidates. Money, the manual promised, could provide that care.

The manual displays the Hadassah organization's usual fine-tuned appreciation for the nuances of pulling in supporters and soliciting contributions. According to the manual, since Youth Aliyah

> is a program which commends itself to all who have the interests of children at heart, there is no need to limit either your committee or your appeal to those who are at present enrolled in Hadassah. As a matter of fact, it has been our invariable experience that the Youth Aliyah program serves as the closest link between the Hadassah members and other women, and that the interest of the latter when aroused for the Youth Aliyah has, in the vast majority of cases, widened to include many if not all of Hadassah's projects. Your committee therefore should be made up of those influential members of your community who can give themselves to the work, or who can successfully stimulate the generosity of others.

A new fundraising method, called the *minyan* (quorum), was recommended. Under this plan, ten women would join together to subsidize the upkeep of one Youth Aliyah child for two years, an act the manual described as "redeeming the child." This choice of language is suggestive. By calling a group of women a *minyan*, the Hebrew term for the quorum of ten men necessary to perform certain religious ceremonies, Hadassah was challenging the male exclusivity of the traditional religious quorum while giving religious significance to the act of supporting a Youth Aliyah child, a significance further emphasized by the allusion to the religious *pidyon ha-ben* (redemption of the first-born son) ceremony.

Finally, the manual defended the productive, Zionist character of its Youth Aliyah work. It closed with a warning that during the *minyan's* meetings,

> the program should be most carefully worked out so that the Youth Aliyah project is presented not as a separate entity divorced from Zionist ideology and accomplishment, but as part and parcel of the program of a Jewish National Home in Palestine. Hadassah's role in Palestine's upbuilding should also be

stressed in order that our contributors may understand the true relationship among all fields of constructive Zionist endeavor.[69]

Years later, Marian Greenberg pointed out that the *minyan* helped to democratize the process of donating to Youth Aliyah since it enabled less well-off women to pool their resources and pay in weekly or monthly installments.[70]

As the war proceeded, immigration to Palestine declined, but Szold's dream of offering Youth Aliyah–style opportunities to the deprived Jewish youth of the Palestinian slums was at last realized. In April 1941, Hadassah contributed $120,000 to launch a new Youth Aliyah program for urban youth in Palestine called "From Town to Village." A group of sixty children were chosen and sent to preparatory training camps to begin the two-year program.[71]

Another of Szold's plans also came to fruition in 1941 when she transferred funds to the Va'ad Leumi to establish the Child and Youth Welfare Association to be supported by the Child and Youth Trust Fund. Szold first proposed the idea for a central fund to pay for services for children and youth in her 1937 plan *The Cry of the Children of Palestine*. Shortly afterward, on a visit to Baltimore, she met with Katherine Lenroot, the chief of the United States Children's Bureau. The Children's Bureau was the institutional voice of child-saving advocates and American Progressive reformers. Five years later, Szold's new organization was modeled on the Children's Bureau and, indeed, Hadassah described this as a "National Children's Foundation" which was, in effect, "a Children's Bureau in Palestine." In a tribute to Szold, Lenroot said:

> The American people will have to make greater sacrifices for the support of community services for health, education and welfare than they have yet known, if the care we give to our children here is to measure up to the vision and the program which Hadassah has developed under Miss Szold's leadership for the children of Palestine.[72]

Just as the war forced Youth Aliyah to shift its efforts from Europe to Palestine and the larger Middle East, it was also compelled to absorb rescued children younger than the adolescent age group for which it was originally designed. One of the most famous episodes in Youth Aliyah's wartime history was the arrival of the Teheran children, a group of nearly one thousand Polish-Jewish refugee children, from infants to teenagers, who had attached themselves to a larger group of adult refugees who somehow wandered across Europe and the Middle East for three years before finally being stranded in a Red Cross displaced persons camp in Teheran, Iran, in September 1942. Fewer than two hundred of the children were accompanied by their parents; most were orphans.

Through the Jewish Agency, Youth Aliyah applied to the British Mandatory government for immigration certificates for the Teheran children. This meant, as Hadassah explained, that Youth Aliyah took on "a financial and a moral responsibility toward the child . . . for a period of two years or up to the age of eighteen." Suddenly Youth Aliyah had to grapple with finding placements for infants and very young children and with finding the money to pay for it all. Szold issued an urgent plea "in the name of the Jewish Women of Palestine, to the Jewish women of the world and through them to all women in the free democratic countries" for donations to help the Yishuv cope with the Teheran children:

> I would have the Jewish women everywhere appeal . . . to the motherhood instinct of all women, the creative instinct that abhors destruction. The women of the world cannot but recognize that the cause of the Jewish child is their cause. . . . Women are the natural protectors of childhood. They are the guardians of the generations. . . . Is not the plea for women to organize a movement to "Save the Child for Civilization" the plea for a supreme peace effort?[73]

Tamar de Sola Pool, Hadassah's national president, replied that "we accepted the challenge that you brought to us of mobilizing American womanhood on behalf of the endangered Jewish children, to save those who may yet be saved." But she explained, "Your specific suggestion of a world women's organization was considered by all whom we consulted as neither feasible nor likely to achieve the purpose you had in mind." De Sola Pool reminded Szold that "overall organizations can serve a useful purpose for channeling public opinion, but they have proved altogether useless in fund raising and intensive practical action." Nonetheless, she promised that Hadassah would undertake an intensive program of fundraising for Youth Aliyah. Hadassah had already enlisted other American organizations to support the cause, including the nonsectarian National Council of Women of the United States (claiming to represent ten million women), the American Friends Service Committee, the Joint Distribution Committee, and the Conference Committee of National Jewish Women's Organizations.[74]

Even while the Youth Aliyah fundraising campaign in the United States still emphasized the careful selection process by which children came to be in Youth Aliyah's care, the reality in Europe was far different. Admission procedures had not only broken down, they had become irrelevant. Escape was the only imperative, and every child who somehow managed to get to Palestine was welcomed whatever the difficulties. The organization decided to sort all the children in their care by age groups and then interview them individually to assess their educational and religious backgrounds as well as to check their medical and mental health. Gisela Wyzanski, Hadassah's National Youth Aliyah Chairman at the time, recalled later: "This was the first time that children came in large groups where there were no relatives, where there were no parents, where nothing of their previous religious background was known and . . . orthodox elements insisted that these children be brought up as orthodox."[75] Szold personally interviewed each child, no matter how young, to ascertain whether their parents and families had been religious. With children too young to understand such questions, she asked simply, "Did your father wear a beard? Did he have sidelocks? Did your grandfather go to synagogue? Did your parents celebrate Jewish holidays?" Mira Bramson, a former Teheran child now living in New York, remembers Szold asking such questions of her older brother (then age eight and a half) and says that in retrospect she appreciates the "wisdom and sensitivity and thoughtfulness" that Szold demonstrated in handling the traumatized Teheran children like herself. Szold described these "intimate and sometimes prolonged" conversations with "every single one" of the children as "mother talk."[76]

These children, as Hadassah saw it, were a test case for Youth Aliyah's ability to handle the many children who would join the flood of refugees expected at the end of the war. In a pamphlet titled *For These We Shall Sacrifice and Work . . . As Though They Were Our Own*, Hadassah warned that the Teheran children

> are the heralds of thousands, of tens of thousands to come, and to come soon!
> . . . Exemplary action is demanded in succoring this advance guard of our
> national re-enforcements—for thus we should regard these Teheran children.
> We must establish model procedures for the reception, the care, the placement
> and the education of these child refugees.[77]

In spite of where Youth Aliyah money was collected, financial responsibility for guaranteeing Youth Aliyah undertakings lay, ultimately, with the Jewish Agency, which was responsible for overseeing all Jewish settlement in the Yishuv. Given that child refugees were expected from all parts of Europe, not just from Germany, the Jewish Agency dissolved the Central Bureau for the Settlement of German Jews in Palestine (of which Youth Aliyah was a part) in January 1943 and replaced it with the Department for Child and Youth Immigration. With Szold carrying on as director, Youth Aliyah retained its own organizational and administrative autonomy although it was now more tightly under the auspices of the Jewish Agency. On March 10, 1943, Hadassah sent a letter to Szold requesting official representation on the soon-to-be-created managing committee of Youth Aliyah:

> You who know our methods of work so well will surely understand that we cannot continue to function effectively if we are to be relegated permanently to purely fundraising functions. As long as you were the sole director of Youth Aliyah, we felt that Hadassah was represented, if not formally, then actually and in fact. Now that the new plan would set up an enlarged committee to share the responsibility, we are all the more insistent upon our right to participate in policy-making and direction.[78]

In October 1943, Hadassah's request was granted, and the new governing body of Youth Aliyah included Tamar de Sola Pool as the representative of Hadassah seated alongside representatives of WIZO and other organizations. Hadassah's Marian Greenberg wrote: "By its insistence upon formal participation in decisions, as well as dollars, Hadassah helped Youth Aliyah prepare for a future without Henrietta Szold."[79] Since other organizations were now officially sharing responsibility for Youth Aliyah, on November 29, 1943, Hadassah gave up the title of "sole sponsor" for a new designation as "official representative" in the United States for Youth Aliyah.

In the United States, Hadassah's national leaders had additional concerns: once the United States entered the war in late 1941, Hadassah joined other Jewish organizations in publicly asserting their patriotism and unqualified support for America's war effort. A copy of a telegram sent to President Roosevelt at the White House was reprinted on the cover of the *Hadassah Newsletter*. The telegram, again linking American values to the Zionist enterprise in Palestine, declared that Hadassah's one hundred thousand members across the United States

> solemnly respond to your stirring call. . . . We who have given every support to the Allied war effort through our work in Palestine and through our active program for the protection of the American way of life in our own country, rededicate ourselves to safeguard the fundamental truths which you have enunciated. . . . We are calm and confident, trusting in your leadership and in your guidance of the destiny of our country and of civilization itself.[80]

Despite the urgency of Youth Aliyah's wartime needs, Hadassah still continued to solicit donations for its medical programs: "When you give your dollars for medical supplies for the people of Palestine you give for democracy's defense," said a 1942 pamphlet, adding that "Hadassah has . . . offered its fullest cooperation to the American government through the War Department." The pamphlet explained:

> There are those who fight with guns and bullets. There are others who help them fight by providing drugs and the equipment needed to administer them, by maintaining high health standards among civilian populations, and supporting long-established institutions of public welfare. This has been Hadassah's job in Palestine for three decades. This is still Hadassah's job today.[81]

In all its wartime publicity material, Hadassah made the case that its ongoing social welfare work in Palestine represented the organization's patriotic contribution to the American war effort. But despite such assurances, many American Jews worried that it might be regarded as unpatriotic to raise money for Zionist causes while the war was on. To assuage such doubts, the *Hadassah Newsletter* offered a feature article by Edward Norman: "There cannot be the slightest doubt," he wrote, "that the first duty of Jewish Americans—as of all Americans in this most serious crisis and time of danger, is to America itself. Whatever we Jews of America can do . . . to help our country to emerge victorious . . . we not only must do—but we, like all Americans, want to do."

And building Palestine was strengthening America. Nobody expected the United States, no matter how generous, to take in all of Europe's refugee Jews after the war: Palestine was the logical option. American Jews and Zionists, explained Norman, could do their bit to assist America by helping build up Palestine to prepare for the resettlement of millions of displaced European Jews. "No intelligent Jewish American should allow hysteria to stampede him into reducing support" for this effort, he argued, for "in aiding Palestine now, he will be helping to realize an integral part of our country's long-range aim of insuring freedom and peace in the world of the future."[82]

Thus, Hadassah sought to reconcile not only Zionist ideology, but Zionist activism, with the demand for wartime American patriotism. Twenty years earlier, American Zionists like Brandeis and Magnes struggled to synthesize Americanism and Zionism. Each ideology, they claimed, embraced the same democratic ideals. A good American, if he or she were Jewish, should therefore feel even more American, they argued, in supporting Zionism. Again, as Hadassah presented it, support for Zionism was itself the patriotic duty of Jewish Americans. Strikingly, Hadassah appealed to American Jews to support its programs in Palestine as Americans, rather than as Jews. Zionist goals in Palestine, claimed Hadassah, were congruent with America's war aims and even with its postwar hopes for a just and lasting peace. Similarly, Hadassah described its own work in Palestine as "a wartime source of strength to the strategy of the United States and of the United Nations."[83]

Those who donated money to Youth Aliyah received a certificate in the mail reading:

> In the name of the Jewish refugee child who has been freed from bondage in ghetto and concentration camp and led through your contribution to a permanent home in Palestine . . . Hadassah sends this expression of heartfelt gratitude. As this child grows to maturity and takes a place in the vanguard of men and women who are fighting to save democracy and keep it a reality, may you know the rewarding experience which comes from the knowledge that you have helped to transform a persecuted, uprooted child into a hopeful, stalwart pioneer.

The language of the certificate weaves together wartime themes with postwar Zionist and Jewish hopes. The opening echoes the incantatory phrases of the Passover Haggadah, which recites the story of the Israelites' escape from Egyptian bondage and describes how they were led to freedom in the Holy Land. Although Youth Aliyah rescues children, the certificate stresses the important role they will later assume as adults in fighting for democracy—language of the American war effort. Finally, in a brief nod to traditional Zionist ideology, and a further echo of the Haggadah story of the journey from "slavery to freedom," the donor is assured that this "persecuted" and "uprooted" child of the Diaspora will be "transformed" via Zionism into a "stalwart pioneer."[84]

From its earliest days, Hadassah fine-tuned its techniques for recruiting members, publicizing its activities, and raising funds. From the first, when it sought a nurse who would take photographs of her work in Palestine for fundraising purposes, Hadassah took its propaganda—and later its publicity—very seriously. Spreading the word about Hadassah's work was vital to raising money and therefore to the organization's continued ability to support both Youth Aliyah and its other projects in Palestine. Sometimes a personal touch was called for and, for example, at Hadassah's behest Szold would send letters to individual American donors to thank them for their contribution. Hadassah also forwarded to Szold many heartbreaking letters from surviving family members searching desperately for lost children who they hoped had been rescued by Youth Aliyah.

The perpetual need for new and original publicity-ready material from Palestine was a subject of constant discussion—and sometimes friction—between Szold and Hadassah. Szold sent Hadassah long descriptive reports of her visits to Youth Aliyah facilities, her meetings with individual youngsters, and general developments in the country. Hadassah did its best to set up interviews for Szold; an interview with a reporter from *Reader's Digest* in 1944, for example, was regarded as a coup, since the magazine reached eight million readers. But Hadassah's huge appetite for information and stories, and its frequent pleas to "send case histories" to use in producing new publicity materials, overwhelmed Szold. In 1944, Szold wrote to Gisela Wyzanski, chairman of the National Youth Aliyah Committee in New York:

> We are suffering here from a lack of a publicity director. We have made every effort imaginable to secure one, especially one who would pursue the track described in your own letter . . . namely to follow up cases and reveal their dramatic characteristics. With every request that comes to us from you and from other sources for material of this sort, we realize anew that our routine forces in this office, including myself, cannot cope with the situation. We need a full-time publicity agent.[85]

At the same time, however, not every suggestion or offer of help was accepted. An offer of assistance from a Hadassah member in California was refused by Szold as too flashy. Wyzanski concurred:

> It seems the Los Angeles air tends to produce Hollywood-like ideas for the promotion of Youth Aliyah which, if launched when and as the promoter wished, might prove inappropriate, as you so tactfully indicate. However, that is the price we must pay for such ardent workers as Mrs. Zion, who has many a miraculous achievement for Youth Aliyah to her credit.[86]

Successful fundraising depended on both an artful use of propaganda and close guidance to ensure that members publicized Hadassah's programs and solicited donations in the most thoughtful and financially effective way. The 1945 revised Hadassah manual mailed to members described itself as the Hadassah "Bible" and, indeed, was prefaced with a series of near-biblical injunctions:

> We are attaching a copy of your Hadassah Manual, your "Bible" for the coming year. It will tell you WHAT your activity is, WHY it is important, HOW you are to promote it, WHEN you are to campaign to get results, and WHO would make up the ideal personnel of your committee. Please use it daily. Refer to it constantly. Get to know it. The Manual is your Handbook and Guide. Make sure that you get the most from it![87]

And "getting the most from it" was increasingly important as Hadassah's wartime financial commitments, already great, would grow still larger.

In 1943, Szold asked Hadassah to consider taking over the ownership of Ben Shemen, the venerable agricultural boarding school that had hosted the very first Youth Aliyah group. With its original source of funding from the Jewish community in Germany gone by 1935, Ben Shemen depended on Youth Aliyah support and its future status was uncertain. Szold wanted Hadassah to assume responsibility for the school. It would mean, said Szold, that Hadassah for the first time would fund an established educational institution, and that "would give Hadassah its foothold, its center, its power-station, so to say, for all its educational undertakings." But, Szold admitted, "I cannot hide from you . . . that the possession and administration of Ben Shemen would entail upon Hadassah a net of responsibilities almost as complicated and as widespread as the medical work."[88]

Hadassah's national president, Judith Epstein, wrote back with a thoughtful summary of Hadassah's reservations about Ben Shemen. First, Hadassah did not want to have to pour all its fundraising energy into a single institution at the expense of its other projects, nor to bear all the responsibility for Ben Shemen's survival. Second, Hadassah "had been effective in laying upon the medical work the impress of American scientific thinking," but the educational field in Palestine was unfamiliar, and "separated as we are from the scene, both physically and psychologically . . . makes us hesitate, as we have not hesitated in the medical field, to exert our influence." Finally, Epstein pointed out:

> Hadassah has consistently introduced projects into Palestine which the Yishuv could not afford to undertake . . . we felt that the Yishuv had a right to look to us for something that Palestine itself could not bring about, either because of lack of funds, or the kind of training and experience in . . . which America excels. In the case of Ben Shemen, we would be taking over a project that is already highly developed, that bears the impress of the thinking of a whole generation, that has been moulded to meet the peculiar needs of Palestine.[89]

Rather than adopting Ben Shemen, Hadassah was more concerned it was losing its singular grip on American-based Youth Aliyah activities. Hadassah asked Szold to intervene in its conflict with some of the other organizations raising funds for Youth Aliyah, including the UPA, Pioneer Women, and the Mizrachi Women's Organization. Epstein complained to Szold that "a multiplicity of appeals . . . has confused the public to such an extent that we fear for the effectiveness not only of our efforts in the field, but for the project itself." Apparently each of the various organizations had announced a different cost for rescuing and supporting a child. Epstein also asked Szold to confirm that $360 was the true yearly cost of "maintenance, education and ordinary medical care" for a child.

In order to coordinate their activities and avoid further confusion, Hadassah and the UPA agreed to set up an advisory committee made up of representatives of each of the organizations involved. In the meantime, Hadassah sent an urgent cable to Szold, demanding that Youth Aliyah provide official confirmation of Hadassah's "special status as 'official Youth Aliyah representative [in] America'" and asking Youth Aliyah to "please instruct other groups accordingly designating them 'supporting agencies.'"[90]

Relations with non-Jewish organizations were less problematic. An American Christian coalition called Children to Palestine, which sought to raise awareness of, and funds for, Youth Aliyah among non-Jews, asked Hadassah to coordinate an exchange of letters between Youth Aliyah children in Palestine and non-Jewish children in the United States. Hadassah willingly complied. But a request from this same organization to bring a group of Youth Aliyah children to the United States "for propaganda purposes" was turned down: both Hadassah and Youth Aliyah administrators in Palestine felt it would be "harmful" to the children themselves.[91]

Another successful venture was Szold's From Town to Country scheme for underprivileged Palestinian Jewish youth. In 1944, two years after it started, Youth Aliyah sent Hadassah glowing descriptions of how From Town to Country had transformed "small, under-sized city children" into "sturdy country youth, prepared to fill the requirements of the Yishuv." At the first graduation ceremony for the program, one young man said:

> Here we have been welded into one group, prepared to face a communal future. These two years have borne fruit. We did not disappoint the hopes placed in us. We have taken root in the farm. Today we are workers with a past. In our studies we have made up lost time until today we are in the proper classes for our age. . . . Little by little we have entered a new life.

The program's first twenty-two graduates were described as the "vanguard" who "have proved that not only the refugee youth, but the under-privileged Palestinian urban youth as well, can make good when given a chance to work the soil."[92]

By 1945, as more and more of Europe stood liberated, Hadassah reported that Youth Aliyah in Palestine was struggling to absorb fifteen thousand young Jewish war refugees from across Europe, the Middle East, and Asia. Hadassah appealed to its supporters: "Help us teach them to laugh, to play, to study and work, to become upstanding men and women, good citizens of a democratic world. Give them back their childhood through Youth Aliyah. Give today!" Would-be donors were assured that they could still count on Hadassah's long-standing "one hundred percent" policy whereby "100% of the Youth Aliyah contribution you give to Hadassah goes intact to Palestine with no deduction for administration in this country." Many responded. By 1948, Hadassah had contributed a staggering sum of nearly fifteen million dollars to Youth Aliyah.[93]

While Hadassah's wartime participation in Youth Aliyah was touted as an unqualified success, questions have since been raised about Szold's role. Some critics have questioned whether her advanced age—she was seventy-five years old when she took charge of Youth Aliyah—and her careful, methodical habits meant that she lacked the flexibility of mind to deal with the prewar crisis in Europe. Freier herself criticized Szold's rigidly bureaucratic approach and believed that Szold was naive—in what Freier thought was a typically American way—about the threat posed by the Nazis.[94] Freier was convinced that Szold should have concentrated less on paperwork and following the rules (both self-imposed and those of the British Mandatory authorities) and more on fieldwork, trying to get as many youngsters out of danger as fast as possible. Indeed, many youngsters denied immigration certificates did not survive the war. Recent historical research supports this view. Historian Sandra Berliant Kadosh argues:

> Unfortunately, there were many deficiencies in Youth Aliyah's response to the Holocaust. The Youth Aliyah leadership in Palestine failed to realize the extent of the tragedy in Europe and showed little flexibility in adjusting the Youth Aliyah program. To 1945 and beyond, Youth Aliyah continued to adhere to the ideology, the methods, the policies and the bureaucratic structures which were first established in 1934.[95]

In 1939, concerned that Szold was moving too slowly, Freier came up with a plan to send a shipload of children without immigration certificates to Palestine. Szold, fearing that any illegal scheme might jeopardize Youth Aliyah's standing with the British authorities, blocked the plan from proceeding. Szold convinced the organizations that had promised to subsidize the venture to renege. A bitter Freier wrote, "Children who might have been saved by this plan perished in Germany."[96]

In early 1942, midwar, Szold was already thinking about the shape Youth Aliyah would take after the war ended. In a confidential letter to Georg

Landauer she suggested that they should begin "to work out a plan for the Youth Aliyah work at the end of the war, in view of the generally expected large immigration, particularly of young people, after the cessation of hostilities." Despite the reports that millions of Jews had already died in Europe by 1942, Szold told a colleague that she believed that "a great mass" of child refugees would arrive in Palestine after the war "and Youth Aliyah must be ready for them. They must plan . . . nothing should been done rashly or superficially, for there was no hurry. Ten thousand children had already been rescued by Youth Aliyah with patience and method and the determination that no one child should become lost in the mass."[97] But Henrietta Szold did not live to see the end of the war or witness its aftermath. She died on February 13, 1945.

For its part, Hadassah, despite its strong membership numbers and success in fundraising for Youth Aliyah in the 1930s and 1940s, remained insecure about its place within American Zionism. Thirty years after its founding, Hadassah still felt obliged to defend the message that its social welfare activities were productive and pioneering, rather than charitable and philanthropic, in character. Given the historical association between women's volunteerism and charity work, Hadassah justifiably feared that as a women's organization, its work would be devalued. As Youth Aliyah combined both maternalism and nation-building pioneering, it was especially important for Hadassah to participate in Youth Aliyah's management and decision-making framework. Ironically, Hadassah, which always fought being relegated to a supporting role as mere fundraisers in the American Zionist movement, was forced to argue this very point with Szold—who had created Hadassah in order to take women out of the auxiliaries and into the center of Zionist action.

Szold's resistance to an enlarged hands-on role for Hadassah in Youth Aliyah was not due to any qualms about women's abilities. Rather it was due to her determination to prevent arms-length American interference in the Yishuv. This tension between Hadassah and Szold echoed the larger conflict in organized Zionism between the American desire for greater control of how American funds were spent in the Yishuv and the Yishuv's demand for autonomy. Szold may have valued American know-how and American money, but once she moved to Palestine she began to argue for all hands-on decision making to remain the property of those in the Yishuv. As far as Szold was concerned, any Hadassah members who moved permanently to Palestine could promptly participate as Palestinians. "If you want representation here, you can have it," Szold told the National Board, "If you sent representatives over here . . . I warrant you that in six months they are Palestinian in outlook, as they should be." Without such local representation, however, Szold pressed Hadassah to abandon its "present method of deciding details of administration at a distance of seven thousand miles."[98]

Palestinian Jews, however, unlike the male-dominated American Zionist organizations, did understand the pioneering impact of Hadassah's social welfare work. They did not need to be convinced. "Your real difficulty is not over here," Szold told Hadassah, "It is in America that you must safeguard your entity. In Palestine you will not lose it."[99] But, for all its worries, Hadassah's status in America, as well as in Palestine, was secure. With Szold's death, Hadassah found its own voice in Palestinian affairs and, at the same time, assumed a larger, more participatory role in the management of Youth Aliyah. Through this involvement, Hadassah eventually played a major role in absorbing not only the scarred remnant of Holocaust survivors but also, shortly after statehood, a previously unexpected mass immigration of Jews from the countries of the Middle East and North Africa.

Notes

1. Louis Brandeis to Emanuel Neumann, 17 August 1930, *Letters of Louis D. Brandeis*, vol. 5, ed. Melvin I. Urofsky and David W. Levy (Albany: State University of New York Press, 1978), 443.

2. Rafael Medoff, *Zionism and the Arabs: An American Jewish Dilemma, 1898–1948* (Westport, Conn.: Praeger, 1997), 66.

3. Rose Jacobs, "Looking Ahead," *Hadassah News Letter*, November 1935, 6–7. Jacobs served two terms as national president: 1930–1932 and 1934–1937.

4. Recha Freier, *Let the Children Come: The Early History of Youth Aliyah* (London: Weidenfeld & Nicolson, 1961), 14.

5. For Georg Landauer's recollections of the obstacles faced in winning cooperation and funding for Freier's plan from Szold as well as from other individuals and organizations, including the Jewish Agency executive and international aid agencies, see his newspaper article, "The Way of Youth Aliyah," *Davar*, 17 and 19 February 1950, RG 1/B 44, HWZOA.

6. Recha Freier, "Chapters by Recha Freier on Youth Aliyah 1932–1935," Jerusalem, October 1952, Chapter One, RG 1/B 1/F 5a, HWZOA.

7. The *Histadrut* (Hebrew for "federation") is the general federation of labor—an umbrella group of the country's trade unions that also offers health and other services to its members.

8. See Freier, *Let the Children Come*, 11–12; Norman Bentwich, *Jewish Youth Comes Home: The Story of Youth Aliyah, 1933–1943* (Westport, Conn.: Hyperion, 1976).

9. See Sandra Berliant Kadosh, "Ideology versus Reality: Youth Aliyah and the Rescue of Jewish Children During the Holocaust Era, 1933–1945" (Ph.D. diss., Columbia University, 1995), and Brian David Amkraut, "Let Our Children Go: Youth Aliyah in Germany, 1932–1939" (Ph.D. diss., New York University, 2000).

10. Yoav Gelber, "The Origins of Youth Aliyah," *Studies in Zionism* 9 (1988): 148. For a description of Ben Shemen as well as other children's villages and educational institutions in Palestine during this period, see Noach Nardi, *Zionism and Education in Palestine* (New York: Bureau of Publications, Teachers College, Columbia University, 1934).

11. For further explanation of how the system worked, see Viscount Edwin Samuel's account of immigration policy after 1934 in Aaron S. Klieman, ed., *The Rise of Israel*, vol. 19, *Zionist Political Activity in the 1920s and 1930s* (New York: Garland, 1987), 155–62. Arab unrest always led to more restrictions on Jewish immigration as the British tried to meet their conflicting obligations to both Jews and Arabs in Palestine. For a discussion of the twists and turns of British policy on Jewish immigration to Palestine, see Gabriel Sheffer, "Political Considerations in British Policy-Making on Immigration to Palestine," *Studies in Zionism* 4 (October 1981): 237, 274; Calvin Goldscheider, *Israel's Changing Society: Population, Ethnicity and Development* (Boulder, Colo.: Westview, 1996), 45–48.

12. Freier, *Let the Children Come*, 39.

13. Freier, *Let the Children Come*, 12.

14. *Hechalutz* ("The Pioneer") was the name of the movement of Socialist Zionist youth activists in the Diaspora who organized themselves to live in communal agricultural settlements in Palestine. The movement began in Russia in the early 1900s.

15. See Joan Dash, *Summoned to Jerusalem: The Life of Henrietta Szold, Founder of Hadassah* (New York: Harper & Row, 1979), 232, 236; Freier, *Let the Children Come*, 14, 31; Marian Greenberg, *There Is Hope for Your Children: Youth Aliyah, Henrietta Szold and Hadassah* (N.p.: Hadassah, the Women's Zionist Organization of America, 1986), 8; and Kadosh, "Ideology versus Reality," 20ff.

16. Freier, *Let the Children Come*, 33.

17. The Jewish Agency was established in 1922 under the terms of the British Mandate for Palestine "as a public body for the purpose of advising and cooperating with the Administration of Palestine in such economic, social and other matters as may affect the establishment of the Jewish National Home and the interests of the Jewish population in Palestine, and, subject always to the control of the Administration, to assist and take part in the development of the country." Raphael Patai, ed., *Encyclopedia of Zionism and Israel* (New York: Herzl Press, 1971), s.v. "Jewish Agency for Israel" by A. Zwergbaum.

18. Freier, *Let the Children Come*, 35; Henrietta Szold to Mrs. Levin, Jerusalem, 12 January 1934, HWZOA; Henrietta Szold, 19 November 1933, aboard SS *Naldera*, in Marvin Lowenthal, *Henrietta Szold: Life and Letters* (New York: Viking, 1942), 257.

19. Freier, *Let the Children Come*, 36; Dash, *Summoned to Jerusalem*, 240; Greenberg, *There Is Hope for Your Children*, 9–10; Henrietta Szold to Rose Jacobs, Jerusalem, 10 February 1934, in Lowenthal, *Life and Letters*, 262.

20. Misha Louvish, "Aliyah," in *Immigration and Settlement* (Jerusalem: Keter, 1973), 31; Kadosh, "Ideology versus Reality," 40; Henrietta Szold, Jerusalem, 2–9 June 1933, in Lowenthal, *Life and Letters*, 248.

21. Kadosh, "Ideology versus Reality," 37.

22. Freier, *Let the Children Come*, 43.

23. Freier, *Let the Children Come*, 41–42. Such rigidity was not unusual among Zionists. Even after the German pogrom of November 1938, says historian Brian Amkraut, most Zionist leaders in Palestine "nonetheless refused to deviate from the commitment to selective immigration aimed at constructing the future Jewish state." Brian David Amkraut, "Zionist Attitudes towards Youth Aliyah from Germany, 1932–1939," *The Journal of Israeli History* 20, no. 2 (Spring 2001): 80.

24. Josephthal immigrated to Palestine in 1938. He held a succession of influential government posts, including head of the Absorption Section in the Immigration Department of the Jewish Agency and, later, minister of labor. See Ben Halpern and Shalom Wurm, eds., *The Responsible Opinion: The Life and Times of Giora Josephthal* (New York: Schocken, 1966).

25. Halpern and Wurm, eds., *The Responsible Opinion*, 95–96.

26. See Chanoch Rinott, "Major Trends in Jewish Youth Movements in Germany," in *Leo Baeck Institute Year Book* 19 (London: Secker & Warburg, 1974), 77–95; Werner Rosenstock, "The Jewish Youth Movement," *Leo Baeck Institute Year Book* 19 (London: Secker & Warburg, 1974), 97–105.

27. Freier, *Let the Children Come*, 33.

28. Dash, *Summoned to Jerusalem*, 254; Greenberg, *There Is Hope for Your Children*, 92; Marlin Levin, *It Takes a Dream: The Story of Hadassah* (Jerusalem: Gefen, 1997), 157.

29. Dash, *Summoned to Jerusalem*, 253.

30. Chanoch Rinott, "Youth Aliyah," in *Immigration and Settlement* (Jerusalem: Keter, 1973), 80; Bentwich, *Jewish Youth Comes Home*, 54; Levin, *It Takes a Dream*, 159.

31. Levin, *It Takes a Dream*, 158; Greenberg, *There Is Hope for Your Children*, 92; Marian Greenberg, "Hadassah and Youth Aliyah," 10, RG 1/B 44/F 326a, HWZOA; Georg Landauer to Mrs. Edward (Rose) Jacobs, 27 August 1935, RG 1/B 1/F 6, HWZOA.

32. Bentwich, *Jewish Youth Comes Home*, 54; Dash, *Summoned to Jerusalem*, 254.

33. Quoted in Dash, *Summoned to Jerusalem*, 255–56.

34. Greenberg, *There Is Hope for Your Children*, 92; Hadassah press release,18 October 1948, RG 1/B 1/F 6, HWZOA.

35. See Levin, *It Takes a Dream*, 159ff, for a blow-by-blow account of how American Zionist leaders reacted to the contract.

36. Louis Lipsky to Mrs. Edward (Rose) Jacobs, New York City, 22 October 1935, RG 1/B 1/F 6, HWZOA. Keren Hayesod continued to compete with Youth Aliyah over fundraising and raised a ruckus not only in the United States, but also in Germany and other countries. For more on Keren Hayesod's efforts to control Youth Aliyah's fundraising schedule, see Brian David Amkraut, "Zionist Attitudes towards Youth Aliyah from Germany, 1932–1939," 72ff.

37. Mrs. Edward (Rose) Jacobs to Morris Rothenberg, 26 November 1935, RG 1/B 1/F 6, HWZOA.

38. Levin, *It Takes a Dream*, 164.

39. Hadassah press release, "Hadassah Convention Adopts Youth Aliyah Project," 9 December 1935, RG 1/B 1/F 6, HWZOA.

40. Levin, *It Takes a Dream*, 165.

41. Jessie Sampter, "The Youth from Germany and the Youth from Palestine," January 1936, RG 1/B 1/F 6, HWZOA.

42. Zena Harman, ed., "Youth Aliyah Letters Written by Henrietta Szold," 53–55, RG 1/B 71, HWZOA.

43. Henrietta Szold, "News Reel Speech," December 1935, RG 7/HS/Sub-series 6, HWZOA.

44. "Birthday Tribute for Miss Szold, 75," *New York Times*, 15 December 1935, sec. 2, 6; Joseph M. Levy, "Honors for Miss Szold," *New York Times*, 15 December 1935, sec. 10, 11.

45. Harman, ed., "Youth Aliyah Letters Written by Henrietta Szold," 13.

46. Hadassah, the Women's Zionist Organization of America, *The Children Speak*, February 1937, RG 1/B 21/F 138, HWZOA.

47. Hadassah press release, "Eddie Cantor at Boston Party," 13 May 1936, RG 1/B 17/F 111, HWZOA; Marian Greenberg, *Joyful Mother of Children: Youth Aliyah under Henrietta Szold* (New York: Hadassah, the Women's Zionist Organization of America, 1960), 14, RG 1/B 44/F 326a, HWZOA.

48. Levin, *It Takes a Dream*, 166. In 1952, Eleanor Roosevelt accepted the title of World Patron of Youth Aliyah. She visited Youth Aliyah facilities in Israel in 1952, 1955, and 1959.

49. Greenberg, *Joyful Mother of Children*, 3.

50. Henrietta Szold, "Speech at the Dinner Given by the Executive Committee, National Council of Jewish Women," 26 December 1935, RG 1/B 18/F 202. HWZOA; Szold to Rose Jacobs, Jerusalem, 23 November 1936, HWZOA; Levin, *It Takes a Dream*, 168; Marian Greenberg, "Youth Aliyah's First Six Years with Hadassah: Address by Mrs. David B. Greenberg to the Youth Aliyah and Vocational Education Committee," 4 December 1957, 5, RG 1/B 39/F 286, HWZOA.

51. Greenberg, *Joyful Mother of Children*, 15.

52. Greenberg, "Youth Aliyah's First Six Years with Hadassah," 5.

53. For excerpts of the Peel report, see Walter Laqueur, *The Israel-Arab Reader: A Documentary History of the Middle East Conflict* (New York: Bantam Books, 1969), 56–58. For a discussion of events leading up to the partition proposal, and its impact, see J. C. Hurewitz, *The Struggle for Palestine* (New York: Schocken, 1950), 72ff.

54. Malcolm MacDonald, the son of British prime minister Ramsay MacDonald, held a post at the Colonial Office, where he was closely involved in Palestine policies. Weizmann to Malcolm MacDonald, London, 7 October 1938, in Klieman, ed., *The Rise of Israel*, vol. 19, *Zionist Political Activity in the 1920s and 1930s*, 461.

55. Harman, ed., "Youth Aliyah Letters Written by Henrietta Szold," 57.

56. Hadassah, the Women's Zionist Organization of America, "Memorandum to Intergovernmental Committee for Refugees, Evian, France," n.d., RG 1/B 12/F 10,

HWZOA; Hadassah, the Women's Zionist Organization of America, "Memorandum to Intergovernmental Committee on Refugees, Washington, D.C.," n.d., RG 1/B 12/F 10, HWZOA. See also Dash, *Summoned to Jerusalem*, 270–71. For an examination of the Evian conference and, in particular, how it dealt with the representatives of Jewish voluntary organizations, see S. Adler-Rudel, "The Evian Conference on the Refugee Question," *Leo Baeck Institute Year Book* 13 (London, Jerusalem, New York: East and West Library, published for the Leo Baeck Institute, 1968): 235–73.

57. Another brief window of opportunity was offered to German Jewish children by the *kindertransport* (children's transports) scheme, whereby the British government agreed to allow entry to thousands of German, Austrian, and Czechoslovakian Jewish children under the age of eighteen beginning in December 1938. These transports stopped with the outbreak of the war in September 1939. For a history of these efforts to rescue young victims of the Nazis, see Walter Laqueur, *Generation Exodus: The Fate of Young Jewish Refugees from Nazi Germany* (Hanover, N.H.: Brandeis University Press, 2001).

58. Naomi Shepherd, *Ploughing Sand: British Rule in Palestine, 1917–1948* (London: John Murray, 1999), 98, 118; Anita Shapira, *Land and Power: The Zionist Resort to Force, 1881–1948* (Stanford: Stanford University Press, 1992), 219ff.; Laqueur, ed., *The Israel-Arab Reader*, 56–58.

59. "Roosevelt Urged to Act for Jews," *New York Times*, 19 May 1939, 6.

60. Greenberg, *Joyful Mother of Children*, 10; Levin, *It Takes a Dream*, 169; Greenberg, *There Is Hope for Your Children*, 37.

61. Mrs. Moses P. Epstein, New York, to Henrietta Szold, Jerusalem, 21 July 1939, RG 1/B 10/F 48, HWZOA.

62. Mrs. David B. Greenberg, New York, to Henrietta Szold, Jerusalem, 15 January 1940, RG 1/B 10/F 48, HWZOA.

63. Hadassah, the Women's Zionist Organization of America, *Hadassah Membership*, 24 October 1938, RG 1/B 9, HWZOA; Kadosh, "Ideology versus Reality," 151; Henrietta Szold to Georg Landauer, Jerusalem, 28 January 1942, RG 1/B 2/F 8, HWZOA.

64. Hadassah, the Women's Zionist Organization of America, *Hadassah and Youth Aliyah*, 1935, RG 1/B 21/F 130, HWZOA.

65. Editorial, "Youth Aliyah," *New York Times*, 8 May 1935, 18.

66. Hadassah, *Hadassah and Youth Aliyah*.

67. The alienation many of these youngsters felt from the self-consciously antibourgeois kibbutzniks and the agricultural, collectivist imperatives of Youth Aliyah overall is documented in Laqueur, *Generation Exodus*, 109–15.

68. Quoted in Kadosh, "Ideology versus Reality," 144.

69. Hadassah, the Women's Zionist Organization of America, *Youth Aliyah Hadassah Manual*, January 1941, 4, 7, RG 1/B 3/F 14, HWZOA.

70. Greenberg, "Hadassah and Youth Aliyah," 32.

71. Greenberg, *There Is Hope for Your Children*, 47, 50.

72. Julia Dushkin, "A Children's Bureau in Palestine," *Hadassah Newsletter*, December 1942–January 1943, 8–10; Hadassah, the Women's Zionist Organization of America, *For Palestine's Children*, 1941, RG 17/B 1, HWZOA.

73. Henrietta Szold, "Save the Child—A Call to Women," Jerusalem, 29 November 1942, RG 1/B 2/F 8, HWZOA.

74. Mrs. David de Sola Pool to Henrietta Szold, New York, 13 January 1943, RG 1/B 2/F 8, HWZOA. De Sola Pool was Hadassah's national president from 1939 to 1943. Her husband, David, was also very active in Zionist organizations and contributed many articles to the Zionist press, including the *Hadassah Newsletter*.

75. Mrs. Charles E. Wyzanski, Address to the National Youth Aliyah Committee of Hadassah, "Vignettes of My Years as Youth Aliyah Chairman," 7 January 1958, 10, RG 1/B 39/F 286, HWZOA.

76. Mira Bramson, telephone interview by author, 4 February 2003; Henrietta Szold, Jerusalem, to Gisela Warburg, 27 July 1943, RG 1/B 2/F 11, HWZOA.

77. Hadassah, the Women's Zionist Organization of America, *For These We Shall Sacrifice and Work . . . As Though They Were Our Own*, December 1942, RG 1/B 21/F 152, HWZOA; Greenberg, *There Is Hope for Your Children*, 54–64; Levin, *It Takes a Dream*, 217–19.

78. Greenberg, "Hadassah and Youth Aliyah," 21–22.

79. Levin, *It Takes a Dream*, 170; Greenberg, *There Is Hope for Your Children*, 64; Henrietta Szold to Mrs. David de Sola Pool, Jerusalem, 22 March 1943, HWZOA; Greenberg, "Hadassah and Youth Aliyah," 23–25.

80. *Hadassah Newsletter*, December 1941–January 1942; Mrs. David de Sola Pool, Sylvia Brody, "Telegram to the President of the United States," *Hadassah Newsletter*, 10 December 1941.

81. Hadassah, the Women's Zionist Organization of America, *How Many Lives Can You Save With the Point of This Needle?* November 1942, RG 17, HWZOA.

82. Edward A. Norman, "Palestine and America's War Aims," *Hadassah Newsletter*, April 1942, 14–16.

83. Tamar de Sola Pool, "American Outpost in the Near East," *Survey Graphic*, October 1942, unpaginated.

84. Hadassah, the Women's Zionist Organization of America, Donor's Certificate, n.d., RG 1/B 78/F 10, HWZOA.

85. Henrietta Szold, Jerusalem, to Mrs. Charles Wyzanski, New York, 27 March 1944, RG 1/B 2/F 11, HWZOA.

86. Mrs. Charles Wyzanski, New York, to Henrietta Szold, Jerusalem, 20 July 1944, RG 1/B 3, HWZOA.

87. Hadassah, the Women's Zionist Organization of America, *Hadassah Manual: Youth Aliyah*, 1945, RG 1/B 3/F 14, HWZOA.

88. Henrietta Szold, Jerusalem, to Mrs. Moses P. Epstein, New York, 7 November 1943, RG 1/B 2/F 11, HWZOA.

89. Mrs. Moses P. Epstein, New York, to Henrietta Szold, Jerusalem, 7 February 1944, RG 1/B 2/F 11, HWZOA. Judith Epstein served two terms as president: 1937–1939 and 1943–1947.

90. Mrs. Moses P. Epstein, New York, to Henrietta Szold, Jerusalem, 22 November 1943, RG 1/B 2/F 11, HWZOA.

91. Letter, Children to Palestine Organization, RG 1/B 17/F 118, HWZOA. See also Tamar de Sola Pool, "Children to Palestine," *The Woman's Press*, June 1948, RG 1/B 21/F 158, HWZOA. For Hadassah's concerns about bringing Youth Aliyah children to the United States, see the letter from Mrs. Siegfried Kramarsky, New York, to Hans Beyth, Jerusalem, 13 November 1945, RG 1/B 3/F 14, HWZOA.

92. Dorothy Kahn Bar-Adon, "The Cedars of Lebanon," February 1944, RG 1/B 3/F 11, HWZOA.

93. Hadassah, the Women's Zionist Organization of America, "Escape to Life: Youth Aliyah," August 1945, RG 1/B 21/F 155, HWZOA; Greenberg, *There Is Hope for Your Children*, 99.

94. See Freier, *Let the Children Come*, Appendix I. For the rest of her life, Freier also remained angry about Szold's initial unwillingness to get involved in Youth Aliyah and about the way that Szold and Hadassah then took credit for starting the Youth Aliyah movement. Freier eventually took Szold to court over the issue. See also Gelber, "The Origins of Youth Aliyah," 149.

95. Kadosh, "Ideology versus Reality," 11, 4. See also Dash, *Summoned to Jerusalem*, 275–76, for her discussion of whether Szold was "obstructionist."

96. Freier, *Let the Children Come*, 62.

97. Henrietta Szold to Landauer, Jerusalem, 28 January 1942, RG 1/B 2/F 8, HWZOA; Dash, *Summoned to Jerusalem*, 312.

98. Henrietta Szold, Jerusalem, to the National Board of Hadassah, New York, 23 March 1929, RG 17/HS/B 17/F 168b, HWZOA.

99. Szold, Jerusalem, to the National Board of Hadassah, New York, 23 March 1929.

CHAPTER SIX

~

"Future Builders of the State": Youth Aliyah and the Rescue of Oriental Jewish Children

The end of the war did not spell the end of the pressure on Hadassah and Youth Aliyah to rescue children from abroad or provide for their care and education in the Yishuv: Hadassah leaders estimated that there were forty-two thousand orphaned children in postwar Europe—Holocaust survivors—who needed to be retrieved.[1] At the same time, Hadassah had an ongoing responsibility for the children already in Youth Aliyah's care. In October 1945, Hadassah delegates met in Chicago and agreed on a budget of one million dollars for the education and maintenance of the 6,500 Youth Aliyah children then in Palestine. "150,000 American Jewish mothers," Hadassah announced, "will become 'foster parents' for another year to thousands of orphaned Jewish children."[2]

To oversee the ingathering of survivor children, in 1946 Youth Aliyah opened ten new offices in cities across Europe including Athens, Stockholm, and Istanbul. Youth Aliyah took these children, many of whom had no known relatives, under its wing and, once in Palestine, provided for their care. The following year, in a report to the United Nations Special Committee on Palestine, the Jewish Agency reported that Youth Aliyah had brought 23,250 young people to Palestine since its inception and that, as of October 1, 1947, there were 8,701 wards "in training" housed in either collective settlements, cooperative villages, or Youth Aliyah institutions.[3]

While many countries might regard an influx of unaccompanied young people as a liability, Zionist leaders in Palestine were enthusiastic about the potential of these youngsters: Moshe Kol, the head of Youth Aliyah in Palestine,

153

often described child and youth aliyah as the country's "richest source of *halutziot*." Moreover, he shared Hadassah's vision of Youth Aliyah as the means by which Jewish women could contribute to the pioneering Zionist cause. Indeed, Kol's pitch for greater international involvement by women was emphatically maternalist:

> Up to the present Hadassah of America has played the foremost part and WIZO and other women's organizations have done their share but now it is imperative that a new phase in our work be opened, a phase that will place responsibility on hundreds of thousands of Jewish women throughout the world. . . . Youth Aliyah is the particular branch of our work which should embrace all the Jewish mothers of the world, who should be asked to assume responsibility for the rescue of thousands of children and their education in Eretz Israel, that they may be transformed into a reservoir of pioneering strength for our future.

The "new phase" to which Kol refers here is the need for Youth Aliyah to ingather thousands of Jewish children from Islamic countries.[4]

Some children from these countries were already under the care of Youth Aliyah. During the war years, although Youth Aliyah concentrated on rescuing Jewish children from European countries under the Nazi heel, it also brought to Palestine groups of children in desperate need from Middle Eastern and North African countries.[5] Now Youth Aliyah faced a double task: the absorption of European war orphans and the urgent need to rescue more youngsters from the increasingly imperiled Jewish communities of the Middle East and North Africa.

European powers had established a foothold in the Middle East and North Africa in the nineteenth and early twentieth centuries: Algeria became a French colony in 1830; Tunisia became a colonial protectorate of France in 1881; Morocco became a colonial protectorate of both France and Spain in 1912; and Egypt became a British protectorate in 1914. The colonial framework provided Jewish communities in these countries with a measure of security and protection. At the same time, because local Jews were perceived as allied with Europe, they were also left vulnerable to the resentment of local Arab populations. As historian Bernard Lewis puts it: "Western influence prepared the downfall of the Islamic Jewries in more ways than one."[6]

With the rise of anti-imperialist sentiment in the countries of the Middle East and the Maghreb, Jews became targets of nationalist riots. Arab anger was also inflamed by European support for Jewish settlement in Palestine. Local Jews were branded as Zionist agents and were attacked. In the 1930s and

1940s there were many outbreaks of anti-Jewish violence in the Arab world. Hundreds were injured and killed, Jewish homes and workplaces destroyed. In the aftermath of the Second World War, as Arab nationalist movements gathered steam, the situation of the Jewish communities of the Middle East became ever more precarious.[7]

According to a 1946 Jewish Agency report, there were an estimated eight to nine hundred thousand Jews in the Middle East and North Africa. Jewish Agency representatives toured some of these Jewish communities and de-scribed the discrimination, poverty, disease, and other hardships suffered by the Jews of the North African ghettos. The report concluded that

> the position of most of the Jewish communities in the East is characterised by a regime of disabilities and by a state of political and economic insecurity. They are denied an effective equality of rights and are at every step made aware of their inferiority. Their precarious status drives them to seek foreign support. When they do so, they are branded as disloyal.

Entire communities would have to be evacuated, Jewish Agency officials said.[8]

A strategy was proposed whereby Youth Aliyah would get the children out first and bring them to Palestine in advance of their parents. Once there, the youngsters could learn Hebrew, begin the process of adjustment, and prepare the way for their parents' later arrival.

But British restrictions on the number and categories of immigrants al-lowed to enter Palestine were still in force, and the absorption capacity of Youth Aliyah's reception facilities in Palestine was already severely strained by survivor admissions. In addition, many of the North African and Middle Eastern children were in poor health; some had trachoma, were pretubercu-lar, or had other contagious diseases. These children needed medical atten-tion and convalescence, but these were not easily provided in Palestine.

With the end of the war it was, however, once again possible to have a pe-riod of preparatory training, education, and physical care for youngsters be-fore they arrived in Palestine. Accordingly, many of the youngsters from Is-lamic countries did not go directly to Palestine. Instead, they were separated from their families and sent to transit camps in Norway or France, some to convalesce and some to begin their Zionist education. The children might spend anywhere from a few months to a year in these locations before mov-ing on. In Norway, Youth Aliyah had the use of a former German army camp near Holmestrand renovated by a coalition of aid organizations and trans-formed into a residential treatment center for children.[9] In France, Youth

Aliyah used several facilities, some of which it managed in cooperation with other Zionist youth movement organizations. One of the largest facilities in France was the Herbert H. Lehman home for children at Cambous, near Montpelier.[10]

Where would Hadassah fit in? With such a major financial commitment to Youth Aliyah, and with Youth Aliyah's mandate expanding, Hadassah wanted a more hands-on role in Youth Aliyah planning. Hadassah's national Youth Aliyah chairman, Bertha Schoolman, arrived in Palestine on November 28, 1947, to begin a five-year post as cochair of the Youth Aliyah Management Committee. Her arrival was a victory for Hadassah after many years of battling, often with Henrietta Szold, for greater participation in Youth Aliyah's day-to-day decision making. Moshe Kol, director of Youth Aliyah, was the committee's chairman. Kol and Schoolman were caught up by the spirit of impending change. The day after Schoolman arrived in Palestine, the United Nations recommended the partition of Palestine and the creation of a Jewish state.

With the end of the British Mandate, the State of Israel was established on May 14, 1948. Fighting off an invasion by neighboring Arab countries, the new state prevailed. If the mood was cautiously upbeat, the problems were severe. Living conditions were difficult, security a concern, and into all this flooded refugees, including orphaned children. Within six months, one hundred thousand immigrants arrived in Israel. "In practical terms," says political scientist Mitchell Cohen, "the government was entirely unprepared to cope with the situation."[11]

The need for social, community, and health services of the kind Hadassah had founded was never greater. But Hadassah faced the imminent loss of jurisdiction over most of its projects to state control as Israel's first prime minister, David Ben-Gurion, began the process of integrating and absorbing various pre-state organizations and institutions into government and generally establishing centralized governmental authority.[12] Over the next few years, in keeping with its policy of devolution, Hadassah's countrywide medical activities (infant welfare stations, school hygiene programs, etc.) would gradually be transferred to the new national government. This inevitable transition was a key element in the Zionist state-building enterprise, but it was also worrisome for Hadassah because it would mean that

> there would be less and less to show to our American visitors and members who, over the years, have grown accustomed to the idea that Hadassah is *the* factor in the medical field of the Yishuv and in Child Welfare. Imagine their disappointment when they come to Israel and see there practically nothing of

Hadassah's activities. . . . Such a situation would . . . sooner or later reflect on Hadassah's fundraising capacity among those of its members who have visited Israel and those at home to whom they relate what they have seen in the country.[13]

Through taking tourists on guided visits to Hadassah projects around the country, Hadassah hoped to impress Americans with its own achievements as well as with the extent of Zionist development overall. It was now vital that Hadassah find a new, and high-profile, focus for its considerable energies and fundraising apparatus.

Hadassah asked the eminent American educational expert Alexander Dushkin to evaluate Youth Aliyah's educational programs and policies with an eye to recommending a new area of concentration for Hadassah. Dushkin visited eleven kibbutzim, fourteen children's villages and other institutions for children, two seminaries for *madrichim* (youth leaders), and an immigrant reception center. He also met with senior Youth Aliyah bureaucrats. On the whole, Dushkin considered Youth Aliyah a resounding success:

As an immigrant to the U.S.A., some of us have experienced the powerful as-similative educational influence of the American public school system. . . . What the American public school did and does for its immigrant children, that Youth Aliyah does amply for . . . its young refugees. . . . We saw these young people transformed; sturdier, healthier, with proud and secure experience as successful workers. For they were much wanted everywhere not only as young Jewish citizens but also as good workers. They were talking Hebrew as fluently as the native "Sabras," and they were achieving an educational standard equal to 85% of the children of the Yishuv.

Dushkin felt that Youth Aliyah had succeeded in giving youngsters in its care a "broad social outlook" and that they were indeed enacting the Youth Aliyah motto, "The absorbed shall become the absorbers."[14] According to Dushkin, Youth Aliyah furthered the Yishuv's "melting pot" approach to im-migrant absorption, which he felt compared favorably with the assimilative thrust of American society—in both cases, education helped immigrants to move to an equal footing, as full citizens, with the native-born.[15]

But Dushkin also found problem areas. Many of the Youth Aliyah *madrichim* were poorly trained, and the education provided to Youth Aliyah wards was often inferior. Moreover, given the agricultural priority of Youth Aliyah's educational program, the young people who preferred to pursue a nonagricultural career were generally unserved or ignored. "Everywhere we . . . heard the frequent voices of individuals crying out their need to learn a

. . . trade or skilled occupation," Dushkin reported. He agreed that an agricultural education was valuable even for those individuals who moved on to industrial occupations, and that agriculture was an important part of developing a self-sufficient economy, but there was still a problem: "The dilemma is therefore how to preserve agricultural life as the aim and ideal for all young people in Youth Aliyah, and at the same time to make possible specialized industrial training for those who can not adjust to agricultural village life or who have an inner need for skilled artisanship." Here was a role for Hadassah. Dushkin recommended that Hadassah "concern itself with maintaining the high educational quality of the program and to help meet those educational needs which aim to prepare the immigrant youth for full and productive life."[16]

Hadassah was receptive to this advice. An internal Hadassah memo noted:

> The figures quoted in his report clearly prove the fact (which we all know) that a very considerable percentage of boys and girls, after having received their educational training through Youth Aliyah, leave the settlements and embark upon a life in town for which, unfortunately, Youth Aliyah has not prepared them at all and in which they have therefore to start right at the bottom as unskilled workers.

Now that industrial development was just as important as agriculture in the overall development of the country, the memo argued, "these children could, with practically the same effort, have become properly trained for their real vocation" rather than joining the many unskilled and semi-skilled workers already competing for scarce jobs.[17]

The solution was obvious: Hadassah should adopt vocational education as its new countrywide project:

> By earmarking its collections for Youth Aliyah for the needs of vocational training among youth immigrants and by providing this training through its own vocational education projects . . . set up all over the country, Hadassah would secure a project impressive to the American visitor in its importance and scope, financeable out of present collections and do at the same time a service of greatest importance to thousands of Youth Aliyah wards and, in the end, to the proper establishment of a high-grade industry in Israel.[18]

This would allow Hadassah to meet a real need among Youth Aliyah's charges and at the same time carve out a distinct role for itself as the patron of vocational education within its overall support for Youth Aliyah. Resolved to accept Dushkin's recommendations, Hadassah moved to implement his proposals in a number of areas. The organization established a special fund to pay for textbooks, audiovisual equipment, musical instruments, and other such items. Another fund was set up to test a vocational training program to help those youngsters who were not interested in agriculture to prepare for other kinds of employment.[19]

But while Hadassah was happy to sponsor vocational education as part of Youth Aliyah programs, Youth Aliyah itself was internally divided over whether it should offer vocational education at all. Those who argued against it claimed that if the organization diluted its focus on agriculture it would lose its raison d'être as a pioneering Zionist educational movement devoted to land settlement. In addition, administrators feared that, given a vocational option, young people would abandon agricultural work much to the detriment of the state. What is more, they pointed out, vocational and technical education was available through other organizations in the country. Dushkin wrote to Hadassah:

> Whereas Youth Aliyah leaders are increasingly aware of the need for adjusting their activities to individual differences, they nevertheless continue to insist that the main stream of Youth Aliyah education must be such as to turn the young people's attention to village life rather than to towns and cities. In view of this, every suggestion of vocational education along the usual lines is met with suspicion and resistance.[20]

This question was debated by Youth Aliyah staff, who acknowledged that "we must not compel a person to work at a trade which he does not want and feels that he was not created for it. We saw at Ben Shemen [agricultural school] that not giving a trade to a given type of youth meant later exposing him to the influence of the street or his joining extreme movements." There were also more serious implications for Israel as a developing society if Youth Aliyah failed to provide young immigrants with the education and training they needed to be able to compete, on equal terms, for jobs with native-born Israelis:

> If Youth Aliyah will not leave as an inheritance to . . . its trainees a knowledge of a vocation we will be confronted with a new class division in Israel. The native Israelis will occupy first place and the new-comers will be the weak ones, as is the case in the army at present; the officers are Israelis, the experts, the ranks are new immigrants. . . . On the one hand, there is native youth that has studied 11 to 12 years and on the other hand, there is the immigrant youth, who are doomed to be workers in the settlement. The Israeli youth is the nucleus, it

is educated and possesses a vocation. If we cannot give the immigrant youth twelve years of learning, we must give it the possibility of acquiring a vocation. And another thing; we must not leave agricultural study at its present level, but we must raise it to a higher professional level.[21]

Although participants at this particular meeting spoke in terms of class distinctions, the debate over vocational education versus agricultural training was soon to acquire a new, ethnic dimension. Inevitably, Youth Aliyah got caught up in the emerging "culture clash" between the European "old-timer"–dominated Israeli establishment and new Jewish immigrants from Islamic countries.

In any case, it was soon apparent that debates over pedagogical issues were part of a larger emerging national debate, a thorny debate that was not easily resolved. But Youth Aliyah workers were also concerned about the social and psychological problems that were now surfacing among many of the young refugees pouring into the country. After a four-month investigatory trip to Israel during this tumultuous period, Marian Greenberg reported to Hadassah's National Board:

> Imagine in terms of American experience, an immigration of 1,500 children a month coming from 30 countries, speaking as many languages, reflecting a variety of social and educational backgrounds—or the lack of them—and harboring an infinite number of experiences totally unrelated to their chronological age. Remember that this is but one part of a mass immigration into a tiny country which is neither at war nor at peace and cannot yet be demobilized. Despite the critical shortage of housing, the inadequate budget furnished by voluntary agencies, the devoted but overworked corps of teachers and a rudimentary staff of professional psychiatrists and social workers, a superhuman job is being done.

Greenberg pointed out that many of the European youngsters now joining Youth Aliyah, Holocaust survivors, had serious psychological problems as a result of their wartime experiences. They were hardened and wary, suspicious of adults and of each other.[22]

These youngsters required professional help, said Greenberg. In particular, "American know-how is needed in Israel in connection with Youth Aliyah." She continued:

> I do not know whether the country is financially or otherwise prepared to take on American trained social workers and psychiatric social workers in anything like the proportion needed. Nevertheless, I am convinced that research and

study of Youth Aliyah problems merits the consideration of American social workers, who are eager to contribute their skills for the solution of a pressing problem.

As always, Hadassah was ready to pitch in and paid to send two Israeli social workers, Shlomit and Asher Hoek, to the New York School of Social Work in order to study the problems of the young war refugees.

The Hoeks prepared a report titled *Helping Post-War European Jewish Adolescents to Adjust in Israel.* They found that many of the young war survivors hid deep psychological disturbances behind a facade of well-being:

> Since physically they responded so quickly to good care, many persons were deceived by their outgoing qualities and seemingly good adjustment and misled into thinking that there was a similar capacity for emotional resilience, and that, given normal and healthy conditions, the newcomers would "forget" their past experiences. Almost invariably this belief was badly shaken.[23]

The Hoeks' report raised an issue about which there was some ambivalence in Youth Aliyah: should the young refugees be helped to overcome their recent traumatic experiences or should they be encouraged to forget their Diasporic past and culture altogether?

This question bespoke tensions in the larger society over the nature of the new national identity that was to be shaped and over how many people in Israel then understood the Holocaust. The Zionist imperative of "negation of the Diaspora" called for all immigrants to shed their Diasporic pasts and subsume themselves, whatever their backgrounds, in a new identity. This entailed discouraging the preservation of memories and cultural traditions associated with Diaspora life. Youth Aliyah led the way in educational efforts to transform young refugees into Hebrew-speaking *sabras.* To rid them of what was termed a *galut* (exilic) mentality, Youth Aliyah wanted youngsters to shed the social habits acquired in other countries and contexts. Some such habits were the product of cultural differences, but some resulted from difficult life experiences.

While all Youth Aliyah youngsters were asked to abandon their cultural traditions, young Holocaust survivors were also expected to forget their recent traumatic experiences. In this, as in other respects, Youth Aliyah served as a social laboratory. For at least fifteen years after the end of the war—until the Eichmann trial in 1961—Israelis avoided public discussion of the Holocaust. Israeli historian Anita Shapira describes it as "repression" and explains that "there was no room in the newly formed heroic state for

exhibitions of weakness and humiliation." As a result, adult Holocaust survivors, with their taint of victimhood, were often treated with hostility and
resentment rather than sympathy.[24] Similarly, Youth Aliyah regarded young
war survivors with a sense of urgency—they must be transformed as quickly
as possible.

The Hoeks regarded this social engineering as problematic. They cautioned that Israelis would have to show more understanding when dealing
with young war refugees and accept that it was unrealistic to expect an in-
stant transformation of their personalities and behavior. For example, they
argued, apparently antisocial traits like lying, stealing, and cheating were in
fact necessary survival skills in the death camps and in wartime conditions:
"The community must be familiarized with the reasons for the apparently
unethical and asocial behavior which may be anticipated in the Youth
Aliyah children. These children fear, hate and resist all authority, and have
still to learn that organized society requires the exercise of authority and
self-discipline."[25]

In some ways, this was familiar terrain. From past experience, Youth
Aliyah's staff knew that children from each European national group had a
different profile: a distinct cultural, social, and educational background.
Rather than something to work with, these differences were marks of inappropriate behavior (un-*halutzic* in the early days, un-Israeli later on) and were
slated for elimination. Each group, it seemed, posed a particular set of problems for the movement. For example, a Youth Aliyah study noted that

> the habits of the adolescent child from Poland were contrary to what prevailed
> among children of the same age in Youth Aliyah. They smoked, played cards,
> went in for modern ballroom dancing and were addicted to the cinema—all
> concepts in direct contrast to Youth Aliyah's emphasis on the rural life and en-
> vironment.[26]

While the Polish youth were thought to suffer from an excess of urbanity,
some of the North African children, it seemed, had the opposite problem. As
Greenberg explained it, "they are unaccustomed to the ordinary amenities of
Western society." As a result, before regular educational programs could begin, these children required "basic instruction in social behavior."[27]

Indeed, Youth Aliyah staff in France were baffled by the behavior of newly
arrived North African Jewish children: "Most of them are young savages with
their own code of honour and a code of forbidden and permitted things
which is very different from that of other children," the director of Youth
Aliyah's French office explained in an interview. He elaborated:

Some of the children seem never to have slept in a bed, they have never eaten with knives and forks, they do not know how to use a lavatory, they have never undressed before going to sleep and they did not know there were such things as sheets. Their manners and customs were—and still are—a matter of absolute bewilderment for our monitors. Some of our young North-African children were not used to sitting on chairs and still take every possible opportunity of sitting cross-legged on their bed or on the floor. In some of our houses the problem of food was almost a tragedy: the children who used to live on olives and black coffee could not digest the ordinary European food we offered to them.

In short, the director said, Youth Aliyah had a formidable task ahead where these children were concerned since it had to "make civilized beings out of them . . . to turn the little savages that we are now receiving into useful human beings, morally and physically healthy, future builders of the state of Israel."[28]

Early reports indicated that Youth Aliyah's efforts to remake these youngsters were successful. The *Palestine Post* reported that two hundred Moroccan children, after spending six months in Norway, were "transformed from little more than 'uncivilized' street urchins into well-behaved young children." The newspaper quoted Moshe Kol that "similar excellent results" had been achieved in the twelve transit homes and a camp in France. In a cable to his colleagues in Israel, Kol suggested that "when the children come to Israel it will be difficult to distinguish them from our own 'sabras.'"[29]

Media coverage in the Jewish, American, and international press also focused on Youth Aliyah's power to transform youngsters. An article in the UNESCO magazine, *Impetus*, drew on resonant biblical imagery for its title, "Exodus via Norway," and described the changes wrought by Youth Aliyah staff working with Moroccan children in their charge. "Are these the same children?" asked a caption under before-and-after photographs of the children. The article described newly arrived Moroccan children as "little gamins with their sullen looks, savage gestures and strange *mellah* [ghetto] slang" who, after eight months of Youth Aliyah's care became "civilized . . . smiling, robust, well-mannered children." With this successful rehabilitation, "these young immigrants from North Africa can begin their new lives on a par with other young Israeli settlers from all over the world."[30]

These results were certainly promising, but it was becoming clear that the children would also need extra help even after they arrived in Israel and that more funding would be needed to support such programs. To raise the funds, a new publicity strategy was necessary. Eva Michaelis, head of public relations at the Jewish Agency's Department for Child and Youth Immigration, informed Hadassah:

> Our publicity and information service, as well as our propaganda, will have to be switched over to North Africa and the Near Eastern countries. It will be your task in future to explain to the Jewish and non-Jewish public alike that the salvation of these children is as urgent and pressing as was the rescue of the European children. Whilst these children are not in immediate danger of life, there is in their present surroundings not the slightest chance for them to develop into healthy and normal human beings and to enjoy the basic conditions of health, education, culture and civilisation.

Michaelis promised to send explanatory material to Hadassah that would provide "all the necessary information about the background and development of Yemenite, North African and Turkish children."[31]

A raft of new background material, meant for circulation among the membership, began arriving at Hadassah headquarters in New York. One booklet, *Our Children, Our Future*, a collection of newspaper articles and essays translated into English and edited by Michaelis, is typical. Michaelis wrote that she hoped the booklet would "assist . . . in achieving a better understanding of our Oriental fellow Jew and the desperate need of his children, who are our children too." The booklet was designed to introduce Americans to the Jews of Islamic countries. But rather than dealing with the rich history and culture of these communities, the booklet focused instead on alarming descriptions of their current impoverished and beleaguered state:

> The Jews of North Africa live under conditions which are wretched even by Middle Eastern standards. Psychologically, too, they are at a very low ebb—a fact which may be attributed to their inferior political and legal status, the contempt in which they are held by their Arab neighbors, and their feeling of physical insecurity resulting from generations of oppression.

Because the booklet was intended to dispel "some prevalent misconceptions" such as that "the Moroccan Jews do not want to work," it emphasized the social causes of what it described as "psychological traits" and "behavioral differences." A description of the squalor in the Marrakesh "ghetto" explains: "It is almost unbelievable that human beings can be born and grow up in such surroundings; it is certainly understandable that they may exhibit certain psychological differences from people living in a more normal environment." Nevertheless, readers are assured that "Moroccan Jews are eager to learn and to work" and that they "react favourably whenever they encounter an attitude which establishes confidence in themselves and makes them feel that they are active and useful members of society."[32] Underlying this analysis was the idea that a shift to a different environment and educational intervention were key.

While the problems of North African Jews as a whole were of interest to Youth Aliyah and Hadassah, the needs of their children were the greatest priority. The push was now on to convince Americans that the Jewish children of the Islamic countries were as endangered by poverty and anti-Jewish oppression as their European brethren had been by the war. Youth Aliyah sent the grim statistics to Hadassah headquarters: faced with state-sanctioned hostility from their Muslim neighbors, Jews endured infant mortality rates of as much as 50 percent, shocking rates of malnourishment and disease, and high rates of illiteracy and child labor. Large families were crowded together in unsanitary living conditions in the Jewish slums. Hadassah issued a press release:

> Fifty percent of the boys of Moroccan Jewish families are dead before their thirteenth year. No statistics even exist about girls. Fifteen thousand are without education of any kind. Some 80–90% are seriously ill. Their surroundings resemble the Middle Ages. Israel is eager to rescue them from a fate which means sure death. They need a preliminary processing period during which they can be cured, properly fed, and prepared for the healthy cooperative living awaiting them under the auspices of the Youth Aliyah movement.[33]

It all sounded familiar to American Jews, who remembered the exposés of tenement life in their own cities earlier in the century. And these images were particularly meaningful for Hadassah—an organization whose earliest influence was the Progressive campaign to improve the lives of America's urban poor.

Suddenly, however, the strategy was different. Instead of trying to improve living conditions in North Africa, efforts focused on transferring the Jewish communities of these countries to Israel, beginning with the children. Moshe Kol told delegates to Hadassah's 1949 convention in San Francisco:

> Jews living in Arab countries are living as prisoners of war, as enemy aliens in countries where their ancestors have resided for centuries. We are faced with terrific pressure from our brethren in these countries to remove the children swiftly. Parents beg us to take them out even if they themselves must remain behind.

The situation was urgent, announced Hadassah, adding that, according to Kol, conditions for Jews in Morocco, Yemen, Iraq, and Tripolitania were so bad that "Buchenwald was the only comparison."[34]

By May 1949 there were eight thousand Oriental youngsters in European transit camps waiting to go to Israel.[35] As large numbers of these children began to arrive in Israel fresh from their rehabilitative stay in Norway or France, Youth Aliyah workers concluded that while the children's health had improved, many still lagged behind their Israeli peers both behaviorally and educationally. Once again, Youth Aliyah had to adjust its programs to meet the distinct needs of a new set of arrivals. The first task was to undertake comprehensive psychological assessments. The experts soon determined that

> these children differ in many ways from those who originate in Europe. . . . [Their] natural intelligence develops at a quicker pace than that of European children, as they are mostly left to themselves. They did not go to school, and at home their parents, who had many children, did not spend much time with them nor devote any time to educating them in the same way that European children are supervised, guided and educated. . . . Owing to the lack of care and loving kindness on the part of their parents, the children did not form the same emotional attachments to them as children from Europe do. . . . Thus they do not know civilization as we know it, but it appears to be quite easy to get them used to civilized ways of life. What is difficult is to restrain their aggressive instincts, to foster in them a sense of social responsibility, and to imbue pleasant relationships with their tutors or their comrades.[36]

Although Youth Aliyah's publicists were anxious to draw parallels between the plight of the children from Islamic countries and the war refugees from Europe, the former group was often described in terms that reflect a startling degree of social, cultural, and even racial estrangement. The Oriental children were described as "savages" who behaved like "little animals." Their behavior, habits, customs, and culture were not just unfamiliar, but "uncivilized" and often shocking. Even their familial relationships were judged to be of a quite different order. Indeed, a psychological assessment of children going to Norway found that

> these children have not the same kind of tie to their parents, as is generally conditioned by European family tradition. The child is not the centre of the family, nor is it given any special care or attention. It is not spoilt in any way. Be it clothes, or food, the parents usually think of themselves first, and then of the little ones. If one wants something from a child, one shouts rather than tries to obtain the result by "love." This fact opens up a big and new field for education. The lack of this familiar shouting and beating will at first arouse a great mistrust and scepticism amongst the children.[37]

Thus, while many of the European children Youth Aliyah had previously taken in were true orphans, these North African children *had* parents but were, it was implied, orphaned by parental neglect and inattention. Youth Aliyah claimed it could do for the children what their parents could not or would not: "In the Children's Colony they have perhaps for the first time met people who understand them, who are capable of giving them the warm kindness they have never known before—people who patiently teach them all those things which are part of the normal and healthy education of other children."[38] Hadassah, of course, would share Youth Aliyah's in loco parentis role. As Youth Aliyah's publicity director, Zena Harman, told delegates at Hadassah's annual conference, Youth Aliyah children "are the children of the Jewish people as a whole. Fate made them other people's children, but they might well have been ours. They are entitled to what we consider our own children should receive in education and upbringing."[39]

In order to learn more about the background of some of the North African youngsters, Youth Aliyah sent its education director, Chanoch Reinhold, to visit the Jewish communities of Morocco. Reinhold visited the schools and looked at the family life of Jews in the *mellah*. Reinhold wrote: "The aimless wandering through the alley-ways of the Mellah, the gloomy rooms in which they must live, and the look in their eyes, point out a social background that casts its shadow of wretchedness over the personality of the child." Reinhold concluded that the Jews of the ghetto "live in a maze of unquestioned beliefs, isolated from the world."[40]

Although Hadassah's publicity materials consistently echoed the themes that appeared in Youth Aliyah's own material, there is some evidence to suggest that Hadassah members occasionally discovered discrepancies between the information they were provided with by the Israeli office of Youth Aliyah and the reality on the ground. After making her own information-gathering trip to Morocco, for example, Hadassah's national Youth Aliyah chairman (from 1953 to 1956) Dr. Miriam Freund decided that "we had mistaken impressions with regard to Moroccan Jewry." She confirmed that "conditions in the mellah are indescribable." But she said, "The impression in this country is that Moroccan Jewry is a completely deprived and depraved Jewry. I came and found that at least seventy-five percent of all the Jewish children are going to school and fifty percent of the seventy-five percent are going to very good schools." Moreover, said Freund, among the community's adults, "It was interesting to see their feeling for Hadassah and to realize Hadassah's influence outside of the United States and Israel."[41]

After meeting with the local representatives of the Jewish Agency and Youth Aliyah, Freund challenged the Israeli government's overall strategy for persuading Moroccan Jews to emigrate: "The [Jewish] Agency and the State are wrong in their attacks on life in Morocco," she said. "They have not found a way to make them want to go to Israel now. It is our business to sell Israel to them properly." For all her doubts, Freund's priority was still to rescue children, and she was sure that Hadassah's approach to the problem was productive: "We are beginning to show a pattern of action and opening up people's minds to what can be done—proving that these children are not depraved, hopeless, lost children, but underprivileged and deprived of certain advantages."[42]

To make its case, Hadassah often used biographies of individual children to represent the movement as a whole—a practice that Szold had previously rejected. One Hadassah brochure offered the portrait of a Moroccan boy named Eliahu that concluded: "There is no doubt about it—Eliahu is going to be a much happier individual in the broad expanses of the Negev, than selling striped satins in the crowded bazaars of Casablanca."[43] This simple contrast between the oppressive life of child labor in the Oriental Diaspora and the opportunity afforded by Youth Aliyah appears repeatedly in the publicity materials. Moroccan Jewish children, declared another pamphlet, "in marked contrast to the happy, fearless children of Israel—have misery and despair stamped upon their faces." The repercussions of this early deprivation are severe and produce "an effect upon their mentality in later life."[44]

Concerned about popular misconceptions that verged on racism, both Youth Aliyah and Hadassah stressed that the social and psychological differences suffered by the Oriental youngsters were not the result of any inherent biological deficiency but rather should be attributed to their ghetto backgrounds. These problems would surely disappear with proper education. Indeed, Youth Aliyah's education director remarked that after only a month or two in a healthy environment, the Oriental children "change beyond all recognition."[45] Assimilation to what might be called a European model of Israeliness was a singular goal of Youth Aliyah education and the yardstick by which success might be measured. "Given the opportunity," said Youth Aliyah publicity director Zena Harman, "these children after two or three years of education and training can scarcely be distinguished from their European brethren."[46]

But what form should that education take? Moshe Kol acknowledged that "the complete change in the type of the new immigrant from Arab countries . . . called for a different form of education."[47] Confronting the problem head-on, Youth Aliyah teachers moved quickly to develop new pedagogical techniques and strategies. A group of educators met in Haifa to discuss this issue, which was assuming some urgency as Oriental children would soon be the majority of wards. Youth Aliyah also established an Education Advisory Council to track emerging educational problems and recommend solutions. The council included representatives of Youth Aliyah, the educational experts Dr. Carl Frankenstein and Alexander Dushkin, and Bertha Schoolman, representing Hadassah.

At its inaugural meeting on October 31, 1949, the council agreed that Youth Aliyah's curriculum was "decidedly outdated." It had been "created under different circumstances and for different types of youth." The council suggested that "for the youth coming from Oriental communities it would be more effective . . . to teach history and geography through the use of materials from Oriental nations and places, rather than from Occidental tradition." Other subjects were also discussed, including the ongoing need to provide better training for *madrichim*, the need to offer students some nonagricultural vocational training, and a new problem: the question of how Youth Aliyah should deal with the parents of children in its care.

The issue of parents and parental access to children arose because Youth Aliyah was now accepting into its program increasing numbers of young people who were neither orphans nor, in many cases, separated from their families. While Youth Aliyah had previously removed groups of children from Morocco, by 1949 it was also working with the children of recently arrived Oriental immigrant families. Why were these children in care? Many of the new immigrant families were large, and in order to ease the burden of transition, some parents requested that Youth Aliyah look after one or two of their children. This presented a dilemma for the organization, which was used to dealing with children but not with their parents.

The matter of accepting these children was debated by Youth Aliyah's management committee in light of the chronic shortage of funding for the children already in care. If these young people were not accepted by Youth Aliyah, they might not get any education at all and, instead, would be pressed by their parents into menial jobs. At least a Youth Aliyah education offered such youngsters a chance to become "valuable members of the pioneer movement." A compromise was worked out with the Aliyah Department (responsible for adult immigration), which agreed to subsidize half of the cost of maintaining up to one hundred children in this new category who would be accepted each month by Youth Aliyah.[48]

A potential rift between Hadassah and Youth Aliyah was in the offing. Hadassah had already concluded that the time-tested methods of Youth Aliyah were fast becoming outmoded and were inappropriate for dealing with the children of the Oriental immigrants. Hadassah was also more attuned than Youth Aliyah to the importance of family relationships among the new immigrants, even as the organization recognized how family ties could impede integration. Anna Tulin, Hadassah's national Youth Aliyah chairman from 1950 to 1953, recalled:

> The Youth Aliyah children who came to us without parents from Europe were a terribly difficult task; they looked upon the Youth Aliyah Home and the *madrichim* as their parents, and their problem was that they had no sure family ties. However, the Oriental Jews, who came with parents, were almost a more difficult problem, because their parents clung to them, as parents would, and not only clung to the children, but had ideas which were quite foreign, and prevented the children from adapting readily. For instance, a boy of 13 was considered by his father as a bread-winner, and was considered a lazy boy if he wanted to continue going to school.[49]

Youth Aliyah's administrators did not know how to deal with parental interference, if not resistance, to their programs. Moreover, the then current thinking among American child psychologists was, said Tulin, "that it would be very bad to separate the child from the parents." Long an advocate for keeping families together, Hadassah asked the eminent American social worker Louis Sobel to visit Israel and write a report on the question of whether Youth Aliyah should continue to remove children from parental authority. "In Israel," Sobel warned, "this question has reached the stage of semi-public debate—on questions of philosophy and principle."[50]

In 1953, Sobel released his report. He began by acknowledging the tension between the American view that "the worst home is better than the best institution" and Israel's need to rescue youngsters from "the deplorable physical conditions, the conflict of the social, economic standards and cultural values—literally out of the middle ages —of the mass of immigrants from the Orient now in the Maabarot [tent camps]." In addition, Sobel recognized that Youth Aliyah was the best existing means of fulfilling the "urgent national need to 'Israelize and productivize' the younger generation." Based on his experience with the Jewish Child Care Association of New York, Sobel concluded that "the question of separation, could not be considered by itself as a principle; that there could only be one valid question from all points of view, that of the interests of the child, his family and total circumstances."[51]

In contrast to public thinking on these matters in the United States, Sobel pointed out, Israeli attitudes toward residential education and community placements were positive. Parents and children alike regarded Youth Aliyah as an opportunity for social and educational advancement—"a desirable experience," said Sobel, "offering positive values sufficient to offset the pain and problem of separation from loved ones." Hence "no theoretical discussion of 'separation' in the light of American experience can be complete or adequate, without giving full effect to this difference."[52]

Nevertheless, Sobel felt that Youth Aliyah was trying to unduly accelerate the integration of Oriental children by removing them from parental influences and weakening family ties. In so doing, Sobel argued, there was a "lack of appreciation on the part of the *madrichim* and administrative staff in the kibbutzim, schools and institutions of the psychological import and meaning of the experience *away from home* for the individual child." As an alternative, Sobel suggested that Youth Aliyah should develop day programs in the *ma'abarot* (tent camps) and other options that would allow children to stay with their families. Overall, he recommended "a total effort to make the whole program more sensitive to the needs of the individual children."[53]

For all his talk of assessing Youth Aliyah in terms of its Israeli social context, rather than imposing American values, Sobel's concern with the individual rather than the collective reflected his American viewpoint. By contrast, for Israelis in an era of nation building, the needs of the collective took priority. Indeed, Youth Aliyah's educational philosophy was originally designed to ensure that the needs of the individual child were conjoined to Zionist imperatives of nation building through collective pioneering. Youth Aliyah's founder, Recha Freier, from the start declared that the primary purpose of Youth Aliyah was to make a priority of rescuing those youngsters who would contribute the most to building the Jewish homeland. This was not kept secret from the youngsters. Indeed, Chanoch Reinhold, the *madrich* of the very first Youth Aliyah group in 1934, said that he was "required to make clear to the youngsters that the needs of the country . . . had to come first and override personal wishes."[54] More than two decades later, despite American recommendations that Youth Aliyah's programs should become more responsive to the individual, Moshe Kol insisted that Youth Aliyah's goal was still "to build up the personality of our pupils as Jews, and as citizens, conscious of the tasks they must undertake . . . to identify themselves with the true needs of Israel, and to integrate their personal happiness in the welfare and happiness of the community."[55]

But the demographic revolution wrought by immigration from Muslim countries gradually forced Youth Aliyah to make fundamental changes to its policies and programs. In this first decade after statehood, Youth Aliyah was swept up in larger currents of change in Israel as massive waves of immigration from dozens of countries doubled the Jewish population and significantly shifted the ethnic balance of the country. In 1948, 85 percent of the Jewish population of Israel and 85 percent of new immigrants were of European origin. By 1951, however, over 70 percent of immigrants to Israel came from

Asia and North Africa. These waves of mass immigration were understood to be the fulfillment of the Zionist program of "ingathering of the exiles" (*kibbutz ha-galuiot*) and the task of the Zionist state was to ensure the absorption (*klita*) and merging or "fusion of the exiles" (*mizug ha-galuiot*).

Both the significance of and the approach to immigrant absorption in the emerging state of Israel were conditioned by Zionist ideology. Classical Zionism was based on the rejection or negation of Diaspora Jewish life and on the spirit of pioneering as the best and perhaps only means to create not just a revolutionary new type of collectivist society but a new type of person—the *halutz*, or Jewish pioneer. Through "self-labor" the *halutz* would work for the "redemption of the land." Prime Minister David Ben-Gurion described the *halutz* as a "new human type such as had not been seen among the Jews in all the lands of the Diaspora."[56]

The principle of open immigration by Jews was enshrined in Israeli law. The 1948 Declaration of the Establishment of the State of Israel announced: "The State of Israel will be open for Jewish immigration and the ingathering of exiles." The 1950 Law of Return and the 1952 Citizenship Law ensured that every Jew was entitled to settle in Israel and receive citizenship immediately. Thus Jewish immigrants were regarded not as refugees but, in effect, as citizens in exile returning to their homeland.[57] Such immigration or ingathering was regarded as the very raison d'être of the Jewish state and was facilitated by a vast range of institutional efforts to accommodate newly arrived citizens.

Throughout the decade, more than half of all new arrivals came from non-European countries; in some cases, such as Yemen, Iraq, and Morocco, almost the entire Jewish population of a country was transplanted to Israel. Because the supply of housing and jobs was inadequate to meet the needs of this huge influx, many newly arrived immigrants of the 1950s were housed in tented transit camps (*ma'abarot*). By May 1952 there were two hundred fifty thousand people in 113 such camps.[58] The transit camps, originally intended as a temporary measure, were generally located in isolated areas, and many inhabitants found it difficult to obtain the employment and housing that would allow them to move out of these sites. Some stayed in these camps for years and remained dependent on the social services provided by the Jewish Agency and a variety of other aid organizations and government departments.

If weaning new immigrants off social assistance was sometimes difficult, the effort to turn them into model Israelis, at least as envisioned by Zionist gatekeepers, was even more difficult. It soon became clear that the Oriental arrivals were not integrating well into Israeli society. Many could not find jobs or permanent housing, many of their children were not in school, and rates of delinquency, violence, and health problems were rising. This was a social problem of enormous proportions and was regarded in many quarters as a crisis. A battery of sociologists and psychologists soon arrived to assess the immigrants in order to determine how best to encourage their assimilation. These scholars did in-depth studies of the problems experienced by Oriental immigrant families as they struggled to integrate into Israeli society in the 1950s, and it was from these families that the majority of Youth Aliyah wards came in that decade.[59]

Many of the sociologists, psychologists, anthropologists, and other social scientists who studied the new immigrants of the 1950s were mandated to advise the government and absorption bureaucracy on how best to facilitate the integration of the immigrants. This was scholarship in support of the nation-building enterprise, and much of the scholarship became the foundation for policy. For the most part, these social scientists began from the premise that the immigrants had to change themselves or be changed in order to meet the needs of the larger society. This premise fit neatly with the Zionist tenet that citizens of the new state must assume a new national identity and subsume their individual needs to the demands of the collective.[60]

Shmuel Eisenstadt was the most prolific and influential of the social scientists studying the new immigrants. He developed theories about what factors contributed to the absorption or nonabsorption of immigrants and concluded that an individual's ability to become successfully integrated depended, in large measure, on his or her ethnic culture and traditions and on the status of Jews in his or her country of origin. In Eisenstadt's view, some ethnic communities were more "backward" than others and people from these communities needed to "modernize" in order to integrate. The understanding of Jewish ethnicity that prevailed in Israel in the 1950s was also shaped, to a large extent, by Eisenstadt and his colleagues.[61]

In the struggle to integrate large numbers of immigrants from diverse backgrounds, the problem of ethnocultural differences loomed large. By the mid-1950s, scholars and politicians spoke of a "crisis of absorption," a "culture clash," and even a "cultural crisis" when describing the situation of Oriental immigrants. In 1955, Columbia University researcher Abraham Shumsky wrote that "today . . . the feeling is widespread that the nation is divided—that there are two Israels."[62] On one side of the divide were the European, secular, Westernized Ashkenazim who also made up the country's economic and political establishment. On the other side were the Oriental immigrants: religiously pious and culturally traditional, and whose social behavior reflected the cultures of the North African and Middle Eastern countries from which they came. If some regarded the Oriental immigrants as a lost generation, in-capable of making the leap from "primitive" and "premodern" thinking to be-come fully integrated as "modern" Israelis, it was imperative that their chil-dren, a generation of hope, be turned into fully integrated Israelis, unbound by the past.

How was this to happen? In the Zionist paradigm, Israel offered an oppor-tunity for Jews to divest themselves of the taint of Diaspora life. An individ-ual immigrant's absorption required that he or she conform to modern, secu-lar, and Western values and reject ethnic particularism in favor of a Zionist commitment to the common cause of Jewish nationhood. But in their tradi-tionalism, Oriental Jews represented exactly those features of Jewish life that the European Jews, many of whom had themselves only recently immigrated, believed they had themselves rejected and transcended. The Oriental immi-grants' apparent refusal to instantly embrace Western and Zionist values was seen as a rejection of those values. From the perspective of the Israeli estab-lishment, the new immigrants' adherence to Diasporic culture, customs, and values posed a threat to social cohesion, national unity, and the Zionist proj-ect altogether.

Because the unabsorbed Oriental immigrants constituted such a large pro-portion of the Israeli population, there was a growing sense of urgency about the situation. Media reports fed public fears about strange and unruly new im-migrants festering in squalid tent camps. A *Ha'aretz* newspaper reporter who spent two months in the *ma'abarot* described people "entirely dominated by savage and primitive instincts."[63] And what of the children? Prime Minister Ben-Gurion warned that the younger generation of immigrants must be im-bued with "the superior moral and intellectual qualities of those who created the State. . . . If, Heaven forbid, we do not succeed, there is a danger that the coming generation may transform Israel into a Levantine state."[64] These con-cerns led Ben-Gurion to design a strong educational component for the newly established Israel Defense Forces (IDF). The IDF provided general and citi-zenship education to new immigrants in its ranks and, as historian E. Michael Perko points out, "early on, *Mizrahim* [Middle Eastern and North African Jews] became the particular targets of Education Corps activity."[65]

As it seemed to many that the Oriental immigrants could not be absorbed, it became common to dismiss the adults among them as a "desert generation"—an analogy to the Israelites of the biblical Exodus whose experience of Egypt-ian slavery had so shaped their characters that they were unfit to enter "the Promised Land." Rather than waste time and resources on the desert genera-tion, efforts should be focused on the children of the immigrants. The catalyst in making them into Israelis was education. Youth Aliyah administrators were particularly receptive to this message. They had long regarded education as the key to immigrant absorption—the means by which society could ensure that the children of immigrants would become fully integrated. As Kol explained to Hadassah: "You cannot educate their parents. Moses waited 40 years in the desert before the Jews came to Israel, before the old generation passed away and the new generation was prepared for the new life. We have no time to wait 40 years. . . . We are living in an atomic age now. We are training the young people."[66]

Although it might seem both callous and unfair to say that adult immigrants could not be reeducated, Hadassah pointed out that "even in the United States . . . educational efforts were directed towards the children of immigrants, rather than toward their parents. Israel, unfortunately, cannot afford an elaborate and costly adult education program at this stage of its development, however desirable."[67] Hadassah also echoed Youth Aliyah's view that parents impeded their children's adjustment. An information kit providing "salient facts to be used for your bulletins, speeches, quizzes" explained to Hadassah members: "The youth, generally eager to learn new things, are often held back by the superstitions and set traditions of their parents, thus making modern education difficult." Nevertheless, turning a blind eye to reality, Hadassah claimed that Youth Aliyah was sensitive to the children's need to preserve their heritage and their ties to their parents: "Youngsters are helped to understand and appreciate their old traditions while they learn to accept the new. A special effort is made to win over the parents, so that they will be able to understand their children's' needs and strivings as they adjust to their new environments."[68]

Putting a best face on Youth Aliyah activities was critical. Hadassah was deeply committed to raising awareness of, and support for, Youth Aliyah programs among both American Jews and the larger American public. These efforts were helped immeasurably when Hadassah enlisted Eleanor Roosevelt, the widow of President Franklin Delano Roosevelt. At a White House meeting with Hadassah representatives, Eleanor Roosevelt agreed to take up the honorary post of World Patron of Youth Aliyah beginning in 1952. Mrs. Roosevelt was a noted humanitarian activist in her own right and had wide popular appeal. In her youth, she taught immigrants girls at the Henry Street Settlement and came to admire the work of Lillian Wald and Florence Kelley.[69] In her capacity as World Patron, Roosevelt made repeated trips to Israel, where she toured the country, visited Youth Aliyah facilities, and held discussions with educators and students. She frequently gave informed speeches at Hadassah and Youth Aliyah conferences. Roosevelt also saw firsthand the Jewish communities of Morocco and went to France to visit Moroccan Jewish children in the transit home at Cambous.[70] Other notables who lent their support to Youth Aliyah included Queen Elizabeth of Belgium, Queen Juliana of Holland, and Lord Balfour of England.

Now, as Youth Aliyah refocused onto Oriental child integration, Hadassah's publicity material made much of Israel as a modern, Western, and democratic society and stressed the importance of introducing these values to new immigrants from both Eastern European and Islamic countries: "A whole new way of democratic living must also be grasped by the young people who formerly lived under such backward political conditions," the organization said.[71] Both Youth Aliyah reports and Hadassah publicity consistently described not only the living conditions of the North African communities but the social and cultural level of the people themselves as mired in the Middle Ages. Hence, said Hadassah, "A gap of several centuries must be bridged by these children that they may fit in and understand modern life in Israel. They must be taught even such elementary social attitudes such as eating habits, ways of dressing and grooming."[72] Without such modernizing influences there was a danger that the Oriental immigrants would overwhelm the fragile social consensus of the new state.

For the American organization, there was a clear connection to be made between the issue of youth education and the question of whether the new state of Israel should reflect Eastern or Western cultural values. Like the Israeli establishment, Hadassah came down firmly on the side of Westernization: "We lost one generation," said Dr. Miriam Freund in 1954, "but we cannot afford to lose the second generation—Israel would be an oriental rather than a western State."[73]

Thus, in this era of mass immigration, and with state support, Youth Aliyah education directed at immigrant children was defined as crucial to social cohesion and to the success of the new state. Youth Aliyah's pedagogy adhered to Zionist principles and was designed to further Zionist nation-building imperatives. Hence it was seen as the ideal instrument of immigrant education—the means by which a child's character, attitudes, and goals could be shaped or reshaped to meet the needs of the new state. The children would in turn teach their parents what they had learned. Thus Youth Aliyah would serve not only to mold the character of individual children into the Zionist ideal of the New Hebrew but also to help accommodate their parents to the Westernized national identity framework of Israeli society.

It was vital that Youth Aliyah succeed in this task. Youth Aliyah director David Umansky acknowledged that "Youth Aliyah is trying to carry out . . . the functions which the State is not yet in a position to undertake."[74] The authorities turned to Youth Aliyah, and Youth Aliyah looked to Hadassah to help provide the financial resources to absorb the Oriental immigrants. As a result, Hadassah was positioned to play a pivotal role in the most critical period following statehood. While Hadassah had so far adhered to its policy of "devolution" and handed over control of many of its services and facilities to the new Israeli government, it was increasingly clear that Youth Aliyah's survival depended on Hadassah's continued social service involvement and financial support where the government was still ill prepared to take control. Thus, just as in the pre-state period, Hadassah was called upon to provide the essential services that the state lacked the means to support.

There were a vast number of school-age children among the immigrants of the 1950s. Many of these children had previously received only religious instruction or, especially in the case of the girls, had never seen the inside of a classroom. Despite Israel's 1949 Compulsory Education Law, which stipulated that all children get nine years of state-supervised primary school education, many children were kept out of school by their parents to help earn money for their families. By 1954 an estimated forty-six thousand boys and girls from fourteen to eighteen years of age, about half of the youth of this age group, were entirely outside the state-approved educational framework. Most of these youth were new immigrants, and they neither went to school nor received vocational training of any sort. At the same time, qualified teachers, schools, and even textbooks and paper were in short supply.[75] Youth Aliyah head Moshe Kol described "the alarming picture of the youth in the Maaboroth [sic], loitering about in gangs, gambling and pilfering orchards and orange-groves; trying to make money the easy way, often by dishonest means, rotting away in an atmosphere of inter-communal hatred, living in tiny cloth-huts or in a single room with a large family."[76] Youth Aliyah administrators recognized that they must make radical changes to their programs if these youngsters were to have a better future. One innovation, based in part on the recommendations made by both Sobel and Dushkin in their respective reports, was to establish day training centers in or near the ma'abarot that could be attended by young people living nearby with their families. The training centers offered intensive educational upgrading and vocational training in carpentry, metalwork, and cooking. According to the Ministry of Labor, after eighteen months of such training, graduates would be qualified as skilled workers. In some cases, a small subsidy was paid to the parents who would otherwise need their children's income. In every respect this represented a major shift from Youth Aliyah's stress on agricultural education in a residential setting.

Even as Youth Aliyah tried to turn young immigrants into Israelis, Youth Aliyah head Moshe Kol voiced a cautionary note in opposition to the prevailing tendency to force Oriental immigrants to accommodate themselves to the dominant European social and cultural milieu of the new state. Sounding a new note for many Israelis, Kol argued: "We do not want to destroy all the values that these Jews are bringing with them." Kol told Hadassah, "The North African Jews are bringing important Jewish and cultural values with them. What we are looking for is a synthesis between Western and Oriental culture."[77] But this must not be read as a call for cultural pluralism. Far from it. For Hadassah, this translated into preservation of colorful customs: "Each group brings its own dances, its own cookery, its own language, its own mores, its own special small skills and crafts," Hadassah's Dr. Miriam Freund told an American radio interviewer. "We try to preserve as much of this special heritage as possible, encouraging the children to present their native dances, music, songs and other art forms whenever there is a festivity or celebration of any kind."[78] Costumes and folk dancing, yes. Retention of an "Oriental" mindset, no.

Thus, despite good intentions, Youth Aliyah could not avoid the culture clash among its wards and staff. In the Zionist youth and the refugees and war orphans who made up the bulk of the Youth Aliyah wards of the 1930s and 1940s, the movement had a captive and willing student population. But the Oriental youths who eventually represented the majority of Youth Aliyah wards in the 1950s were less willing to harness themselves to Zionism's agricultural goals and more troubled by the separation from their families and ethnic cultures. Without a background in the Zionist youth movements, they were unfamiliar with the pioneering ideals so central to Youth Aliyah's doctrine. In addition, they did not want to be farmers: one report after another described their aversion to doing agricultural work, which was, Kol acknowledged, "looked upon in their countries of origin as one of the most degraded of occupations."[79] This opposition to agriculture put Oriental youngsters in conflict with the principles on which Youth Aliyah education was based. As Freund explained in a radio interview:

> Youth Aliyah teaches its children to work with their hands, and to be proud of it. We teach them to become farmers. Many of the Oriental people have contempt for those who work with their hands—and especially for farmers. Others feel that when their children are old enough they should try to make money by whatever means are at hand, rather than take time off to learn a skill.[80]

From Youth Aliyah's perspective, agricultural training provided the best opportunity for these youngsters to escape a life of poverty and gain self-respect by becoming contributing members of society and taking an active role in nation building. Kol argued that to allow some young people to opt out of agriculture would make them second-class citizens. "Who has the right to permit these young people . . . to grow up as the hewers of wood and drawers of water of Israeli society?" Kol asked.

> And why shouldn't Youth Aliyah give these youngsters a proper training and a chance to rid themselves of their inferiority complexes and to become equal citizens in the State of Israel? To draw any distinction between young people coming from the squalor and repression of the Moslem countries and their brothers and sisters from the free world, runs counter to the very basis of Zionist ideology. We want the latter to come as pioneers motivated by ideals of *hagshama atzmit*—self-realization—to be integrated into Jewish society. We seek to rescue the former from Levantine degradation, to convert them into pioneers and builders of the new Jewish life.[81]

For all his insistence on the benefits of imposing Youth Aliyah's pioneering values on reluctant Oriental youth, however, Kol did admit to a concern about how assimilatory pressures might impact these youngsters and affect their chances of social integration: "I would urge a cautious approach to, and a thorough study of, the problems of youth from the oriental communities," Kol told his colleagues.

> We must not let them develop a feeling that values they brought with them from the countries of origin and their communities have become worthless. There are customs which had better be abandoned, but there are values which are worth preserving and even cultivating. Do not let us believe that all that existed in Europe and what exists here is the height of perfection. We must blend the values of the working population and the productive elements of Israel with the positive values brought here by the youth from the countries of the Diaspora. We shall never succeed in planting our ideals in the hearts of the young if we destroy all that was dear to them before. No structure can be built in a vacuum.[82]

Still, in the hierarchy of values, assimilation took precedence over cultural respect. Nevertheless, Youth Aliyah bureaucrats optimistically assured Hadassah that Youth Aliyah educational programs would bridge the ethnic gap by helping young people adjust to Israeli society. In a letter to Hadassah's Bertha Schoolman, Chanoch Reinhold wrote: "Youth Aliyah serves as an outstanding, pioneering, unifying force in creating an understanding and close ties between the east and west in Israel."[83] Here, of course, Reinhold is referring not to international relations, but to relations between Eastern and Western Jews in Israel. Similarly, Kol claimed that Youth Aliyah was the best means of ensuring the absorption of immigrants from Muslim countries: "Their sons and daughters must be the full equals of all other boys and girls in Israel. We are eradicating feelings of discrimination and inferiority and constructing a bridge over the gap separating us from the new immigrants from these countries."[84]

Zena Harman told Hadassah that Youth Aliyah helped "children of forty different nationalities obliterate the past in their proud new Jewishness."[85] Hadassah leaders were apparently persuaded not only that Youth Aliyah could indeed "obliterate the past" but that it should do so, and regularly affirmed their support for Youth Aliyah's efforts. Dr. Freund, perhaps inspired by Youth Aliyah's motto, "The absorbed shall be the absorbers," declared: "When you see the North African and Moroccan children as the teachers of Polish youth, then you understand that Israel will become one. Perhaps that is the greatest message that Youth Aliyah can bring us." By 1956, 74 percent of Youth Aliyah's thirteen thousand wards were young people with Oriental backgrounds, either immigrants themselves or children of immigrants.[86]

But it was one thing to declare a principled tolerance for ethnic diversity and quite a different thing, as Youth Aliyah staff discovered, to grapple with cultural differences as they arose in day-to-day life. Despite Kol's warnings, and Hadassah's conviction that Youth Aliyah should be trying to protect the trappings of children's cultural heritage, an internal report by a Youth Aliyah psychologist revealed a more troubling picture. The psychologist, Reuven Feuerstein, described his meeting with a group of sixteen-year-old Moroccan boys in a Youth Aliyah group who "spoke to me eloquently of their progress and emancipation and of their primitive parents and how they could never go back to them." Their German-born *madrich* readily admitted that he had prevented the boys from singing, or even listening to, Arabic music. When Feuerstein pleaded with the boys to sing a traditional liturgical song, their reaction was so negative that he reported: "I felt that these children hated themselves and they hated me."[87]

Similar problems resulted from Youth Aliyah's effort to train young people from the new *moshavim* (cooperative agricultural settlements) on which new immigrants were being settled by the government. Since most of the adults in these *moshavim* had no farming background, the survival of such communities was in doubt. Once again, Youth Aliyah broke with its traditional policies in order to start a new program designed for young people from these *moshavim*. The aim of this program was to provide the young people with enough agricultural training to enable them to return to their *moshav* and then spend the few years before their army service instructing their parents in modern agricultural techniques.

In order to encourage the graduates to go back to the *moshav*, the program focused on individualized education and tried to preserve ties between the youth and their families. From 1950 to 1960, three thousand young people went through this type of training. But a study conducted in 1960 described the difficulties experienced by the young graduates when they returned home after their agricultural training. The study used the term "return-crisis." After two years away, the graduates were "very critical of the persistence of the traditional social structure in the *moshavim*, which is opposed to the social values absorbed in their schools." The youths also complained that "despite their keen interest in reading and further education," their return to the *moshav* had "virtually closed all avenues of further study."[88] Nonetheless, as Moshe Kol pointed out, "With the best intentions in the world Youth Aliyah can nevertheless not guarantee that its educational and training courses will not create a gap between the parents and their children. The very object of the education it imparts is to develop new standards in the lives and outlook of its pupils."[89]

Clearly, Youth Aliyah's policy of educating young people apart from their parents, when carried out among immigrant families in the 1950s, had unintended effects. One of these was that it intensified the feelings of alienation between the generations that often occur in immigrant families. Youth Aliyah wards received not only general education but also an ideological indoctrination in Zionism that exacerbated this estrangement from their parents. In the case of Oriental youth, the generation gap took on negative cultural dimensions, as the youth learned to see their parents' difficulties in integrating as a result of backwardness stemming from traditionalism and religious beliefs. Another major problem was that many Youth Aliyah graduates, unwilling to do agricultural work, were ill equipped to take up alternate occupations and so were unprepared for the urban environment into which most drifted.

The ideological certainties that shaped Youth Aliyah pedagogy in the 1930s reflected the European cultural milieu of early Zionism. This Zionist ideology may have been foreign to some middle-class German Jewish youth without Zionist training in the late 1930s, but it was entirely alien to most of the Oriental youth in Youth Aliyah in the 1950s. At the same time, some of these Zionist principles, especially those that focused on agricultural development, were themselves losing relevance in the face of wider Israeli industrialization and urbanization.

Youth Aliyah administrators, as if blinkered to change, were unwilling to compromise on what they regarded as the core principles of the movement. As late as 1959, Moshe Kol, who spoke of cultural respect, still believed that

Youth Aliyah should prepare young Israelis to advance national interests, rather than their own personal interests—that is, make them agricultural pioneers rather than citizens of an increasingly urban society:

> We live in a period when it is vital for us to build up a new man in Israel. We must begin with the younger people . . . if we do not succeed in convincing them that their own future and happiness is indissolubly bound up with the future and happiness of the people of Israel, we cannot hope to advance towards economic independence, or towards the creation of a new nation by the fusion of the diverse Jewish communities in this country.[90]

Nevertheless, over the course of the decade Youth Aliyah's ideological rigidity began to weaken as the Israeli-born youth in the movement's care demanded a greater range of educational and vocational choices. By the decade's end, Youth Aliyah had been transformed into a giant network of social services and programs serving thirteen thousand children and youth. Day centers even made it possible for some young people to access Youth Aliyah educational programs without leaving home.

For all its problems, Youth Aliyah remained Hadassah's prize program. In 1958, the cost to Hadassah members of supporting each Youth Aliyah child for one year reached six hundred dollars. Members who contributed this sum were awarded the honorary title of *Ima* (mother).[91] To coincide with Youth Aliyah's twenty-fifth anniversary that year, Hadassah orchestrated a nationwide publicity campaign on behalf of Youth Aliyah and got media coverage from magazines, newspapers, radio, and television across the United States. An educational kit was sent out to Jewish schools across the United States with a "Youth Aliyah Unit of Instruction." Neither the culture clash nor the debate about agricultural versus vocational education were mentioned. Instead, Hadassah promised that the kit would provide "a wealth of exciting ways to introduce our American children to the magic of Israel" through the "superb educative values" of the Youth Aliyah "story":

> Youth Aliyah—the child rescue movement—contains all the elements which appeal to a child's imagination: the thrill of adventure, plus the deep emotional involvement with the persecuted youngsters who are saved from sorrow and misery and brought to Israel to live with hope again. Because it is a true story, and not a fairy tale, their identification with Youth Aliyah wards is even more poignant. For as they take in the moving Youth Aliyah story with their eyes and ears, they also absorb the intangible spirit of Judaism—the ethical precepts, the long struggle for survival, the precious sense of "belonging."

Like the Penny Luncheons campaign of an earlier era, this was an effort to enlist American schoolchildren in the cause: the kit prompted youngsters to ask "what can we do to help, to do *our* share in this work?"[92] Also echoing the past was the promise that American children would be enriched by learning about Youth Aliyah and brought closer to an understanding of Judaism, Jewish history, and pride in Israel.

Eleanor Roosevelt spoke at Hadassah's annual conference in 1959. She described her visits to the Cambous transit home, in which Moroccan Jewish youngsters prepared to go to Israel, and lauded Youth Aliyah's achievements in working with young immigrants. In a reflection of emerging Cold War concerns, Roosevelt also mentioned the difficulty of educating immigrant children from Eastern European countries "who have already been indoctrinated in Communism." But she described Israel as a bulwark of the West:

> The one state in the Middle East where you know you are developing a Democratic State, a state where people . . . want to be free and act for themselves. I have always felt that that was the hope of the Near East, really; that some day . . . it would be Israel that could be the beacon of light—the one country that really understood democracy. There is no understanding of it in most of the countries around it.[93]

Roosevelt's remarks were significant enough to headline a *New York Times* column about the conference: "Mrs. Roosevelt Warns on Communism."[94]

By the late 1950s Hadassah also enjoyed a closer relationship with Youth Aliyah administrators in Israel than was the case when Henrietta Szold was alive. During Szold's lifetime she juggled Youth Aliyah and Hadassah, keeping them both moving separate from one another. Hadassah had to press hard to have its voice heard in Youth Aliyah's policymaking process. With Moshe Kol now at the helm of Youth Aliyah, however, Hadassah finally received its due. Kol forged a close and direct relationship with Hadassah leaders that made the women's organization feel like an equal, rather than a junior, partner in running the program. In keeping with a tradition established by Szold, Kol kept Hadassah leaders in the United States informed of developments in Israel in long, detailed letters he wrote describing his visits to and observations about Youth Aliyah programs, facilities, staff, and students. More than that, Kol regularly solicited Hadassah's advice on policy and decision making.

Dr. Freund responded that Hadassah appreciated both Kol's openness and his efforts to make his Israeli colleagues "understand that this American women's group, six thousand miles away, could think with them although we were not sitting with them in Jerusalem."[95] Kol reciprocated with generous praise for Hadassah:

> I cannot think about Youth Aliyah without Hadassah. Hadassah is an integral part of Youth Aliyah, and we know it, and our children know it, and everybody in the country knows it. There are other women's organizations; but there is no comparison between what they do and what Hadassah does for Youth Aliyah. We look upon Hadassah as our second hand. One hand are the educators; the other is Hadassah. With those two hands we can succeed.[96]

A few years later, Kol told Hadassah's board at a preconvention meeting: "You are completely right . . . when you say that Hadassah influences the policy of Youth Aliyah . . . you are really partners in Youth Aliyah." He summed up: "This cooperation of Youth Aliyah and Hadassah, I think, is one of the most fruitful cooperative pieces of work not only in Zionism but in the history of our people."[97]

Certainly, Hadassah helped pay the bills. By 1959 Hadassah had 318,000 members who had contributed a cumulative total of $36.5 million to Youth Aliyah—the largest contribution made by any single organization. The money had supported a total of seventy-five thousand children.[98] Hadassah continued to fund Youth Aliyah programs and facilities, and to participate in policymaking and decision making. Gone was all criticism of Hadassah for preserving its organizational autonomy against the centralizing impulse of American Jewish and Zionist organizations. Youth Aliyah was widely regarded as a jewel in Zionism's crown, and Hadassah's supportive involvement with Youth Aliyah contributed to a general acceptance of the idea that, as Giora Josephthal told a World Youth Aliyah conference, "It is natural that the Jewish woman throughout the world regards this enterprise as her special province."[99] Reflecting on Hadassah's influence on both Israeli society and American Jewry, Dr. Freund told members of her organization:

> It was with a surge of pride that I realized that Hadassah was no longer just an agency for raising money and sending it on to Youth Aliyah . . . we were becoming a partner in the decisions of . . . Youth Aliyah. In other words, not only were we educating the women of America . . . we have educated the entire Jewish population to the word Youth Aliyah, but we were doing more than that. We were helping to shape the life of Israel through the life of thousands upon thousands of young people who are being graduated and going into every post and corner of the land.[100]

If Hadassah shared governance of Youth Aliyah, it also shared in Youth Aliyah's failings. Hadassah's approach to its Youth Aliyah work from the immediate post–World War II period through the 1950s was heavily influenced by the organization's prior experience dealing with Jewish immigrants in the Yishuv. These earlier immigrants, whether from Eastern Europe, North Africa, or the Middle East, brought with them a bewildering variety of sociocultural traditions. Given this firsthand experience with what it perceived to be the backwardness of non-Western cultures and societies, Hadassah readily accepted the view, promulgated by Israeli social scientists twenty years later, that just like earlier arrivals, the Oriental immigrants of the 1950s also needed to be modernized, civilized, and Westernized. With its long-standing commitment to education and convinced by the Israeli authorities that the country's future was at stake, Hadassah accepted that Youth Aliyah's leadership knew best when it tried to accelerate the assimilation of Oriental children and conscript them to the Zionist pioneering ethos.

Through its support of Youth Aliyah, Hadassah played a crucial role in Israel's effort to cope with the ethnic and educational problems presented by the mass immigration of the 1950s. In the first decade of statehood, as in the pre-state period, Hadassah brought American traditions of social idealism to its work with a new generation of young immigrants to the Jewish homeland. In other ways, too, Hadassah's approach to Youth Aliyah was consistent with its own early history—for example, Hadassah continued to believe in the unparalleled quality of American "know-how" and to supply American consultants to offer advice to Youth Aliyah administrators. Similarly, Hadassah persistently deferred to expert opinion—whether offered by Americans or Israelis—on the psychological problems, cultural characteristics, and educational needs of young immigrants.

Hadassah's unwavering faith not only in the power of education to integrate immigrants but also in the desirability of the "melting pot" model of encouraging different ethnic groups to assimilate into the mainstream was also born of its American background and experience. A similar view held sway in Israel during the 1950s, where the consensus was that ethnic differences were a transitory aspect of the immigrant experience and would disappear with assimilation. "Ethnic," in short, was for Israelis synonymous with "immigrant," "outsider," and un-Israeli.

But efforts to force the acculturation of Oriental Jews succeeded only in destroying the social and cultural fabric of immigrant ethnic groups and so ultimately obstructed, rather than advanced, their entrance into the mainstream of society. This process was duplicated, in microcosm, by Youth Aliyah, which was supposed to educate young immigrants and prepare them to take their place in Israeli society. For those youngsters who resisted being forced into the role of pioneering farmers or who found the separation from their families and home cultures unbearable, however, Youth Aliyah offered scant alternatives. Sadly, many of the youngsters who left Youth Aliyah before graduating also lost out on their only chance at an education.[101]

Despite the high hopes of Israelis and Hadassah alike that Youth Aliyah education could help to close the "ethnic gap," there is ample evidence of continuing tensions and social disparities between ethnic groups in Israel to-day—the responsibility for which Hadassah must share in part. Nevertheless, with Hadassah's ongoing support, Youth Aliyah continues to serve both disadvantaged native-born youth and young immigrants to Israel through residential education and related programs. In serving both groups, Youth Aliyah fulfills Henrietta Szold's vision of providing education to all needy youngsters, not just immigrants. Although Youth Aliyah—and the Hadassah organization—have survived long past the demise of the American Progressive movement, the Progressive and maternalist ideals that inspired Hadassah's first foray into Palestine continue to influence Hadassah's child welfare work in Israel today.

Notes

1. Hadassah press release, 25 February 1946, RG 1/B 3/F 14, HWZOA.

2. The Jewish Agency for Palestine, Department for Child and Youth Immigration, "Facts and Figures on Youth Aliyah," October 1945, RG 1/B 6, HWZOA; A. Fuerst, "The Absorption of Child Immigrants in the Yishuv: An Investigation into Problems and Proposals Relating to Absorptive Capacity," January 1945, RG 1/B 3/F 11, HWZOA; Hadassah press release, 10 October 1945, RG 1/B 3/F 13, HWZOA.

3. The Jewish Agency for Palestine, Department for Child and Youth Immigration, *Children and Youth Aliyah: An Outline*, December 1947, 7, RG 1/B 21/F 157, HWZOA.

4. Moshe Kol, *Child and Youth Aliyah: The Richest Source of Chalutziuth*, 25 August 1948, 3, RG 1/B 17/F 111, HWZOA. This is the published version of Kol's address to a meeting of the Zionist Actions Committee in Tel Aviv.

5. In contrast to the Ashkenazi, or European Jews, these Eastern Jews were called "Levantines" (*Levantinim*) or "Orientals" in that period and are referred to now as *Mizrahim* or "Easterners." The term *Sephardi* is sometimes incorrectly used interchangeably with *Mizrahi*. In fact, *Sephardim* denotes those Jews who trace their origins to Spain or Portugal, whereas *Mizrahim* denotes those Jews who trace their origins to North African and Middle Eastern countries.

6. Bernard Lewis, *The Jews of Islam* (Princeton, N.J.: Princeton University Press, 1984), 184.

7. For a discussion of Zionism among Middle Eastern Jews, see Michael M. Laskier, "The Evolution of Zionist Activity in the Jewish Communities of Morocco, Tunisia and Algeria: 1897–1947," *Studies in Zionism* 8 (1983): 205–23; for a brief survey of anti-Jewish riots and decrees, see Martin Gilbert, *The Jews of Arab Lands: Their History in Maps* (London: Board of Deputies of British Jews, 1976).

8. The Jewish Agency for Palestine, Information Office, *The Position of the Jewish Communities in Oriental Countries*, Jerusalem, 1947, 20, RG 1/B 21/F 157, HWZOA.

9. For a unique retrospective glimpse of the children's perspective on their stay in Norway, see the article by Doris Aflalo, "The Pied Piper of Norway," *Ha'aretz*, English edition, 20 May 1999, 12–15.

10. Y. Naari, "Child and Youth Aliyah in France," February 1949, 2, RG 1/B 33/F 240, HWZOA.

11. Mitchell Cohen, *Zion and State: Nation, Class and the Shaping of Modern Israel* (New York: Columbia University Press, 1992), 228. A comprehensive portrait of the new society of Israel, under siege from within and without, is provided by Tom Segev, *1949: The First Israelis* (Markham, Ontario: Fitzhenry & Whiteside, 1998).

12. Ben-Gurion's term for this process was *mamlachtiut* (statism). See the essays by Alan Dowty, "Israel's First Decade: Building a Civic State," and Ernest Stock, "Philanthropy and Politics: Modes of Interaction between Israel and the Diaspora," in *Israel: The First Decade of Independence*, ed. Ilan Troen and Noah Lucas (Albany: State University of New York Press, 1995).

13. Mr. Solmsen to Mrs. Agonsky, "Hadassah's Role in Youth Aliyah," 23 November 1948, RG 1/B 44, HWZOA.

14. Alexander Dushkin, *Educational Achievements and Problems of Youth Aliyah in Eretz Israel, Report Submitted to Hadassah*, October 1947, 4, 6, RG 1/B 17/F 114, HWZOA. Dushkin moved permanently to Israel in 1949 and thereafter served as an educational consultant to Hadassah.

15. In both the United States and Israel, schools have been on the front lines of the effort to assimilate and integrate immigrant children. See Shlomo Swirski, *Politics and Education in Israel: Comparisons with the United States* (London: Falmer, 1999); Walter Ackerman, "Making Jews: An Enduring Challenge in Israeli Education," *Israel Studies* 2, no. 2 (Fall 1997): 1–20; Chaim Adler, "Thirty-five Years of Israeli Schooling: The Perspective of Absorption," in *Cultural Transition: The Case of Immigrant Youth*, ed. Meir Gottesman (Jerusalem: Magnes Press, 1988).

16. Dushkin, *Educational Achievements and Problems*, 8, 21.

17. Mr. Solmsen to Mrs. Agonsky, "Hadassah's Role in Youth Aliyah."

18. Mr. Solmsen to Mrs. Agonsky, Hadassah's Role in Youth Aliyah."

19. Chanoch Reinhold, "The Hadassah Fund for Special Educational Purposes," Jerusalem, 10 September 1955, RG 1/B 21/F 157, HWZOA.

20. A. M. Dushkin to Dr. Miriam Freund, New York City, 6 October 1950, RG 1/B 27/F 198, HWZOA.

21. Minutes, "Discussion on Vocational Education in Youth Aliyah in which Members of the Training Department Participated," 13 December 1948, RG 1/B 33/F 244, HWZOA.

22. Marian Greenberg, "Youth Immigration to the State of Israel," 16 June 1949, RG 1/F 249/B 34, HWZOA.

23. Greenberg, "Youth Immigration to the State of Israel."

24. Anita Shapira, "The Holocaust: Private Memories, Public Memory," *Jewish Social Studies* 4, no. 2 (Winter 1998): 40. For an account of the debate in Youth Aliyah, see Reuven Feuerstein, "On the Desirability of Preserving Family and Communal Traditions," in *The Integration of Adolescents: A Selection of Articles Drawn from the Publications of Youth Aliyah* (Jerusalem: Jewish Agency, 1984).

25. Greenberg, "Youth Immigration to the State of Israel."

26. A. S. Super, *New Children of the New Israel: Ten Years of Youth Aliyah*, 1958, 15, RG 1/Subgroup 4/B 44, HWZOA.

27. Greenberg, "Youth Immigration to the State of Israel."

28. Y. Naari, "Child and Youth Aliyah in France."

29. "Moroccan Urchins Made into Citizens," *Palestine Post*, 5 October 1949, RG 1/B 29/F 217, HWZOA; Child and Youth Aliyah, Public Relations Department, "Facts and Figures," 19 September 1949, RG 1/B 29/F 215, HWZOA.

30. Charlotte Weber, "Exodus via Norway," *Impetus*, June-July-August 1950, 4–9, RG 1/Subgroup 4/B 33/F 243, HWZOA.

31. Eva Michaelis, Jerusalem, to Mrs. S. Kramarsky, New York, 6 October 1949, RG 1/B 33/F 243, HWZOA.

32. Eva Michaelis, ed., *Our Children, Our Future* (Jerusalem: Public Relations Department, Child and Youth Aliyah, 1950), RG 1/B 75, HWZOA.

33. Hadassah press release, 11 November 1949, RG 1/B 33/F 242, HWZOA.

34. Hadassah press release, 11 November 1949.

35. Greenberg, "Youth Immigration to the State of Israel."

36. Otto Zarek, "North African Problem Children," in Michaelis, ed., *Our Children, Our Future*.

37. Fritz Salomon, "Psychological Observation Amongst the 200 Children Going to Norway," Paris, 19 May 1949, RG 1/Subgroup 4/B 33/F 243, HWZOA.

38. Randi Istre, "Children Remoulded," in Michaelis, ed., *Our Children, Our Future*, 34.

39. "Advance Quotes on Mrs. Zena Harman's Speech at the Youth Aliyah Conference at the Waldorf Astoria," 17 April 1950, RG 1/F 246/B 33, HWZOA.

40. Chanoch Reinhold, *In the Country of Origin of Our Youth*, [1954?], 11, 7, RG 1/B 36/F 261, HWZOA. The Jewish community of Morocco—estimated at about 240,000 in 1952—was the largest in the Arab world (Swirski, *Politics and Education in Israel*, 66).

41. Dr. Miriam Freund, "Report to Youth Aliyah and Vocational Education Committee of Hadassah," 23 June 1954, 2, RG 1/B 37/F 280, HWZOA.

42. Freund, "Report to Youth Aliyah and Vocational Education Committee."

43. Molly Lyons Bar-David, "Hope in Thy Future," in Michaelis, ed., *Our Children, Our Future*, 6.

44. "Moroccan Jewry," in Michaelis, ed., *Our Children, Our Future*, 6.

45. Reinhold, *In the Country of Origin of Our Youth*.

46. "Advance Quotes on Mrs. Zena Harman's Speech at the Youth Aliyah Conference at the Waldorf Astoria."

47. Public Relations Department, Child and Youth Aliyah, "Facts and Figures," 6 December 1949, RG 1/B 29/F 215, HWZOA.

48. Eva Michaelis, Publicity Department, Child and Youth Aliyah, "Newsreel No. 10," 10 February 1949, RG 1/F 215, HWZOA.

49. Mrs. Abraham Tulin, Address to the National Youth Aliyah Committee of Hadassah, "My Years as Youth Aliyah Chairman," 3 September 1958, 2, RG 1/B 39/F 278, HWZOA.

50. Louis H. Sobel, "Report on a Visit to Israel in Connection with Youth Aliyah," 6 October 1953, 3, RG 1/Subgroup 4/B 39, HWZOA. Sobel was the executive director of the Jewish Child Care Association in New York City and was also the chairman of Hadassah's Youth Reference Board.

51. Sobel, "Report on a Visit to Israel," 8.

52. Sobel, "Report on a Visit to Israel," 9–10.

53. Sobel, "Report on a Visit to Israel," 15 (italics in original), 22, 18.

54. Chanoch Reinhold (Rinott), "Dynamics of Youth Aliyah Groups," in *Between Past and Future: Essays and Studies on Aspects of Immigrant Absorption in Israel*, ed. Carl Frankenstein (Jerusalem: Henrietta Szold Foundation for Child and Youth Welfare, 1953), 246.

55. Moshe Kol, "The Tasks of Youth Aliyah," 1959, RG 1/B 39/F 287, HWZOA.

56. For Ben-Gurion, see Segev, *1949: The First Israelis*, 291. For an analysis of Zionist discourse, see Laurence J. Silberstein, *The Postzionism Debates: Knowledge and Power in Israeli Culture* (New York: Routledge, 1999).

57. For this reason, it is not entirely accurate to refer to Jews who move to Israel as either "immigrants" or "refugees." Israelis use the Hebrew term *olim* (from *aliyah*, "ascent"). Nonetheless, for clarity and ease of reading, the term "immigrant" is used here.

58. Calvin Goldscheider, "Creating a New Society: Immigration, Nation-Building, and Ethnicity in Israel," *Harvard International Review* (Spring 1998): 67–68; Israel Prime Minister's Office, *Background Paper: Aliyah* (Jerusalem: Prime Minister's Office, 1998); Avraham Shama and Mark Iris, *Immigration without Integration: Third World Jews in Israel* (Cambridge, Mass.: Schenkman, 1977), 50.

59. See, for example, Rivka Weiss Bar-Yosef, "Desocialization and Resocialization: The Adjustment Process of Immigrants," in *Studies of Israeli Society: Migration, Ethnicity and Community*, ed. Ernest Krausz (New Brunswick, N.J.: Transaction, 1980); S. N. Eisenstadt, "The Process of Absorption of Immigrants in Israel," and Carl Frankenstein, "The Problem of Ethnic Differences in the Absorption of Immigrants," in Frankenstein, ed., *Between Past and Future*, 341–67 and 13–32.

60. For discussion of what has been called Israel's "conscripted scholarship," see Uri Ram, *The Changing Agenda of Israeli Sociology: Theory, Ideology and Identity* (Albany, N.Y.: SUNY Press, 1995), and Deborah Bernstein, "Immigrants and Society: A Critical View of the Dominant School of Israeli Sociology," *British Journal of Sociology* 31, no. 2 (June 1980): 246–64. Foremost among the "conscripted scholars" were S. N. Eisenstadt and Carl Frankenstein.

61. For an elaboration of Eisenstadt's "modernization thesis," see S. N. Eisenstadt, *The Absorption of Immigrants: A Comparative Study* (Westport, Conn.: Greenwood, 1975; originally published 1954 by Routledge & Kegan Paul); S. N. Eisenstadt, *An Introduction to the Sociological Structure of Oriental Jewry* (Jerusalem: Szold Foundation, 1948); S. N. Eisenstadt, *The Transformation of Israeli Society: An Essay in Interpretation* (Boulder, Colo.: Westview, 1985).

62. Abraham Shumsky, *The Clash of Cultures in Israel: A Problem for Education* (New York: Bureau of Publications, Teachers College, Columbia University, 1955), 18. See also Raphael Patai, *Israel Between East and West* (Philadelphia: Jewish Publication Society, 1953). A small but growing body of literature dealing with this period from an Oriental perspective has begun to emerge among Israelis of Oriental background. This material reflects ongoing anger and resentment about how Oriental immigrants were regarded and treated by the Ashkenazi establishment of the time. Some of this writing is autobiographical and personal; for an example, see Henriette Dahan-Kalev, "You're So Pretty—You Don't Look Moroccan," *Israel Studies* 6 (2001): 1–14. Such criticisms have, in turn, triggered a backlash from those who feel accused. For an example, see Moshe Shokeid, "On the Sins We Did Not Commit in the Research of Oriental Jews," *Israel Studies* 6 (2001): 15–33.

63. Segev, *1949: The First Israelis*, 291. For a discussion of how public fears became focused on Moroccans in particular, see Yaron Tsur, "Carnival Fears: Moroccan Immigrants and the Ethnic Problem in the Young State of Israel," *The Journal of Israeli History* 18 (1997): 73–103. For an example of how these problems were presented to American Jews, see the two colorful firsthand accounts of burgeoning ethnic tensions in Israel written by the American-trained Israeli anthropologist Alex Weingrod, "One Morning in a Maabera: From the Israeli Scene," *Commentary* 28, no. 2 (August 1959): 118–21, and "The Two Israels," *Commentary* 4, no. 33 (April 1962): 313–19.

64. Shama and Iris, *Immigration without Integration*, 50.

65. E. Michael Perko, "'Regimentation Everywhere': *Mizrahim*, Education and Cultural Dissonance in the Israel Defense Forces, 1948–1975" (paper presented at the annual meeting of the Association for Israel Studies, Tel Aviv, Israel, June 2000), 2. The IDF has long been popularly regarded as a "melting pot" institution where Israelis of all ethnic backgrounds and social classes meet on common ground, but social scientists have found that the IDF suffers from the same social divisions and inequalities as the rest of Israeli society. The IDF's shortcomings as an integrative force are outlined in Swirski, *Politics and Education in Israel*, 126–32.

66. "Address of Moshe Kol to Youth Aliyah Conference," New York City, 17 December 1952, 2, RG 1/B 36/F 265, HWZOA.

67. Mrs. Abraham Tulin, "Memorandum on Some Aspects of the Youth Aliyah Education Program," 4 October 1953, RG 1/B 39/F 284, HWZOA.

68. Hadassah, the Women's Zionist Organization of America, *Factually Speaking on Youth Aliyah*, December 1958, 5, RG 1/F 49, HWZOA.

69. Mrs. Abraham Tulin, "My Years as Youth Aliyah Chairman," 2; Paul Boyer, ed., *The Oxford Companion to United States History* (Oxford: Oxford University Press, 2001), s.v. "Eleanor Roosevelt" by Blanche Weisen Cook.

70. Hadassah Youth Aliyah Annual Report, September 1954–September 1955, 11, RG 1/B 34/F 254, HWZOA; Mrs. Franklin D. Roosevelt, Presentation at Conference of National Youth Aliyah Committee of Hadassah, New York City, 3 April 1957, RG 1/B 36/F 269, HWZOA.

71. Hadassah, *Factually Speaking on Youth Aliyah*, 5.

72. Hadassah, *Factually Speaking on Youth Aliyah*, 5.

73. Freund, "Report to Youth Aliyah and Vocational Education Committee."

74. David Umanski, "Absorption Problems of Youth Aliyah," 1959, RG 1/B 39/F 287, HWZOA. David Umanski (or Umansky) was Youth Aliyah department director (working under Moshe Kol) from 1948 to 1967.

75. Amos Eilon, "New Paths for 'Youth Aliyah,'" 1954, 1–2, RG 1/B 44, HWZOA. Israel's educational system was run along complicated, partisan political, religious, and ethnic lines. See Swirski, *Politics and Education in Israel*; Aharon Fritz Kleinberger, *Society, Schools and Progress in Israel* (Oxford: Pergamon, 1969).

76. Address of Moshe Kol, "Activities Among the Youth of Israel," educators' meeting in Jerusalem, 28 April 1953, 2, RG 1/B 36/F 265, HWZOA.

77. "Address of Moshe Kol to Youth Aliyah Conference," 2. Kol was Youth Aliyah department head from 1947 to 1966. Kol was also an MK (Member of the Knesset) in 1949, 1951, and 1955 and held several government posts in the 1960s, including chairman of the Parliamentary Education, Sports and Culture Committee.

78. Transcript, Dr. Miriam Freund interview with Estelle Sternberger, WLTB Radio, New York, 22 March 1954, RG 1/B 34/F 249, HWZOA.

79. Kol, "Activities Among the Youth of Israel," 2.

80. Transcript, Dr. Miriam Freund interview with Estelle Sternberger.

81. Moshe Kol, *Youth Aliyah: Past, Present and Future* (Jerusalem: UNESCO, 1957), 74.

82. Kol, "Activities Among the Youth of Israel," 5.

83. Chanoch Reinhold, Jerusalem, to Mrs. Albert Schoolman, New York, 3 April 1953, RG 1/B 39/F 284, HWZOA.

84. Moshe Kol, "The Future of Youth Aliyah," 26 March 1959, RG 1/B 36/F 272, HWZOA.

85. "Advance Quotes on Mrs. Zena Harman's Speech at the Youth Aliyah Conference at the Waldorf Astoria," 17 April 1950, RG 1/B 33/F 246, HWZOA.

86. Miriam Freund Rosenthal quoted in Mrs. Edward Jacobs, Address to the Youth Aliyah and Vocational Education Committee, "The History of Hadassah's Association with Youth Aliyah," 7 May 1957, RG 1/B 39/F 286, HWZOA.

87. Reuven Feuerstein, "On the Desirability of Preserving Family and Communal Traditions" (1957), in *The Integration of Adolescents: A Selection of Articles Drawn from the Publications of Youth Aliyah* (Jerusalem: Jewish Agency, 1984), 28.

88. Tikvah Honig-Parnass, *Training Youth from New Immigrant Settlements: A Study in Youth Aliyah Education* (Jerusalem: Child and Youth Immigration Department of the Jewish Agency for Israel/Henrietta Szold Institute for Child and Youth Welfare, 1960), 50–51, RG 1/B 39/F 287, HWZOA.

89. Kol, *Youth Aliyah: Past, Present and Future*, 70.

90. Kol, "The Future of Youth Aliyah."

91. Hadassah, *Factually Speaking on Youth Aliyah*, 14.

92. Mrs. Henry Goldman, letter to principals of Jewish schools, "Youth Aliyah Unit of Instruction," 25 September 1958, RG 1/B 78/F 25, HWZOA; David Kuselewitz, *Youth Aliyah: A Unit of Instruction for the Jewish School*, 1954, RG 1/B 34/F 249, HWZOA.

93. Mrs. Franklin D. Roosevelt, Presentation to Youth Aliyah 25th Anniversary Conference, New York, 4 February 1959, RG 1/B 36/F 273, HWZOA.

94. "Women Zionists End Talks Here, Hadassah Cites Body Aiding Refugees—Mrs. Roosevelt Warns on Communism," *The New York Times*, 5 February 1959, 7.

95. Dr. Miriam Freund, "My Years as Youth Aliyah Chairman," Address to the National Youth Aliyah Committee of Hadassah, 7 January 1959, 2, RG 1/B 39/F 276, HWZOA.

96. "Address of Moshe Kol to Youth Aliyah Conference," 5.

97. Address by Moshe Kol, Pre-Convention National Board Meeting of Hadassah, 13 October 1956, Houston, Texas, 1, 5, RG 1/B 39/F 285, HWZOA.

98. Bertha Schoolman, "Hadassah's Share in the Mitzvah of Redemption," March 1959, 1, RG 1/B 36/F 272, HWZOA.

99. Hadassah Youth Aliyah Annual Report, September 1955–September 1956, 1, 14, RG 1/B 34/F 254, HWZOA. The German-born Josephthal was a Youth Aliyah representative in Germany until 1938; he later worked for the Jewish Agency and in 1960 became Israel's minister of labor.

100. Freund, "My Years as Youth Aliyah Chairman," 2.

101. S. Ben Eliezer, *The Dimensions of Absorption: A Study of Needs and Responsibilities* (Jerusalem: Treasury Department, Jewish Agency for Israel, 1964), RG 1/B 46, HWZOA.

CHAPTER SEVEN

~

Conclusion

Hadassah brought to Palestine an American faith in modern scientific advances, organizational efficiency, and sound management practices. Throughout its history, but especially in the pre-state era, when it came to medical and social service delivery, Hadassah proudly served as an outpost of the United States and a conduit for American values. As Hadassah president Tamar de Sola Pool proclaimed: "In the case of Hadassah, it is hard to tell where America leaves off and Palestine begins. The funds that the women of Hadassah have sent overseas can be reckoned in millions. With them go American ideals and standards."[1]

Before 1948, however, Hadassah's work in Palestine was shaped not just by American values in general but by the maternalist ideas of Progressive-era women's organizations in particular. Hadassah's emphasis on child welfare, health, and sanitarian reform was typical of the many domestic American women's voluntary associations that were active during the Progressive era in the United States. Such groups opened settlement houses and hospitals, sent public health nurses into the community, educated immigrants, helped young women in trouble, and organized school lunch programs and playgrounds. By the 1930s, Hadassah had established in Palestine, with some modifications for local cultures and conditions, a similar network of maternity and child welfare services and programs. Thus we might describe Hadassah's arrival in the Yishuv as the moment when American Progressive maternalists went to Palestine.

But Hadassah tied its maternalist agenda to the Zionist goal of building a Jewish state. Keeping this aim always in view, the organization designed services and established institutions that it hoped would promote the development of a modern, egalitarian, and cohesive Jewish society. At the heart of Hadassah's Zionist maternalism was a principled commitment to democratic values, including equal rights for women as well as for different ethnic and religious groups, and a belief that freely available and comprehensive social welfare services were the necessary foundation of a healthy democratic society. These convictions, shared by maternalist reformers working in the United States and Europe, meant that Hadassah often had more in common with other women's organizations than with the male-dominated American or European Zionist organizations.

Under Szold's guidance, Hadassah maintained not only that women had specific interests within the Zionist movement but that they should be allowed to support those interests independently of the centralized Zionist umbrella organizations or fundraising appeals. Despite the desire of Hadassah's leaders to remain apart from the political fray and infighting of the conflict-ridden organized American Zionist movement, this insistence on Hadassah's independence itself caused more conflicts to develop.

Nevertheless, Hadassah's successful battles for autonomy, especially fiscal autonomy, bolstered the organization's credibility and won it the loyalty of ever-greater numbers of American Jewish women. Their support, reinforced by Hadassah's skillful propaganda, made Hadassah the largest American Zionist organization in the interwar period. An expanding membership base, in conjunction with a finely tuned fundraising apparatus, allowed Hadassah to accomplish many of its goals in the Yishuv. Project by project, Hadassah slowly won acceptance in Zionist circles for its social and political priorities.

Many American Jewish women were profoundly affected by their involvement in Hadassah. For them, the organization became a training ground for learning new skills. Hadassah work gave these women confidence in themselves as political activists and organizers and opened the way for them to find a public voice not only in the Jewish community but in the larger American community, as well as a role in the Zionist movement. This was particularly important early in the twentieth century, when many professions were closed to women and there was often little scope even for educated women in public life. As early as 1930, founding member Lotta Levensohn described the transformation wrought on women by their Hadassah activities:

Women accustomed to nothing more than simple housekeeping accounts became expert in financial affairs; leaders of small clubs learned to apply large-scale organization methods to Hadassah chapters with hundreds of members; girls too timid to stand up in open meeting became platform speakers; office workers became presiding officers; teachers, as well as writers, produced leaflets of all sorts and press material; lawyers led study groups . . . and a great army of housewives expanded their sympathies and their activities beyond their own homes and their local charities.[2]

Hadassah's ongoing commitment to women's rights in the context of organized Zionism made it inevitable that the organization would actively support the struggle for suffrage and equality rights in the Yishuv. This support was reinforced by Szold's publicly articulated view that full legal and political equality for women was not only the measure of a society's progress but the very essence of the Zionist ideal. Hadassah's ongoing concern about social inequalities led the organization to battle against what it regarded as the most egregious cultural traditions affecting girls and women in the Yishuv—polygamy and child marriage. Then, during the 1920s and 1930s, as young single women flowed into Palestine, Hadassah moved quickly to respond to their pressing need for accommodation and paying work. Hadassah also led efforts to establish indigenous Palestinian women's organizations that would give Jewish women in the Yishuv a political voice.

Hadassah hoped that the future Jewish state would be both politically and financially independent. Hence the devolution policy whereby Hadassah undertook to hand over responsibility for each of its programs to local government control. In this, Hadassah followed the same practice as American maternalist organizations. But unlike its American counterparts, Hadassah was operating in the absence of stable government authority and therefore had to be uniquely flexible, willingly stepping aside when local government seemed able to take over and, at the same time, always available to step back in and share the financial and administrative burden when necessary.

When Hadassah first sent its nurses to the Yishuv, it did so in a climate of hostility toward any activities that the American Zionist movement defined as charitable or philanthropic. For this reason, over the years, Hadassah took great pains to distinguish its projects in the Yishuv from traditional forms of charity work. Szold worked hard to implement American-style professional models of organized welfare casework, which she hoped would make begging and indigence obsolete. Hadassah also wished to wean the Yishuv from its unhealthy dependence on foreign donations and help it to become economically self-sufficient. Ironically, Hadassah's own fundraising techniques—emphasizing the Yishuv's neediness—helped to subvert this goal. Because Hadassah's publicity stressed the obligation of American Jews to support their impoverished brethren, it helped to perpetuate the very culture of dependence that it sought to eradicate.

At the same time, however, Hadassah's fundraising pitches successfully promoted a strong bond with the Yishuv (and later Israel) among American Jews. This began with Hadassah's earliest efforts to cultivate among American Jews—even those who did not share Zionist goals—a feeling of responsibility for the welfare of Jews in the Yishuv. Educational programs were designed in concert with fundraising campaigns directed at American Jewish schoolchildren to inculcate this sense of fellow feeling at an early age. Whether the audience was schoolchildren or adults, Hadassah said that donating money was a spiritually enriching act and consistently reminded American Jews of their duty to share the bounty of American life with their fellows in the Jewish homeland.

Ultimately, Hadassah's fundraising campaigns in the United States reinforced a broader trend of commitment to philanthropic support of Israel as a core element of American Jewish life. Among successive generations of American Jews, increasingly distant both from religious traditions and their immigrant past, this approach had great appeal. Thus Hadassah contributed to the evolution of a new American Jewish identity with support for Israel rather than religious observance as its central value.

Also on the home front, Hadassah gave American Jewish women a sense that even their nonmonetary contributions to Zionism were both distinct and valuable. The sewing circles that sent thousands of handmade garments and linens to the Yishuv, for example, provided women with a vehicle for the public application of their domestic skills. Hadassah dignified such activities by describing them as "pioneering" work that offered women a chance to "serve Palestine with the labor of your hands."[3] By such means, Hadassah reinterpreted Zionist participation so that members could stay in America but still regard themselves, through their volunteer work for the organization, as having "a personal part of the pioneer effort." Personal realization through *aliyah* was an option, not an end. As Szold explained to the 1929 Hadassah Convention in New York:

> Hadassah must gather in our well-educated, our finely organized, our idealistic youth in America . . . the young women who can be stimulated to give their all, even if they do not go to Palestine as Chalutzim [*sic*]. Chalutzim, pioneers of an idea, can remain in all countries of the world and still contribute to the realization of the idea.[4]

Hadassah members were encouraged to believe that through their many activities in America, they not only made a significant contribution to achieving Zionist goals but, in the process, actively shared the noble struggles of the *halutzim*. The result, as Irma Lindheim explained, was that "on Jewish women, seeing themselves now as belonging to a band of pioneers venturing forth on new frontiers, the effect was positive and creative. Pride and confidence grew."[5] Thus Hadassah contributed to the development of a distinctive *American* Zionist ideology that minimized the importance of immigrating to the land of Israel as the sine qua non of an individual's Zionist commitment and emphasized, instead, the importance of political and financial support for the Zionist cause.

Hadassah's agreement to sponsor Youth Aliyah in 1935 positioned the organization for its vital role in providing for the absorption of young refugees fleeing Nazi advances in Europe. This sponsorship was the natural outcome of the organization's interest in child welfare work, and Youth Aliyah benefited from Hadassah's twenty years of experience working with children in the Yishuv. Appeals to women's maternal instincts remained the cornerstone of Hadassah's Youth Aliyah fundraising and publicity campaigns from the 1930s through the 1950s. Women were asked not simply to donate money to support Youth Aliyah in general, but to take on the responsibility of supporting a single child. They were told to regard themselves as foster mothers of Youth Aliyah children and, to reinforce the message, Hadassah awarded them the title of *Ima* or "Mother in Israel" for doing so. A wealth of similarly well-developed publicity strategies proved to be powerfully persuasive and made Hadassah's Youth Aliyah fundraising campaigns an astounding success.

Youth Aliyah's ideologically derived pedagogy, which sought to make Zionist pioneers out of the children of the German Jewish bourgeoisie, was warmly received by Hadassah. This form of education, with its emphasis on individual submission to the peer group and the development of a strong sense of social responsibility, seemed, to Hadassah leaders, the best possible solution to the needs of, on the one hand, European war orphans and, on the other, the Zionist movement as it struggled to build a new society. Hadassah's attitude toward Youth Aliyah was influenced both by its own organizational background in immigrant education as well as by a familiarity with the effectiveness of educational programs in helping immigrants assimilate to American life.

Although statehood represented the fulfillment of Zionist goals, Hadassah's support was still necessary to sustain Israel's social welfare system during the 1950s, when the fragile new state was confronted by an influx of immigrants from North African and Middle Eastern countries. Along with continuing to fund medical programs and services, Hadassah raised more funds for Youth Aliyah, which was suddenly thrust into the forefront of efforts to educate and integrate the children of the mass immigration.

A continuity of approach between the pre-state and post-1948 eras was evident in Hadassah's response to Israel's problems with the absorption and integration of Oriental immigrants in the 1950s. When it was first faced with "Eastern" (meaning, at that time, East European, Middle Eastern, and North African) Jews in Palestine a few decades before, Hadassah had then defined its campaign to improve public health and sanitary conditions in the Yishuv as a battle between modernity and backwardness and between West and East. In 1927, rather prematurely, Hadassah declared victory, claiming that "Palestine is no longer an eastern land. It is being penetrated by the western sunlight and transformed by western methods of hygiene."[6] Given that many of the new immigrants of the 1950s brought with them characteristically nineteenth-century types of social problems like illiteracy, child labor, child marriage, high rates of infant mortality, and communicable diseases, it is not surprising that Hadassah once again saw the solution in terms of modernization and Westernization through assimilative education.

This time around, however, the Israeli establishment deemed the parents ineducable or at least unreachable and, with scarce resources available, decided to focus on removing the children from their "backward" home environments. Hadassah did not contest this overall strategy, but it did push for some modifications to the rigidly ideological education offered by Youth Aliyah and some respect for the cultural heritage of Youth Aliyah's charges. Along with providing substantial funding, Youth Aliyah sent many American-trained educational and psychological consultants to advise Youth Aliyah over the years. Under their influence, Youth Aliyah moved, albeit slowly and reluctantly, toward offering education programs tailored more to individual and diverse needs.

It is not clear whether Hadassah leaders understood the extent of the burgeoning culture clash in Israel. Dr. Freund's eye-opening trip to Morocco, where she recognized that the situation of Moroccan Jewry had been misrepresented by Israeli authorities, did not translate into a broader consciousness, among Hadassah leaders, of ethnic problems in Israel or, indeed, within Youth Aliyah. Certainly, Hadassah leaders did not anticipate that these problems would persist for decades to come.

Youth Aliyah's leaders and administrators were no more bigoted than the times they lived in, but from today's vantage point, attitudes toward Oriental Jews in Israel during the 1950s often veered dangerously close to racism. Oriental Jews were routinely described as primitive or backward, and were subjected to extensive anthropological and psychological scrutiny. Hence some questions remain about the role of Youth Aliyah's assimilatory mandate in reinforcing such attitudes as well as about Hadassah's endorsement of that aim.

But Hadassah's support for Youth Aliyah's modernizing mission must also be understood in the context of the historical experience of American Jewry. In the late nineteenth century, longer-established German Jews felt threatened by a massive influx of East European Jewish immigrants. These immigrants, they worried, were backward and incapable of "fitting in" to American society. German Jews—like Henrietta Szold with her night school classes for Russian immigrants—provided educational programs to help the immigrants learn English and adjust to life in America. The public school system also played a major role in making immigrant children into Americans.[7]

Over the years, as the East Europeans and their descendents assimilated, the intraethnic tensions among American Jews were all but forgotten. By the 1950s most American Jews felt that they shared a common European background. Most importantly, American Jews were, as a community, acculturated to the surrounding society. Thus the Jewish experience of immigration, acculturation, and integration in the United States shaped Hadassah's attitude toward Oriental immigrants in Israel. They, too, were expected to willfully jettison their ethnic cultures and traditions in order to join Israel's "modern" and "Western" society. That many did not or would not, at least on terms that Hadassah and Youth Aliyah held up as an assimilative model, still confounds the Israeli social and political scene.

From the beginning, Hadassah sought a distinct place for women in organized Zionism and, through their participation in Hadassah, American Jewish women indeed played a decisive role in the development of the social welfare infrastructure that made statehood possible in 1948. Throughout the 1950s, the new state continued to rely on the essential programs and services that Hadassah had established in the Yishuv. Although the Progressive movement in the United States was no longer an active force by this time, the Progressive and maternalist ideals first embedded in each Hadassah program in the pre-state era were enshrined in the social welfare infrastructure of Israel. As a result, Hadassah, more than any other Diaspora Zionist organization, shaped the political culture of Israel as a social welfare state.

Notes

1. Tamar de Sola Pool, "American Outpost in the Near East," *Survey Graphic*, October 1942, unpaginated.

2. Lotta Levensohn, "Miss Szold as a Leader of Women," 17 November 1930, 2, RG 1/B 2/F 17, HWZOA.

3. Hadassah, the Women's Zionist Organization of America, *Serve Palestine with the Labor of Your Hands*, February 1934, RG 17, HWZOA.

4. Henrietta Szold, Address, Hadassah Convention, 14 November 1929, New York City, in Aaron S. Klieman, ed., *The Rise of Israel*, vol. 19, *Zionist Political Activity in the 1920s and 1930s* (New York: Garland, 1987), 27–28.

5. Irma Lindheim, *Parallel Quest: A Search of a Person and a People* (New York: Thomas Yoseloff, 1962), 217.

6. Rose K. Malmud, "The Story of Hadassah," *Hadassah Newsletter*, March 1927, 5.

7. See, for example, Gerald Sorin, "Mutual Contempt, Mutual Benefit: The Strained Encounter Between German and Eastern European Jews in America, 1880–1920," *American Jewish History* 81, no. 1 (1992–1993): 34–59. For an exploration of how American public schools transformed Jewish immigrant children early in the twentieth century, see Stephen Brumberg, "Teaching America: East European Jewish Immigrants and the Public School Curriculum," in *Going to America, Going to School: The Jewish Immigrant Public School Encounter in Turn-of-the-Century New York City* (New York: Praeger, 1986), 71–94.

~

Postscript

Almost a century has passed since the first Hadassah nurses set foot in Jerusalem. While many other service organizations of that era have since faded into obscurity, Hadassah is still flourishing. With a program budget of $125 million, Hadassah provides vital funding for Israeli medical facilities and supports a host of other health, educational, and vocational programs in Israel and the United States. The key to Hadassah's survival—and success—has been the organization's ability to adapt and change without compromising its mandate.

The path has not always been easy. In the wake of Israel's achievement of statehood, American Zionist organizations went through their share of soul-searching. With statehood—the major goal of Zionism—accomplished, some questioned what it meant to be a Zionist and what continuing role there was for American Zionists in Israel's nation-building enterprise. Would young people, born after the Jewish struggle for statehood, also find a place for themselves in the Zionist fold? But even as many Zionists searched for a niche, Hadassah never doubted its purpose. Its goal had always been more than statehood. It was service. Thus, the establishment of an Israeli state did not mean Hadassah's job was done. So long as there was need on the ground, there was a role for Hadassah.

The question for the organization was how to confront the mounting financial pressures of maintaining and expanding its activities in Israel. In order to take on new projects, it was at first thought essential to free up funds by divesting from some long-standing ventures. This was, after all, in keeping with Hadassah's policy of devolution. With this in mind, Hadassah began negotiating the transfer of responsibility for some community health centers to the Israeli government. After two years of talks, however, the State of Israel refused to assume responsibility for the programs. Echoing Szold's frustration with the Yishuv leadership decades earlier, an exasperated Lola Kramarsky, Hadassah president, wrote:

> This situation emphasizes the necessity of restating Hadassah's view of its role as an American voluntary organization in Israel. . . . Hadassah never thought of itself as the constant supplier of all the services it initiated in the medical, or any other field. On the contrary, it has been and still is our policy to transfer Hadassah-initiated services to responsible local authorities. . . . We think our policy represents both sound statesmanship and sound economics.[1]

But whatever its policies, Hadassah could not simply abandon its projects. And it didn't. The dispute proved a watershed in the relationship between Hadassah and the State of Israel: the women's organization was forced to acknowledge that, in spite of its commitment to devolution, some projects would have to remain permanently in Hadassah's hands.

Hadassah also expanded into new areas of activity. In the international arena, Hadassah stepped beyond social service and into political lobbying on Israel's behalf. For example, Hadassah regarded the 1973 United Nations resolution equating Zionism with racism as a particularly low blow and one that demanded a response. As a nongovernmental organization, or NGO, Hadassah was officially represented at the UN and had long been a strong supporter of the UN's human rights agenda. Hadassah also took pride in its commitment to offering health services on a nondiscriminatory basis to people of all races and religions. The effort to label Zionism as racism was thus regarded by Hadassah as not just an attack on Israel but also as an attack on Hadassah and its work. By joining the campaign to repudiate the resolution, Hadassah assumed an international profile as an advocate for Israel.

Other challenges arose in the 1970s and 1980s as Hadassah scrambled to stay relevant in the lives of a new generation of American Jewish women. As more and more women entered the workforce, fewer had the time and energy to devote to volunteer activities. Interest in specifically Jewish organizations or, for that matter, women's organizations, was waning.[2] Forced to reorient itself in this new social climate, Hadassah adopted a more corporate-style approach to recruiting members and soliciting donations.

With feminism on the rise, and with the inauguration of the UN-sponsored Decade of Women in 1975, Bernice Tannenbaum (Hadassah president from 1976 to 1980) says, "I became convinced that we had to be part of the women's movement." Tannenbaum represented Hadassah at several international women's conferences during the following years. "We never said we were feminist," she admits, "but we still are, in my opinion, feminist."[3] The pragmatism was typical of Hadassah: by not formally branding itself as a feminist organization but still allying itself with feminist causes, Hadassah mobilized women who might be afraid of the stigma of radicalism.

Similarly, in an effort to increase membership and expand Hadassah's base of support, the organization decided in 1983 to jettison the unwritten Hadassah–Women's International Zionist Organization (WIZO) agreement that Hadassah would operate solely in the United States, and promptly began setting up Hadassah affiliates worldwide. Soon after, the Hadassah International Medical Relief Association (now called Hadassah International) was established to allow non-Zionists, non-Jews, and men to fundraise for, and otherwise support, Hadassah's medical work.

Tannenbaum describes the era as a "period of opening up" for Hadassah. Members demanded more participation in the American social and political scene even as they called for Hadassah to act on the world stage. In response, Hadassah expanded its domestic and international initiatives. The organization is now deeply engaged in lobbying and advocacy related to a broad range of social policy issues touching on health, education, equality, and social justice, including everything from reproductive choice and health care to gun control, environmental protections, and immigration policy.

Although Hadassah now operates on a scale that its founders could scarcely have imagined, Szold's Progressive-era notions of how to run an efficient, effective organization still guide her organizational heirs. Hadassah remains at heart practical, innovative, and, above all, responsive to its membership, without whom the organization could not function. This union of committed women is also Szold's legacy: "It's the most secure, steady force," Tannenbaum says. "Women are very steadfast." In other ways, too, Tannenbaum has no doubt that the organization today, despite its expanded mandate, reflects Szold's original plan. "There's a voice there on behalf of human rights, the well-being of society, of trying to lift women and girls' lives, and of being one of the strongest advocates for Israel's well-being and maybe survival," she says. "I see Hadassah as playing a key role in keeping the visions of Henrietta Szold alive."

With about three hundred thousand members in the United States, Hadassah is still the largest single Jewish organization—and the largest women's organization—in the United States. Now expanding onto a worldwide stage, Hadassah has affiliates in more than thirty countries. And the organization's work on behalf of women, children, and the sick in Israel stands out as a model of service beyond challenge. That many Israelis think of Hadassah not as an American women's organization, but rather as a street-level part of the local scene, is a testament to Hadassah's successful integration into Israeli society, and the fulfillment of Henrietta Szold's dream for the organization she created almost a century ago.

Notes

1. Lola Kramarsky, "President's Column," *Hadassah Magazine*, February 1963.

2. Daniel J. Elazar, *Community and Polity: The Organizational Dynamics of American Jewry* (Philadelphia: Jewish Publication Society, 1976; rev. ed. 1995), 262ff.

3. Bernice Tannenbaum, New York, telephone interview by author, 9 December 2004.

~

Glossary

aliyah Hebrew for "ascent," the term used to describe Jewish immigration to the land of Israel.

Arbeitsgemeinschaft für Kinder und Jugendaliyah German for "Joint Movement for Children and Youth Aliyah."

Asefat Ha-Nivharim Hebrew for "National Assembly," also called "Elected Assembly" or "Representative Assembly," the representative body of the Jewish community in Palestine under the British Mandate.

Ashkenazi, Ashkenazim (pl.) Hebrew and Yiddish term describing Jews of European ancestry.

Blau-Weiss German for "Blue-White," a Jewish youth group in Germany that started before World War I.

Brit Shalom Hebrew for "Covenant of Peace," a group established in Palestine in 1925 that advocated binationalism and Jewish-Arab reconciliation.

galut: Hebrew for "exile."

hachshara, hachsharot (pl.) Hebrew for "training," used to refer to Zionist camps that prepared Jewish young people for agricultural pioneering in Palestine.

hagshama atzmit Hebrew for "self-realization."

Ha-Isha Hebrew for "The Woman," the name of a Hebrew-language periodical for women in Palestine.

Ha-Kibbutz Ha-Meuchad One of several kibbutz movements, or federations of kibbutzim, which is identified with a particular ideology.

halukah Hebrew for "distribution," the system of charitable almsgiving from Jews abroad that supported early Jewish communities in Palestine.

halutz (m. sing.), **halutza** (f. sing.), **halutzim** (m. pl.), **halutzot** (f. pl.) Hebrew for "pioneer(s)."

halutzic Hebrew-English amalgam meaning "pioneering."

halutziot Hebrew for "pioneering."

haver, haverim (pl.) Hebrew for "comrade."

Hechalutz Hebrew for "The Pioneer," a Zionist youth movement that promoted pioneering in Palestine.

hevrat noar Hebrew for "youth group."

Hibbat Zion Hebrew for "Love of Zion," a late-nineteenth-century Eastern European proto-Zionist movement that encouraged immigration to the Land of Israel.

Histadrut Hebrew for "federation," the short form of the name for the General Federation of Jewish Workers in the Land of Israel, established in 1920 as an umbrella organization of labor unions.

Histadrut Nashim Ivriot (HNI) Hebrew for "Federation of Hebrew Women," a group set up in 1924 by Henrietta Szold as an umbrella organization for Jewish women in Palestine.

Ihud Hebrew for "union." Along with Judah Magnes, Henrietta Szold was a founding member of this group, which was established in 1942 to promote binationalism in Palestine.

ima Hebrew for "mother."

Jüdische Jugendhilfe German for "Aid to Jewish Youth."

kibbutz, kibbutzim (pl.) A cooperative community in which property is communally owned.

kibbutz ha-galuiot Hebrew for "ingathering of the exiles."

kindertransport German for "children's transports," a scheme that brought European Jewish children to Britain shortly before the outbreak of World War II.

klita Hebrew for "absorption."

kollel, kollelim (pl.) Hebrew for "community."

landsmannschaften Yiddish term for the Jewish mutual aid societies for immigrants organized according to shared community of origin in Europe.

ma'abara, ma'abarot (pl.) Hebrew for "tents," refers to the tent or transit camps set up in Israel to house immigrants in the 1950s.

madrich, madrichim Hebrew for "guide" or "instructor," the term for youth group leaders.

mamlachtiut Hebrew for "statism."

mellah Arabic term for the Jewish quarter or ghetto in Morocco.

minyan Hebrew for "quorum," the ten men required for some prayers and religious observances.

Mizrahi, Mizrahim (pl.) Hebrew for "East" or "Easterners," describing Jews of Middle Eastern and North African origins.

mizug ha-galuiot Hebrew for "fusion of the exiles."

Moezet Ha-Poalot Hebrew for "Women Workers' Council." Established in 1922 as part of the Histadrut, it was allied with the Pioneer Women organization in the United States.

moshav, moshavim (pl.) Hebrew for "dwelling," this term refers to small cooperative agricultural settlements.

muskeljudentum German for "muscular Jews," referring to the Zionist concept that Jews should develop their physical prowess.

Noar Oved Hebrew for "working youth," a Zionist youth movement.

pidyon ha-ben Hebrew for "redemption of the [first-born] son," a religious ceremony.

pushke Yiddish term for the small donation boxes kept in the home into which coins were dropped for charity.

sabra Hebrew term for native-born Israeli.

Sephardic, Sephardim (pl.) Term for descendants of Jews expelled from Spain and Portugal in 1492, ofter used to refer to Jews from the Middle East and North Africa.

shaliach Hebrew for "emissary."

Talmud Torah Hebrew name for a Jewish religious school.

Tipat Halav Hebrew for "drop of milk."

Wandervogel An early-twentieth-century German Jewish youth movement that took its name from the German for "migratory bird" or "vagabond."

Yishuv From the Hebrew for "settlement," the term for the Jewish community of Palestine before the establishment of the State of Israel in 1948.

~

Bibliography

Archives

The Hadassah Archives at the American Jewish Historical Society (All Hadassah materials are reprinted by permission of Hadassah, the Women's Zionist Organization of America, Inc.)
Central Zionist Archives, Jerusalem, Israel
The Jane Addams Papers, Sophia Smith Collection, Smith College Archives
Straus Historical Society, Smithtown, New York

Interviews

Mrs. Mira Bramson, New Rochelle, New York, by telephone, 4 February 2003.
Ms. Alisa Poskanzer, Toronto, 20 May 1999.
Professor Yaffa Schlesinger, Forest Hills, New York, by telephone, 2 January 2002.
Mrs. Bernice Tannenbaum, New York, by telephone, 9 December 2004.
Mrs. June Walker, New York, by telephone, 11 January 2005.
Mrs. Edna Warsawe, Fort Lauderdale, Florida, by telephone, 1 May 2003.

Books, Articles, Pamphlets

Ackerman, Walter. "Making Jews: An Enduring Challenge in Israeli Education." *Israel Studies* 2, no. 2 (Fall 1997): 1–20.
———. "Varieties of Jewishness." *The Journal of Israeli History* 18 (1997): 47–55.
Addams, Jane. *Twenty Years at Hull-House*. Boston: Bedford/St. Martin's, 1999. (Originally published 1910.)

Adiel, S., ed. *On Youth Aliyah Literature: Selected, Classified and Annotated Bibliography.* Jerusalem: Jewish Agency, 1984.

Adler, Chaim. "Israeli Education Addressing Dilemmas Caused by Pluralism: A Sociological Perspective." Pp. 21–44 in *Education in a Comparative Context,* edited by Ernest Krausz. New Brunswick, N.J.: Transaction, 1989.

Aflalo, Doris. "The Pied Piper of Norway," *Ha'aretz* (English edition), 20 May 1999, 12–15.

Almog, Oz. *The Sabra: The Creation of the New Jew.* Translated by Haim Watzman. Berkeley: University of California Press, 2000.

Amkraut, Brian David. "Let Our Children Go: Youth Aliyah in Germany, 1932–1939." Ph.D. diss., New York University, 2000.

Apple, Rima D. "Constructing Mothers: Scientific Motherhood in the Nineteenth and Twentieth Centuries." *Social History of Medicine* 8, no. 2 (1995): 161–78.

———. *Mothers and Medicine: A Social History of Infant Feeding, 1890–1950.* Madison: University of Wisconsin Press, 1987.

Arad, Gulie Ne'eman, ed. *Israeli Historiography Revisited.* Bloomington: Indiana University Press, 1995.

Ashby, LeRoy. *Endangered Children: Dependency, Neglect, and Abuse in American History.* New York: Twayne, 1997.

Avidor, Moshe. *Education in Israel.* Jerusalem: Youth and Hechalutz Department of the Zionist Organization, 1957.

Avineri, Shlomo. *The Making of Modern Zionism: The Intellectual Origins of the Jewish State.* New York: Basic Books, 1981.

Axman, Sophie C. "Child-Life, Its Needs and Its Training." Pp. 25–58 in *Proceedings of the First Convention of the National Council of Jewish Women at New York.* Philadelphia: Jewish Publication Society, 1897.

Azaryahu, Sarah. *The Union of Hebrew Women for Equal Rights in Eretz Ysrael: Chapters in the History of the Women's Movement of Eretz Ysrael.* Translated by Marcia Freedman. Jerusalem: Union of Hebrew Women for Equal Rights in Israel, 1948. Reprint, Haifa: Women's Aid Fund, n.d.

Baker, Paula. "The Domestication of Politics: Women and American Political Society, 1780–1920." Pp. 55–91 in *Women, the State, and Welfare,* edited by Linda Gordon. Madison: University of Wisconsin Press, 1990.

Baker, S. Josephine. *Fighting for Life.* New York: Macmillan, 1939.

Barbuto, Domenica M. *American Settlement Houses and Progressive Social Reform: An Encyclopedia of the American Settlement Movement.* Phoenix, Ariz.: Oryx, 1999.

Batker, Carol J. *Reforming Fictions: Native, African, and Jewish American Women's Literature and Journalism in the Progressive Era.* New York: Columbia University Press, 2000.

Beekman, Daniel. *The Mechanical Baby: A Popular History of the Theory and Practice of Child Raising.* London: Dennis Dobson, 1977.

Ben-Horin, Meier. "Israel's Educational Frontiers." *Education Digest* 22, no. 4 (December 1956): 14–16.

Ben-Porat, Amir. *Between Class and Nation: The Formation of a Jewish Working Class in the Pre-State Period.* Westport, Conn.: Greenwood, 1986.

Ben-Rafael, Eliezer. "Critical Versus Non-Critical Sociology: An Evaluation." *Israel Studies* 2, no. 1 (Spring 1997): 174–93.

———. *The Emergence of Ethnicity: Cultural Groups and Social Conflict in Israel.* Contributions in Ethnic Studies, no. 7. Westport, Conn.: Greenwood, 1982.

———. *Language, Identity and Social Division: The Case of Israel.* Oxford: Clarendon, 1994.

Bentwich, Joseph. *Education in Israel.* Philadelphia: Jewish Publication Society of America, 1965.

Bentwich, Norman. *Jewish Youth Comes Home: The Story of the Youth Aliyah, 1933–1943.* Westport, Conn.: Hyperion, 1976.

Berg, Gerald M. "Zionism's Gender: Hannah Meisel and the Founding of the Agricultural Schools for Young Women." *Israel Studies* 6, no. 3 (Fall 2001): 135–65.

Berkowitz, Michael. *The Jewish Self-Image in the West.* New York: New York University Press, 2000.

———. "Transcending 'Tsimmes and Sweetness': Recovering the History of Zionist Women in Central and Western Europe, 1897–1933." Pp. 42–62 in *Active Voices: Women in Jewish Culture,* edited by Maurie Sacks. Urbana: University of Illinois Press, 1995.

———. *Western Jewry and the Zionist Project, 1914–1933.* Cambridge: Cambridge University Press, 1997.

Bernstein, Deborah. "Immigrants and Society: A Critical View of the Dominant School of Israeli Sociology." *British Journal of Sociology* 31, no. 2 (June 1980): 246–64.

———, ed. *Pioneers and Homemakers: Jewish Women in Pre-State Israel.* Albany: State University of New York Press, 1992.

———. *The Struggle for Equality: Urban Women Workers in Prestate Israeli Society.* New York: Praeger, 1987.

Bernstein, Deborah, and Shlomo Swirski. "The Rapid Economic Development of Israel and the Emergence of the Ethnic Division of Labour." *British Journal of Sociology* 33, no. 1 (March 1982): 64–85.

Bernstein, Judith, and Aaron Antonovsky. "The Integration of Ethnic Groups in Israel." *Jewish Journal of Sociology* 23, no. 1 (June 1981): 5–23.

Bogen, Boris D. *Jewish Philanthropy: An Exposition of Principles and Methods of Jewish Social Service in the United States.* New York: Macmillan, 1917.

Boylan, Anne M. *The Origins of Women's Activism: New York and Boston, 1797–1840.* Chapel Hill: University of North Carolina Press, 2002.

Bremner, Robert H. *American Philanthropy.* Chicago: University of Chicago Press, 1960.

Brown, Michael. "Henrietta Szold." Pp. 1368–73 in *Jewish Women in America: An Historical Encyclopedia,* edited by Paula E. Hyman and Deborah Dash Moore. New York: Routledge, 1997.

———— "Henrietta Szold's Progressive American Vision of the *Yishuv*." Pp. 60–80 in *Envisioning Israel: The Changing Ideals and Images of North American Jews*, edited by Allon Gal. Jerusalem: Magnes Press, 1996.

———— *The Israeli-American Connection: Its Roots in the Yishuv, 1914–1945*. Detroit: Wayne State University Press, 1996.

Brumberg, Stephen. *Going to America, Going to School: The Jewish Immigrant Public School Encounter in Turn-of-the-Century New York City*. New York: Praeger, 1986.

Buhler-Wilkerson, Karen. *False Dawn: The Rise and Decline of Public Health Nursing, 1900–1930*. London: Garland, 1989.

Bulmer, Martin, Kevin Bales, and Kathryn Kish Sklar. "The Social Survey in Historical Perspective." Pp.1–48 in *The Social Survey in Historical Perspective, 1880–1940*. Cambridge: Cambridge University Press, 1991.

Carson, Mina. *Settlement Folk: Social Thought and the American Settlement Movement, 1885–1930*. Chicago: University of Chicago Press, 1990.

Cavallo, Dominick. *Muscles and Morals: Organized Playgrounds and Urban Reform, 1880–1920*. Philadelphia: University of Pennsylvania Press, 1981.

Chambers, Clarke A. *Seedtime of Reform: American Social Service and Social Action, 1918–1933*. Minneapolis: University of Minnesota Press, 1963.

Chambré, Susan. "Philanthropy." Pp. 1049–54 in *Jewish Women in America: An Historical Encyclopedia*, edited by Paula E. Hyman and Deborah Dash Moore. New York: Routledge, 1997.

Charities and the Commons, January 1905–April 1909.

Cohen, Mitchell. *Zion and State: Nation, Class and the Shaping of Modern Israel*. New York: Columbia University Press, 1992.

Cohen, Naomi W. *American Jews and the Zionist Idea*. New York: Ktav, 1975.

Cohen, Ronald D. "Child-Saving and Progressivism, 1885–1915." Pp. 273–309 in *American Childhood: A Research Guide and Historical Handbook*, edited by Joseph M. Hines and N. Ray Hiner. Westport, Conn.: Greenwood, 1985.

Confino, Alon. "Collective Memory and Cultural History: Problems of Method." *American Historical Review* 102, no. 5 (December 1997): 1386–1403.

Conway, Jill. "Women Reformers and American Culture, 1870–1930." *Journal of Social History* 5, no. 2 (Winter 1971–1972): 164–77.

Cott, Nancy. "What's in a Name? The Limits of 'Social Feminism' or, Expanding the Vocabulary of Women's History." *The Journal of American History* 76, no. 3 (December 1989): 809–29.

Cravens, Hamilton. "Child-Saving in the Age of Professionalism, 1915–1930." Pp. 415–88 in *American Childhood: A Research Guide and Historical Handbook*, edited by Joseph M. Hines and N. Ray Hiner. Westport, Conn.: Greenwood, 1985.

Dahan-Kalev, Henriette. "You're So Pretty—You Don't Look Moroccan." *Israel Studies* 6 (2001): 1–14.

Daley, Ira. *The Hadassah Medical Organization Papers in the Hadassah Archives, 1918–1981*. New York: Hadassah, the Women's Zionist Organization of America, 1984.

Daniels, Doris Groshen. *Always a Sister: The Feminism of Lillian Wald.* New York: Feminist Press at the City University of New York, 1989.

Dash, Joan. "Doing Good in Palestine: Magnes and Henrietta Szold." Pp. 99–111 in *Like All the Nations? The Life and Legacy of Judah L. Magnes,* edited by William M. Brinner and Moses Rischin. Albany: State University of New York Press, 1987.

———. *Summoned to Jerusalem: The Life of Henrietta Szold, Founder of Hadassah.* New York: Harper & Row, 1979.

Davis, Allen F. *Spearheads for Reform: The Social Settlements and the Progressive Movement 1890–1914.* New York: Oxford University Press, 1967.

Deshen, Shlomo. "Social Organization and Politics in Israeli Urban Quarters." *The Jerusalem Quarterly* 22 (1982): 21–37.

Deshen, Shlomo, and Moshe Shokeid. *The Predicament of Homecoming: Cultural and Social Life of North African Immigrants in Israel.* Ithaca, N.Y.: Cornell University Press, 1974.

Diamond, Stanley. "Kibbutz and Shtetl: The History of an Idea." *Social Problems* 5, no. 2 (Fall 1957): 71–99.

Diner, Hasia R. "A Political Tradition? American Jewish Women and the Politics of History." Pp. 54–69 in *Jews and Gender: The Challenge to Hierarchy,* edited by Jonathan Frankel. Oxford: Oxford University Press, 2000.

Dorey, Annette K. Vance. *Better Baby Contests: The Scientific Quest for Perfect Childhood Health in the Early Twentieth Century.* London: McFarland, 1999.

Dror, Rahel. "Educational Research in Israel." *Studies in Education* 13 (1963): 156–86.

Druyan, Nitza. "Yemenite Jews on the Zionist Altar." Pp. 153–70 in *Review Essays in Israel Studies,* edited by Laura Zittrain Eisenberg and Neil Caplan. Albany: State University of New York Press, 2000.

Duffy, John. *The Sanitarians: A History of American Public Health.* Urbana and Chicago: University of Illinois Press, 1990.

Dushkin, Alexander. "Henrietta Szold as Educator." Pp. 143–57 in *Jewish Education: Selected Writings,* edited by Abraham P. Gannes. Jerusalem: Magnes Press, 1980.

Dushkin, Alexander M., and Carl Frankenstein, eds. *Studies in Education.* Jerusalem: Magnes Press, Hebrew University, 1963.

Eaton, Joseph W., and Michael Chen. *Influencing the Youth Culture: A Study of Youth Organizations in Israel.* Beverly Hills, Calif.: Sage, 1970.

Edelheit, Hershel, and Abraham J. Edelheit. *History of Zionism: A Handbook and Dictionary.* Boulder, Colo.: Westview, 2000.

Edelston, H. "Uprooting and Resettlement: A Survey of the 'Youth Aliyah' Program in Israel." *Journal of Educational Sociology* 32, no. 8 (April 1959): 392–401.

Ehrenreich, Barbara, and Deirdre English. *For Her Own Good: 150 Years of the Experts' Advice to Women.* New York: Anchor, 1978.

Eisenstadt, S. N. *The Absorption of Immigrants: A Comparative Study.* Westport, Conn.: Greenwood, 1975. (Originally published 1954 by Routledge & Kegan Paul.)

———. *An Introduction to the Sociological Structure of Oriental Jewry.* Jerusalem: Szold Foundation, 1948.

———. *Israeli Society*. New York: Basic Books, 1967.

———. "The Oriental Jews in Israel." *Jewish Social Studies* 12, no. 3 (1950): 199–222.

———. "Some Comments on the 'Ethnic' Problem in Israel." *Israel Social Sciences Research* 1, no. 2 (1983): 20–29.

———. *The Transformation of Israeli Society: An Essay in Interpretation*. Boulder, Colo.: Westview, 1985.

Eisenstadt, S. N., Rivkah Bar Yosef, and Chaim Adler, eds. *Integration and Development in Israel*. New York: Praeger, 1970.

Eiskovits, R. "Children's Institutions in Israel as Mirrors of Social and Cultural Change." *Child & Youth Services* 7, no. 3/4 (1985): 26–29.

Eiskovits, Rivka, and Robert H. Beck. "Models Governing the Education of New Immigrant Children in Israel." *Comparative Education Review* 34 (1990): 177–95.

Elazar, Daniel. *Community and Polity: The Organizational Dynamics of American Jewry*. Philadelphia: Jewish Publication Society, 1976; revised edition, 1995.

———. "Education in a Society at a Crossroads: An Historical Perspective on Israeli Schooling." *Israel Studies* 2, no. 2 (Fall 1997): 40–65.

———. *Israel: Building a New Society*. Bloomington: Indiana University Press, 1986.

Elboim-Dror, Rachel. "Gender in Utopianism: The Zionist Case." *History Workshop Journal* 37 (Spring 1994): 99–116.

——— "Israeli Education: Changing Perspectives." *Israel Studies* 6, no. 1 (Spring 2001): 76–100.

Even-Zohar, Itamar. "The Emergence of a Native Hebrew Culture in Palestine: 1882–1948." *Studies in Zionism* 4 (1981): 167–84.

Ewen, Elizabeth. *Immigrant Women in the Land of Dollars: Life and Culture on the Lower East Side, 1890–1925*. New York: Monthly Review Press, 1985.

Fee, Elizabeth, and Roy M. Acheson, eds. *A History of Education in Public Health: Health That Mocks the Doctors' Rules*. Oxford: Oxford University Press, 1991.

Feige, Michael. "Introduction: Rethinking Israeli Memory and Identity." *Israel Studies* 7 (Summer 2002): 5–14.

Fein, Isaac M. "Baltimore Jews during the Civil War." Pp. 323–52 in *The Jewish Experience in America*, vol. 3, edited by Abraham J. Karp. Waltham, Mass.: American Jewish Historical Society, 1969.

Fineman, Irving. *Woman of Valor: The Life of Henrietta Szold, 1860–1945*. New York: Simon & Schuster, 1961.

Frankenstein, Carl, ed. *Between Past and Future: Essays and Studies on Aspects of Immigrant Absorption in Israel*. Jerusalem: Henrietta Szold Foundation for Child and Youth Welfare, 1953.

———. "The School Without Parents." *Studies in Education* 13 (1963): 105–38.

Freier, Recha. *Let the Children Come: The Early History of Youth Aliyah*. London: Weidenfeld & Nicolson, 1961.

Gal, Allon. "Brandeis, Judaism, and Zionism." Pp. 65–98 in *Brandeis and America*, edited by Nelson L. Dawson. Lexington: University Press of Kentucky, 1989.

Gal, Allon. "Hadassah and the American Jewish Political Tradition." Pp. 89–114 in *An Inventory of Promises: Essays in American Jewish History in Honor of Moses Rishin*, edited by Jeffrey S. Gurock and Marc Lee Raphael. Brooklyn, N.Y.: Carlson, 1995.

Gazi'el, Hayim. *Politics and Policy-Making in Israel's Education System*. Brighton, UK: Sussex Academic Press, 1996.

Gedi, Noa, and Yigal Elam. "Collective Memory—What Is It?" *History & Memory* 8, no. 1 (1986): 30–50.

Gelber, Yoav. "The Origins of Youth Aliyah." *Studies in Zionism* 9 (1988): 147–71.

Geller, L. D. *The Alice L. Seligsberg and Rose G. Jacobs Papers in the Hadassah Archives, 1918–1957*. New York: Hadassah, the Women's Zionist Organization of America, 1985.

Geller, Lawrence D. *The Archives of Youth Aliyah, 1933–1960*. New York: Hadassah, the Women's Zionist Organization of America, 1983.

Geller, Lawrence D. *The Henrietta Szold Papers in the Hadassah Archives, 1875–1965*. New York: Hadassah, the Women's Zionist Organization of America, 1982.

Geller, L. D. and Ira Daley. *Zionist Political History in the Hadassah Archives, 1894–1957*. New York: Hadassah, the Women's Zionist Organization of America, 1984.

Gere, Anne Ruggles. *Intimate Practices: Literacy and Cultural Work in U.S. Women's Clubs, 1880–1920*. Urbana: University of Illinois Press, 1997.

Gilbert, Martin. *Israel: A History*. London: Doubleday, 1998.

Gillis, John R., ed. *Commemorations: The Politics of National Identity*. Princeton, N.J.: Princeton University Press, 1994.

Goldberg, Harvey. "Introduction: Culture and Ethnicity in the Study of Israeli Society." *Ethnic Groups* 1 (1977): 163–86.

———, ed. *Sephardi and Middle Eastern Jewries: History and Culture in the Modern Era*. Bloomington: Indiana University Press, 1996.

Goldscheider, Calvin. "Creating a New Society: Immigration, Nation-Building, and Ethnicity in Israel." *Harvard International Review* (Spring 1998): 64–69.

———. *Israel's Changing Society: Population, Ethnicity, and Development*. Boulder, Colo.: Westview, 1996.

Goldstein, Eric L. "Between Race and Religion: Jewish Women and Self-Definition in Late Nineteenth Century America." Pp. 182–200 in *Women and American Judaism: Historical Perspectives*, edited by Pamela S. Nadell and Jonathan Sarna. Hanover, N.H.: Brandeis University Press, 2001.

———. "The Unstable Other: Locating the Jew in Progressive-Era American Racial Discourse." *American Jewish History* 89 (December 2001): 383–409.

Golomb, Deborah Grand. "The 1893 Congress of Jewish Women: Evolution or Revolution in American Jewish Women's History?" *American Jewish History* 70 (September 1980): 52–67.

Gordon, Linda. "The Progressive-Era Transformation of Child Protection, 1900–1920." Pp. 543–48 in *Childhood in America*, edited by Paula S. Fass and Mary Ann Mason. New York: New York University Press, 2000.

Goren, Arthur A. *The Politics and Public Culture of American Jews*. Bloomington: Indiana University Press, 1999.

Gorney, Yosef. "The 'Melting Pot' in Zionist Thought." *Israel Studies* 6, no. 3 (Fall 2001): 54–70.

———. *The State of Israel in Jewish Public Thought: The Quest for Collective Identity*. Basingstoke, UK: Macmillan, 1994.

Goron, Arthur. "Celebrating Zion in America." Pp. 41–59 in *Encounters with the "Holy Land": Place, Past and Future in American Jewish Culture*, edited by Jeffrey Shandler and Beth S. Wenger. Hanover, N.H.: University Press of New England, 1998.

Gottesman, Meir, ed. *Cultural Transition: The Case of Immigrant Youth*. Jerusalem: Magnes Press, 1988.

Grant, Julia. "Modernizing Mothers: Home Economics and the Parent Education Movement, 1920–1945." Pp. 55–74 in *Rethinking Home Economics: Women and the History of a Profession*, edited by Sarah Stage and Virginia B. Vincenti. Ithaca, N.Y.: Cornell University Press, 1997.

Greenberg, Marian G. *There Is Hope for Your Children: Youth Aliyah, Henrietta Szold and Hadassah*. N.p.: Hadassah, the Women's Zionist Organization of America, 1986.

Haber, Samuel. *Efficiency and Uplift: Scientific Management in the Progressive Era, 1890–1920*. Chicago: University of Chicago Press, 1964.

Hacohen, Dvora. "Mass Immigration and the Israeli Political System, 1948–1953." *Studies in Zionism* 8 (1987): 99–113.

Hadassah Bulletin, September 1914–August 1918.

Hadassah Magazine, March 1961–February 2005.

Hadassah Newsletter, March 1920–March 1961 (*Hadassah News Letter* before October 1938).

Halper, Jeff. "The Absorption of Ethiopian Immigrants: A Return to the Fifties." Pp. 112–139 in *Ethiopian Jews and Israel*, edited by Michael Ashkenazi and Alex Weingrod. New Brunswick, N.J.: Transaction, 1987.

Halperin, Samuel. *The Political World of American Zionism*. Detroit: Wayne State University Press, 1961.

Halpern, Ben. *A Clash of Heroes: Brandeis, Weizmann, and American Zionism*. Oxford: Oxford University Press, 1987.

Halpern, Ben, and Shalom Wurn, eds. *The Responsible Attitude: The Life and Opinions of Giora Josephthal*. New York: Schocken, 1966.

Harrison, Robert. "Patterns of Social Reform, 1890–1920." Pp. 115–43 in *State and Society in Twentieth-Century America*. London: Longman, 1997.

Hartogensis, Benjamin H. "The Russian Night School of Baltimore." *American Jewish Historical Society* 31 (1928): 225–29.

Haskell, Guy. "The Development of Israeli Anthropological Approaches to Immigration and Ethnicity: 1948–1980." *Jewish Folklore and Ethnology Review* 11, no. 1/2 (1989): 19–26.

Hayden, Dolores. *The Grand Domestic Revolution: A History of Feminist Designs for American Homes, Neighborhoods, and Cities.* Cambridge, Mass.: MIT Press, 1981.

Hazan, Bertha, and A. I. Rabin, eds. *Collective Education in the Kibbutz: From Infancy to Maturity.* New York: Springer, 1973.

Heller, Celia. "Emerging Consciousness of the Ethnic Problem." Pp. 313–332 in *Israel: Social Structure and Change,* edited by Michael Curtis and Mordechai S. Chertoff. New Brunswick, N.J.: Transaction, 1973.

Henrietta Szold Foundation. "A Roof Over Their Heads." *International Child Welfare Review* 6, no. 2 (1952): 59–78.

Herman, Felicia. "From Priestess to Hostess: Sisterhoods of Personal Service in New York City, 1887–1936." Pp. 148–81 in *Women and American Judaism: Historical Perspectives,* edited by Pamela S. Nadell and Jonathan Sarna. Hanover, N.H.: Brandeis University Press, 2001.

Herzog, Hanna, and Ofra Greenberg. *A Voluntary Women's Organization in a Society in the Making: WIZO's Contribution to Israeli Society.* Tel Aviv: Tel Aviv University Institute of Social Research, 1978.

Hoag, Ernest Bryant, and Lewis M. Terman. *Health Work in the Schools.* Boston: Houghton Mifflin, 1914.

Hofstadter, Richard. *The Age of Reform: From Bryan to F.D.R.* New York: Knopf, 1963.

Honig-Parnass, Tikvah. *Training Youth from New Immigrant Settlements: A Study in Youth Aliyah Education.* Jerusalem: Henrietta Szold Institute for Child and Youth Welfare/ Child and Youth Immigration Department of the Jewish Agency for Israel, 1960.

Horowitz, Tamar Ruth. "Integration and the Social Gap." *The Jerusalem Quarterly* 15 (1980): 133–44.

Hurewitz, J. C. *The Struggle for Palestine.* New York: Schocken, 1950.

Hoy, Suellen M. "'Municipal Housekeeping': The Role of Women in Improving Urban Sanitation Practices, 1880–1917." Pp. 173–98 in *Pollution and Reform in American Cities, 1870–1930,* edited by Martin V. Melosi. Austin: University of Texas Press, 1980.

Hyman, Paula E. "Feminist Studies and Modern Jewish History." Pp. 120–39 in *Feminist Perspectives on Jewish Studies,* edited by Lynn Davidman and Shelly Tenenbaum. New Haven, Conn.: Yale University Press, 1994.

———. "Gender and the Shaping of Modern Jewish Identities." *Jewish Social Studies* 8 (Winter/Spring 2002): 153–61.

Hyman, Paula E., and Deborah Dash Moore, eds. *Jewish Women in America: An Historical Encyclopedia.* New York: Routledge, 1997.

Iram, Y. "Changing Patterns of Immigrant Absorption in Israel: Educational Implications." *Canadian and International Education* 16 (1987): 55–72.

Iram, Yaacov, and Mirjam Schmida. *The Educational System of Israel.* Westport, Conn.: Greenwood, 1998.

Isaac, J. "Israel—A New Melting Pot?" Pp. 234–66 in *The Cultural Integration of Immigrants: A Survey Based upon the Papers and Proceedings of the Unesco Conference Held in Havana, April 1956,* edited by W. D. Borrie. Paris: UNESCO, 1959.

Izraeli, Dafna N. "The Zionist Women's Movement in Palestine, 1911–1917: A Sociological Analysis." *Signs* 7, no. 11 (1981): 87–114.

Jacobs, Rose. "Alice L. Seligsberg," *American Jewish Year Book* 43 (1941–1942): 431–36.

Jacobs, Rose G. "Beginnings of Hadassah." Pp. 228–44 in *Early History of Zionism in America*, edited by Isidore S. Meyer. New York: American Jewish Historical Society, 1958.

Jaffe, Eliezer David. *Child Welfare in Israel*. New York: Praeger, 1982.

Jewish Agency. *The Integration of Adolescents: A Selection of Articles Drawn from the Publications of Youth Aliyah*. Jerusalem: Jewish Agency, 1984.

———, Youth and Children's Aliyah Department. *Report of Child and Youth Aliyah to the Zionist General Council*. Jerusalem: Public Relations Dept. of Child and Youth Aliyah, 1950.

———. *Report of the World Conference of Youth Aliyah on the Occasion of the Thirtieth Anniversary*. Jerusalem: Jewish Agency Youth Aliyah Department, 1964.

Kadosh, Sandra Berliant. "Ideology vs. Reality: Youth Aliyah and the Rescue of Jewish Children during the Holocaust Era, 1933–45." Ph.D. diss., Columbia University, 1995.

Kafkafi, Eyal. "Changes in Ideology during Two Generations of a Zionist Youth Movement." *The Journal of Israeli History* 17 (1996): 283–99.

Karp, Abraham J. *Haven and Home: A History of the Jews in America*. New York: Schocken, 1985.

Kashti, Yitzhak. *The Socializing Community: Disadvantaged Adolescents in Israeli Youth Villages*. Tel Aviv: School of Education, Tel Aviv University, 1979.

Katznelson-Rubashow, Rachel, ed. *The Plough Woman: Records of the Pioneer Women of Palestine*. Translated by Maurice Samuel. Westport, Conn.: Hyperion, 1976.

Kerber, Linda K. "Separate Spheres, Female Worlds, Women's Place: The Rhetoric of Women's History." *Journal of American History* 75 (June 1988–March 1989): 9–39.

Kessler, Barry, ed. *Daughter of Zion: Henrietta Szold and American Jewish Womanhood*. Hagerstown: Jewish Historical Society of Maryland, 1995.

Kleinberger, Aharon Fritz. *Society, Schools and Progress in Israel*. Oxford: Pergamon, 1969.

Klieman, Aaron S., ed. *The Rise of Israel*, vol. 19, *Zionist Political Activity in the 1920s and 1930s*. New York: Garland, 1987.

Klieman, Aaron S., and Adrian L. Klieman, eds. *American Zionism: A Documentary History*, vol. 5, *My Brother's Keeper: Fostering Projects in the Jewish National Home*. New York: Garland, 1990.

Koenig, Samuel. "The Crisis in Israel's Collective Settlements." *Jewish Social Studies* 14, no. 1 (1952): 145–66.

Kohen-Raz, Reuven. *From Chaos to Reality: An Experiment in Reeducation of Emotionally Disturbed Immigrant Youth in a Kibbutz*. New York: Gordon Breach, 1972.

Kohut, Rebekah. "Jewish Women's Organization in the United States." *American Jewish Year Book* 33 (1931): 165–201.

Kol, Moshe. *Mentors and Friends*. Translated by Yael Guiladi. London: Cornwall Books, 1983.

———. *Youth Aliyah: Past, Present and Future*. Jerusalem: UNESCO, 1957.

Kotzin, Daniel P. "An Attempt to Americanize the Yishuv: Judah L. Magnes in Mandatory Palestine." *Israel Studies* 5, no. 1 (Spring 2000): 1–23.

Koven, Seth, and Sonya Michel, eds. *Mothers of a New World: Maternalist Politics and the Origins of Welfare States*. New York and London: Routledge, 1993.

———. "Womanly Duties: Maternalist Politics and the Origins of Welfare States in France, Germany, Great Britain, and the United States, 1880–1920." *American Historical Review* 95, no. 4 (October 1990): 1076–1108.

Kraus, Alisa. *Every Child a Lion: The Origins of Maternal and Infant Health Policy in the United States and France, 1890–1920*. Ithaca, N.Y.: Cornell University Press, 1993.

Krausz, Ernest. *On Ethnic and Religious Diversity in Israel*. Ramat-Gan, Israel: Institute for the Study of Ethnic and Religious Groups, Bar-Ilan University, 1975.

———. *Studies of Israeli Society: Migration, Ethnicity and Community*. New Brunswick, N.J.: Transaction, 1980.

Kressel, Gideon. "Arabism (Urubah): A 'Concealed' Cultural Factor in the Ethnic 'Gap' in Israel." *Israel Social Sciences Research* 2, no. 1 (1984): 66–79.

Kutscher, Carol. "Hadassah, The Women's Zionist Organization of America, Part I." Pp. 151–74 in *Jewish American Voluntary Organizations*, edited by Michael N. Dobkowski. New York: Greenwood, 1985.

Kutscher, Carol Bosworth. "The Early Years of Hadassah, 1912–1921." Ph.D. diss., Brandeis University, 1976.

Kuzmack, Linda Gordon. *Women's Cause: The Jewish Women's Movement in England and the United States, 1881–1933*. Columbus: Ohio State University Press, 1990.

Ladd-Taylor, Molly. *Mother-Work: Women, Child Welfare, and the State, 1890–1930*. Urbana and Chicago: University of Illinois Press, 1994.

Laqueur, Walter. *Generation Exodus: The Fate of Young Jewish Refugees from Nazi Germany*. Hanover, N.H.: Brandeis University Press, 2001.

———. *A History of Zionism*. New York: Holt, Rinehart and Winston, 1972.

Laskier, Michael M. "The Evolution of Zionist Activity in the Jewish Communities of Morocco, Tunisia and Algeria: 1897–1947." *Studies in Zionism* 8 (1983): 205–36.

Lawrence, Jon, and Pat Starkey, eds. *Child Welfare and Social Action in the Nineteenth and Twentieth Centuries: International Perspectives*. Liverpool, UK: Liverpool University Press, 2001.

Leshem, Elazar, and Judith T. Shuval, eds. *Immigration to Israel: Sociological Perspectives*. New Brunswick, N.J.: Transaction, 1998.

Levensohn, Lotta. "Henrietta Szold," *American Jewish Year Book* 47 (1945–1946): 51–70.

Levin, Alexandra, ed. *Henrietta Szold and Youth Aliyah: Family Letters, 1934–1944*. New York: Herzl Press, 1986.

Levin, Marlin. *It Takes a Dream: The Story of Hadassah*. Jerusalem: Gefen, 1997.

Levin, Marlin. *Women of Valor: The Story of Hadassah, 1912–1987*, edited by Yossi Avner. Tel Aviv: Beth Hatefutsoth, The Nahum Goldmann Museum of the Jewish Diaspora, 1987.

Levine, Murray, and Adeline Levine. *Helping Children: A Social History*. Oxford: Oxford University Press, 1992.

Levy, David W. "Brandeis and the Progressive Movement." Pp. 99–117 in *Brandeis and America*, edited by Nelson L. Dawson. Lexington: University Press of Kentucky, 1989.

Levy, Hortense. "Hadassah and Other Women's Organizations." Pp. 277–297 in *Modern Palestine: A Symposium*, edited by Jessie Sampter. New York: Hadassah, the Women's Zionist Organization of America, 1933.

Lewis, Arnold. "Educational Policy and Social Inequality in Israel." *The Jerusalem Quarterly* 21 (1979): 101–11.

———. "Phantom Ethnicity: 'Oriental Jews' in Israeli Society." Pp. 133–57 in *Studies in Israeli Ethnicity: After the Ingathering*, edited by Alex Weingrod. New York: Gordon and Breach Science Publishers, 1985.

Lichtenberg, Naomi Ann. "Hadassah's Founders and Palestine, 1912–1925: A Quest for Meaning and the Creation of Women's Zionism." Ph.D. diss., Indiana University, 1996.

Lindheim, Irma. *Parallel Quest: A Search of a Person and a People*. New York: Thomas Yoseloff, 1962.

Lipstadt, Deborah E. "The History of American Zionist Organizations: An Ideological and Functional Analysis." Pp. 531–44 in *Jewish American Voluntary Organizations*, edited by Michael N. Dobkowski. New York: Greenwood, 1985.

Lissak, Moshe. "Images of Immigrants: Stereotypes and Stigmata." Pp. 236–49 in *David Ben-Gurion: Politics and Leadership in Israel*, edited by Ronald W. Zweig. London: Frank Cass, 1981.

———. "Pluralism in Israeli Society." Pp. 363–78 in *Israel: Social Structure and Change*, edited by Michael Curtis and Mordechai S. Chertoff. New Brunswick, N.J.: Transaction, 1973.

———. *Social Mobility in Israeli Society*. Jerusalem: Israel Universities Press, 1969.

Lissak, Rivka Shpak. *Pluralism and the Progressives: Hull House and the New Immigrants, 1890–1919*. Chicago: University of Chicago Press, 1989.

Litt, Jacquelyn S. *Medicalized Motherhood: Perspectives from the Lives of African-American and Jewish Women*. New Brunswick, N.J.: Rutgers University Press, 2000.

Lowenthal, Marvin. *Henrietta Szold: Life and Letters*. New York: Viking, 1942.

Lubove, Roy. *The Professional Altruist: The Emergence of Social Work as a Career, 1880–1930*. Cambridge, Mass.: Harvard University Press, 1965.

Maccabaean, July 1903–March 1918.

Maimon, Ada. *Women Build a Land*. Translated by Shulamith Schwarz-Nardi. New York: Herzl Press, 1962.

Maon, Mary Ann. "The State as Superparent." Pp. 549–54 in *Childhood in America*, edited by Paula S. Fass and Mary Ann Mason. New York: New York University Press, 2000.

McCarthy, Justin. *The Population of Palestine: Population History and Statistics of the Late Ottoman Period and the Mandate*. New York: Columbia University Press, 1990.

McCune, Mary. "Social Workers in the *Muskeljudentum*: 'Hadassah Ladies,' 'Manly Men' and the Significance of Gender in the American Zionist Movement, 1912–1928." *American Jewish History* 86, no. 2 (June 1998): 135–65.

Mead, Elwood, ed. *Reports of the Experts Submitted to the Joint Palestine Survey Commission*. Boston, Mass.: Daniels Printing, 1928.

Mechling, Jay E. "Advice to Historians on Advice to Mothers." *Journal of Social History* 9, no.1 (Fall 1975): 44–63.

Meckel, Richard A. *Save the Babies: American Public Health Reform and the Prevention of Infant Mortality, 1850–1929*. Baltimore: Johns Hopkins University Press, 1990.

Medoff, Rafael. *Zionism and the Arabs: An American Jewish Dilemma, 1898–1948*. Westport, Conn.: Praeger, 1997.

Medoff, Rafael, and Chaim I. Waxman. *Historical Dictionary of Zionism*. London: Scarecrow, 2000.

Migdal, Joel. *Through the Lens of Israel: Explorations in State and Society*. Albany: State University of New York Press, 2001.

Miller, Donald Herbert. "A History of Hadassah, 1912–1935." Ph.D. diss., New York University, 1968.

Moore, Deborah Dash. "Hadassah." Pp. 571–83 in *Jewish Women in America: An Historical Encyclopedia*, edited by Paula E. Hyman and Deborah Dash Moore. New York: Routledge, 1997.

———. "Jewish Ethnicity and Acculturation in the 1920s: Public Education in New York City." *Jewish Journal of Sociology* 18, no. 2 (December 1976): 96–104.

Muncy, Robyn. *Creating a Female Dominion in American Reform, 1890–1935*. Oxford: Oxford University Press, 1991.

Nadad, A. *Reeducation of Wayward Youth*. Jerusalem: Szold Foundation, 1946.

Nardi, Noach. *Zionism and Education in Palestine*. New York: Bureau of Publications, Teachers College, Columbia University, 1934.

Nardi, Noah. *Education in Palestine*. Washington, D.C.: Zionist Organization of America, 1945.

Near, Henry. "The End of Pioneering? The Kibbutz in the 1950s." Pp. 168–95 in *The Kibbutz Movement: A History*, vol. 2. Portland, Ore.: Vallentine Mitchell, 1997.

Newmayer, S. Weir. "The School Nurse as Teacher of Health and Hygiene." *The Trained Nurse and Hospital Review* 79, no. 3 (September 1927): 279–81.

New Palestine, 14 January 1921–27 December 1935.

New York Times, 1 March 1913–31 January 1938.

Nini, Yehuda. "Immigration and Assimilation: The Yemenite Jews." *The Jerusalem Quarterly* 21 (1981): 85–98.

Nora, Pierre. "Between Memory and History." *Representations* 26 (Spring 1989): 7–25.

Nordau, Max. *Max Nordau to His People: A Summons and a Challenge*. New York: Scopus, 1941.

Okkenhaug, Inger Marie. *The Quality of Heroic Living, of High Endeavour and Adventure: Anglican Mission, Women and Education in Palestine, 1888–1948*. Boston: Brill, 2002.

Palestine Bulletin, 12 January 1925–30 November 1932.

Palestine Post, 1 December 1932–21 April 1950.

Palestine Weekly, 26 December 1919–2 August 1931.

Patai, Raphael, ed. *Encyclopedia of Zionism and Israel*. New York: Herzl Press, 1971.

——. *Israel Between East and West*. Philadelphia: Jewish Publication Society, 1953.

——. "Western and Oriental Culture in Israel." Pp. 307–311 in *Israel: Social Structure and Change*, edited by Michael Curtis and Mordechai S. Chertoff. New Brunswick, N.J.: Transaction, 1973.

Paul, Kathleen. "Changing Childhoods: Child Emigration since 1945." Pp. 121–43 in *Child Welfare and Social Action in the Nineteenth and Twentieth Centuries: International Perspectives*, edited by Jon Lawrence and Pat Starkey. Liverpool, UK: Liverpool University Press, 2001.

Paz, Ruth. *Paths to Empowerment: Ten Years of Early Childhood Work in Israel*. The Hague: Bernard van Leer Foundation, 1990.

Penslar, Derek. "Narratives of Nation Building: Major Themes in Zionist Historiography." Pp. 104–27 in *The Jewish Past Revisited: Reflections on Modern Jewish Historians*, edited by David Ruderman and David Myers. New Haven, Conn.: Yale University Press, 1998.

Perko, F. Michael. "'Regimentation Everywhere': *Mizrahim*, Education and Cultural Dissonance in the Israel Defense Forces, 1948–1975." Paper presented at the annual meeting of the Association for Israel Studies, Tel Aviv, June 2000.

Pincus, Chasya. *Come from the Four Winds: The Story of Youth Aliyah*. New York: Herzl Press, 1970.

Porat, Reuven. *The History of the Kibbutz: Communal Education, 1904–1929*. Kibbutz Studies Book Series, no. 10. Ramat Efal, Israel: Yad Tabenkin, Institute for Kibbutz and Labor Movement Studies, 1985.

Rabin, Else. "The Jewish Woman in Social Service in Germany." Pp. 174–200 in *The Jewish Library*, vol. 3, *Woman*, edited by Leo Jung. London: Soncino, 1970.

Raider, Mark A. *The Emergence of American Zionism*. New York: New York University Press, 1998.

Raider, Mark A., and Miriam Raider-Roth. *The Plough Woman: Records of the Pioneer Women of Palestine, A Critical Edition*. Lebanon, N.H.: University Press of New England, 2002.

Ram, Uri. *The Changing Agenda of Israeli Sociology: Theory, Ideology and Identity*. Albany, N.Y.: SUNY Press, 1995.

Raphael, Marc Lee. "The Origins of Organized National Jewish Philanthropy in the United States, 1914–1939." Pp. 213–23 in *The Jews of North America*, edited by Moses Rischin. Detroit: Wayne State University Press, 1987.

Raphael, Marc Lee, ed. *What Is American about the American Jewish Experience?* Williamsburg, Va.: Department of Religion, College of William and Mary, 1993.

Reich, Bernard, and David H. Goldberg. *Political Dictionary of Israel.* London: Scarecrow, 2000.

Reinharz, Shulamit. *Timeline of Women and Women's Issues in the Yishuv and Israel.* Waltham, Mass.: Hadassah International Research Institute on Jewish Women at Brandeis University, 1999.

Reinhold, Hanoch. *Youth Aliyah: Trends and Developments.* Jerusalem: Jewish Agency Youth Aliyah Department, 1957.

Reinhold, Hanoch, and Carl Frankenstein. "The Transfer of Homeless Jewish Children to Israel." *International Child Welfare Review* 5, no. 1 (1951): 65–72.

Reshef, Shimon. "Ben-Gurion and Public Education." Pp. 251–73 in *David Ben-Gurion: Politics and Leadership in Israel,* edited by Ronald W. Zweig. London: Frank Cass, 1981.

Rettig, Salomon, and Benjamin Pasamanick. "Some Observations on the Moral Ideology of First and Second Generation Collective and Non-Collective Settlers in Israel." *Social Problems* 2, no. 2 (Fall 1963): 165–78.

Rich, Adrienne. *Of Woman Born: Motherhood as Experience and Institution.* New York: W. W. Norton, 1976.

Richards, Ellen H. *Euthenics: The Science of Controllable Environment.* Boston: Whitcomb & Barrows, 1912.

Riemer, Yehuda. "Interaction between Youth Movements and Kibbutz: The Case of Kfar Blum." *The Journal of Israeli History* 17 (1996): 167–77.

Rinott, Chanoch. "Major Trends in Jewish Youth Movements in Germany." Pp. 77–95 in *Leo Baeck Institute Year Book 19.* London: Secker & Warburg, 1974.

Rogow, Faith. *Gone to Another Meeting: The National Council of Jewish Women, 1893–1993.* Tuscaloosa: University of Alabama Press, 1993.

Rosen, George. *A History of Public Health.* New York: MD Publications, 1958.

———. *Preventive Medicine in the United States, 1900–1975: Trends and Interpretations.* New York: Prodist, 1977.

Rosenstock, Werner. "The Jewish Youth Movement." Pp. 97–105 in *Leo Baeck Institute Year Book 19.* London: Secker & Warburg, 1974.

Rothman, Sheila M. *Woman's Proper Place: A History of Changing Ideals and Practices, 1870 to the Present.* New York: Basic Books, 1978.

Ruppin, Arthur. *Three Decades of Palestine.* Westport, Conn.: Greenwood, 1975.

Sachar, Howard M., ed. *The Rise of Israel: A Documentary Record from the 19th Century to 1948,* vol. 15, *Practical Zionism, 1920–39.* New York: Garland, 1987.

Sarna, Jonathan. "The Henrietta Szold Era." Pp. 47–94 in *JPS: The Americanization of Jewish Culture, 1888–1988.* Philadelphia: Jewish Publication Society, 1989.

Schneider, Dorothy, and Carl Schneider. *American Women in the Progressive Era, 1900–1920.* New York: Facts on File, 1993.

Schulz, Michael. *Israel between Conflict and Accommodation: The Transformation of Collective Identities: A Study of the Melting Pot Process.* Goteborg, Sweden: Department of Peace and Development Research, Goteborg University, 1996.

Schweid, Eliezer. "The Rejection of the Diaspora in Zionist Thought: Two Approaches." *Studies in Zionism* 15 (1984): 43–70.

Scott, Anne Firor. *Natural Allies: Women's Associations in American History.* Urbana and Chicago: University of Illinois Press, 1991.

Segev, Tom. *1949: The First Israelis.* Markham, Ontario: Fitzhenry & Whiteside, 1998.

Shaked, Joseph. "The Education of New Immigrant Workers in Israel." Pp. 30–46 in *Some Studies in Education of Immigrants for Citizenship 16.* UNESCO: Education Clearing House, 1955.

Shalev, Michael. "Time for Theory: Critical Notes on Lissak and Sternhell." *Israel Studies* 1, no. 2 (Fall 1996): 170–83.

Shama, Avraham, and Mark Iris. *Immigration without Integration: Third World Jews in Israel.* Cambridge, Mass.: Schenkman, 1977.

Shapira, Anita. "The Holocaust: Private Memories, Public Memory." *Jewish Social Studies* 4, no. 2 (Winter 1988): 40–57.

———. "The Origins of 'Jewish Labor' Ideology." *Studies in Zionism* 5 (1982): 93–113.

Shapira, Rina, and Rachel Peleg. "From Blue Shirt to White Collar." *Youth and Society* 16, no. 2 (December 1984): 195–216.

Shapiro, Yonathan. *Leadership of the American Zionist Organization, 1897–1930.* Urbana, Chicago, London: University of Illinois Press, 1971.

Shargel, Baila Round. "American Jewish Women in Palestine: Bessie Gotsfeld, Henrietta Szold, and the Zionist Enterprise." *American Jewish History* 90, no. 2 (2002): 141–60.

Sharon, Nachman. "A Policy Analysis of Issues in Residential Care for Children and Youth in Israel: Past. Present, Future." *Child & Youth Services* 7, no. 3/4 (Summer 1985): 111–22.

Shavit, Yaacov. *The New Hebrew Nation: A Study in Heresy and Fantasy.* London: Frank Cass, 1987.

Shepherd, Naomi. *Ploughing Sand: British Rule in Palestine, 1917–1948.* London: John Murray, 1999.

———. *A Price Below Rubies: Jewish Women as Rebels and Radicals.* London: Weidenfeld & Nicolson, 1993.

Shilo, Margalit. "The Women's Farm at Kinneret, 1911–1917: A Solution to the Problem of the Working Woman in the Second Aliya." Pp. 246–83 in *The Jerusalem Cathedra*, edited by Lee I. Levine. Jerusalem: Yad Izhak Ben Zvi Institute, 1981.

Shokeid, Moshe. "On the Sins We Did Not Commit in the Research of Oriental Jews." *Israel Studies* 6 (2001): 15–33.

Shumsky, Abraham. *The Clash of Cultures in Israel: A Problem for Education.* New York: Bureau of Publications, Teachers College, Columbia University, 1955.

Shuval, Judith T. *Immigrants on the Threshold.* New York: Prentice Hall, 1963.

Shuval, Judith T., and Elazar Shuval, eds. *Immigration to Israel: Sociological Perspectives.* New Brunswick, N.J.: Transaction, 1998.

Shvarts, Shifra. "The Development of Mother and Infant Welfare Centers in Israel, 1854–1954." *Journal of the History of Medicine* 55 (October 2000): 398–425.

Shvarts, Shifra, and Theodore M. Brown. "Kupat Holim, Dr. Isaac Max Rubinow, and the American Zionist Medical Unit's Experiment to Establish Health Care Services in Palestine, 1918–1923." *Bulletin of the History of Medicine* 72, no. 1 (1998): 28–46.

Silberstein, Laurence J., ed. *New Perspectives on Israeli History: The Early Years of the State*. New York: New York University Press, 1991.

———. *The Postzionism Debates: Knowledge and Power in Israeli Culture*. New York: Routledge, 1999.

Simon, Rachel. "Between the Family and the Outside World: Jewish Girls in the Modern Middle East and North Africa." *Jewish Social Studies* 7 (Fall 2000): 81–108.

Sklar, Kathryn Kish. "Organized Womanhood: Archival Sources on Women and Progressive Reform." *Journal of American History* 75 (June 1988–March 1989): 176–83.

Smilanski, Moshe. *Child and Youth Welfare in Israel*. Jerusalem: Henrietta Szold Institute for Child & Youth Welfare, 1960.

Smilanski, Moshe, and L. Adar, eds. *Evaluating Educational Achievements: Summaries of Some Studies Carried Out by the Henrietta Szold Institute on Schooling in Israel*. Educational Studies and Documents, no. 42. Paris: UNESCO, 1961.

Smillie, Wilson G. *Public Health: Its Promise for the Future: A Chronicle of the Development of Public Health in the United States, 1607–1914*. New York: Macmillan, 1955.

Smooha, Sammy. *Israel: Pluralism and Conflict*. London: Routledge & Kegan Paul, 1978.

Sochen, June. *Consecrate Every Day: The Public Lives of American Jewish Women, 1880–1980*. Albany: State University of New York Press, 1981.

———. "Some Observations on the Role of American Jewish Women as Communal Volunteers." *American Jewish History* 70 (September 1980): 23–34.

Sommerfeld, Rose. "Organization in Charity." Pp. 236–45 in *Proceedings of the First Convention of the National Council of Jewish Women at New York*. Philadelphia: Jewish Publication Society, 1897.

Spender, Stephen. *Learning Laughter*. New York: Greenwood, 1969.

Spiro, Melford E. *Children of the Kibbutz*. Cambridge, Mass.: Harvard University Press, 1975.

Spiro, Melford E. "The Sabras and Zionism: A Study in Personality and Ideology." *Social Problems* 5, no. 2 (Fall 1957): 100–110.

Stage, Sarah. "Ellen Richards and the Social Significance of the Home Economics Movement." Pp. 17–33 in *Rethinking Home Economics: Women and the History of a Profession*, edited by Sarah Stage and Virginia B. Vincenti. Ithaca, N.Y.: Cornell University Press, 1997.

Stahl, Abraham. "Teachers' Prejudices: A Perennial Problem in Israeli Education." *Urban Education* 25, no. 4 (January 1991): 440–53.

Steir, Oren B. "Memory Matters: Reading Collective Memory in Contemporary Jewish Culture." *Prooftexts* 18 (1998): 67–94.

Sternhell, Ze'ev. *The Founding Myths of Israel: Nationalism, Socialism and the Making of the Jewish State*. Princeton, N.J.: Princeton University Press, 1998.

———. "A Response to Gorny and Sharkansky." *Israel Studies* 1, no. 2 (Fall 1996): 304–13.

Stillman, Norman. *The Jews of Arab Lands in Modern Times*. Philadelphia: Jewish Publication Society, 1991.

———. "The Moroccan Jewish Experience: A Revisionist View." *The Jerusalem Quarterly* 9 (1978): 111–23.

Straus, Lina Gutherz. *Disease in Milk, the Remedy Pasteurization: The Life Work of Nathan Straus*. New York: Arno, 1977.

Strum, Philippa. "Zionism and the Ideal State." Pp. 100–115 in *Brandeis: Beyond Progressivism*. Lawrence: University Press of Kansas, 1993.

Sufian, Sandra. "Healing the Land and the Nation: Malaria and the Zionist Project in Mandatory Palestine, 1920–1947." Ph.D. diss., New York University, 1999.

Survey, vol. 30, 1913.

Swain, Shurlee. "Child Rescue: The Emigration of an Idea." Pp. 101–19 in *Child Welfare and Social Action in the Nineteenth and Twentieth Centures: International Perspectives*, edited by Jon Lawrence and Pat Starkey. Liverpool, UK: Liverpool University Press, 2001.

Swirski, Shlomo. *Politics and Education in Israel: Comparisons with the United States*. New York: Falmer, 1999.

Szold, Henrietta. "Recent Jewish Progress in Palestine," *American Jewish Year Book* 17 (1915–1916): 25–158.

Tapper, Lawrence. *Hadassah-WIZO Organization of Canada: Finding Aid No. 1235*. Ottawa: National Archives of Canada, 1994.

Tartakower, Aryeh. "The Sociological Implications of the Present-Day Aliyah." *Jewish Social Studies* 13, no. 3 (1951): 291–310.

Toll, William. "A Quiet Revolution: Jewish Women's Clubs and the Widening Female Sphere, 1870–1920." *American Jewish Archives* 41, no. 1 (1989): 9–26.

Tomes, Nancy. *The Gospel of Germs: Men, Women and the Microbe in American Life*. Cambridge, Mass.: Harvard University Press, 1998.

———. "The Private Side of Public Health: Sanitary Science, Domestic Hygiene, and the Germ Theory, 1870–1900." *Bulletin of the History of Medicine* 64, no. 4 (Winter 1990): 509–39.

———. "Spreading the Germ Theory: Sanitary Science and Home Economics, 1880–1930." Pp. 34–54 in *Rethinking Home Economics: Women and the History of a Profession*, edited by Sarah Stage and Virginia B. Vincenti. Ithaca, N.Y.: Cornell University Press, 1997.

Troen, S. Ilan, and Noah Lucas, eds. *Israel: The First Decade of Independence*. Albany: State University of New York Press, 1995.

Tsur, Yaron. "Carnival Fears: Moroccan Immigrants and the Ethnic Problem in the Young State of Israel." *The Journal of Israeli History* 18 (1997): 73–103.

Urofsky, Melvin I. *American Zionism from Herzl to the Holocaust.* Lincoln: University of Nebraska Press, 1975.

Urofsky, Melvin I. *We Are One! American Jewry and Israel.* New York: Anchor / Doubleday, 1978.

Urofsky, Melvin I. "Zionism: An American Experience." Pp. 245–55 in *The American Jewish Experience* , edited by Jonathan Sarna. London: Holmes & Meier, 1986.

Urofsky, Melvin I., and David W. Levy, eds. *Letters of Louis D. Brandeis.* Albany: State University of New York Press, 1978.

Wald, Lillian. *The House on Henry Street.* New York: Dover, 1971.

———. *Windows on Henry Street.* Boston: Little, Brown, 1941.

Waldstein, A. S. *Modern Palestine: Jewish Life and Problems.* New York: Bloch, 1927.

Walkowitz, Daniel J. "The Making of a Feminine Professional Identity: Social Workers in the 1920s." *American Historical Review* 95, no. 4 (October 1990): 1051–95.

Waserman, Manfred, and Samuel S. Kottek, eds. *Health and Disease in the Holy Land: Studies in the History and Sociology of Medicine from Ancient Times to the Present.* Queenston, Ontario: Edwin Mellen, 1996.

Waxman, Chaim I. "Critical Sociology and the End of Ideology in Israel." *Israel Studies* 2, no. 1 (Spring 1997): 194–210.

Weiker, Walter F. "Studies on Ethnicity." Pp. 107–119 in *Critical Essays on Israeli Social Issues and Scholarship*, edited by Russel A. Stone and Walter P. Zenner. New York: State University of New York Press, 1994.

Weiner, Anita. "Institutionalizing Institutionalization: The Historical Roots of Residential Care in Israel." *Child & Youth Services* 7, no. 3/4 (Summer 1985): 3–19.

Weingarten, Michael A. *Changing Health and Changing Culture: The Yemenite Jews in Israel.* Westport, Conn.: Praeger, 1992.

Weingrod, Alex. "How Israeli Culture Was Constructed: Memory, History and the Israeli Past." *Israel Studies* 2, no. 1 (1996): 228–37.

———. *Israel: Group Relations in a New Society.* London: Praeger, 1965.

———. "One Morning in a Maabera." *Commentary* 28, no. 2 (August 1959): 118–21.

———. *Reluctant Pioneers: Village Development in Israel.* Ithaca, N.Y.: Cornell University Press, 1966.

———, ed. *Studies in Israeli Ethnicity: After the Ingathering.* New York: Gordon and Breach, 1985.

———. "The Two Israels." *Commentary* 4, no. 33 (April 1962): 313–19.

Weiss, Sol. "Educating the Disadvantaged, Israeli Style." *Urban Education* 7, no. 2 (July 1972): 181–97.

Weitz, Yechiam. "The Holocaust on Trial: The Impact of the Kasztner and Eichmann Trials on Israeli Society." *Israel Studies* 1, no. 2 (Fall 1996): 1–26.

Wenger, Beth S. "Jewish Women and Voluntarism: Beyond the Myth of Enablers." *American Jewish History* 79, no. 1 (Autumn 1989): 16–36.

———. *New York Jews and the Great Depression*. New Haven, Conn.: Yale University Press, 1996.

Wiebe, Robert H. *The Search for Order, 1877–1920*. New York: Hill & Wang, 1967.

Wigoder, Geoffrey, ed. *New Encyclopedia of Zionism and Israel*. London: Associated University Presses, 1994.

Wishy, Bernard. *The Child and the Republic: The Dawn of Modern American Child Nurture*. Philadelphia: University of Pennsylvania Press, 1968.

Wistrich, Robert, and David Ohana, eds. *The Shaping of Israeli Identity: Myth, Memory and Trauma*. London: Frank Cass, 1995.

Wolins, Martin, and Meir Gottesman, eds. *Group Care: An Israeli Approach; The Educational Path of Youth Aliyah*. New York: Gordon and Breach, 1971.

Woodroofe, Kathleen. *From Charity to Social Work in England and the United States*. Toronto: University of Toronto Press, 1968.

Yanai, Nathan. "The Citizen as Pioneer: Ben-Gurion's Concept of Citizenship." *Israel Studies* 1, no. 1 (Spring 1996): 127–43.

Yiftachel, Oren, and Avinoam Meir, eds. *Ethnic Frontiers and Peripheries: Landscapes of Development and Inequality in Israel*. Boulder, Colo.: Westview, 1998.

Yonah, Yossi. "Cultural Pluralism and Education: The Israeli Case." *Interchange* 25, no. 4 (1994): 349–65.

Zameret, Zvi. *Fifty Years of Education in the State of Israel*. Jerusalem.

Zeitlin, Rose. *Henrietta Szold: Record of a Life*. New York: Dial, 1952.

Zelizer, Viviana A. *Pricing the Priceless Child: The Changing Social Value of Children*. New York: Basic Books, 1985.

Zerubavel, Yael. "The 'Mythological Sabra' and Jewish Past: Trauma, Memory and Contested Identities." *Israel Studies* 7 (Summer 2002): 115–44.

———. *Recovered Roots: Collective Memory and the Making of Israeli National Tradition*. Chicago: University of Chicago Press, 1995.

Index

~

About the Author

Erica B. Simmons received her Ph.D. in history from the University of Toronto. She was awarded a Hannah Postdoctoral Fellowship in the History of Medicine for 2004–2006 at York University in Toronto, Canada.